250 Best
Canadian
Bread
Machine
Baking Recipes

250 Best Canadian Bread Machine Baking Recipes

Donna Washburn
Heather Butt

Robert ROSE

For complete cataloguing information, see page 381.

Disclaimer
The recipes in this book have been carefully tested by our kitchen and our tasters. To the best of our knowledge, they are safe and nutritious for ordinary use and users. For those people with food or other allergies, or who have special food requirements or health issues, please read the suggested contents of each recipe carefully and determine whether or not they may create a problem for you. All recipes are used at the risk of the consumer. Consumers should always consult their bread machine manufacturer's manual for recommended procedures and baking times.

We cannot be responsible for any hazards, loss or damage that may occur as a result of any recipe use.

For those with special needs, allergies, requirements or health problems, in the event of any doubt, please contact your medical advisor prior to the use of any recipe.

Design & Production: PageWave Graphics Inc.
Editor: Sue Sumeraj
Photography: Mark T. Shapiro
Food Styling: Kate Bush
Prop Styling: Charlene Erricson
Index: Belle Wong

We acknowledge the financial support of the Government of Canada through the Book Publishing Industry Development Program (BPIDP) for our publishing activities.

Published by Robert Rose Inc.
120 Eglinton Avenue East, Suite 800, Toronto, Ontario, Canada M4P 1E2
Tel: (416) 322-6552; Fax: (416) 322-6936

Printed in Canada

1 2 3 4 5 6 7 8 9 FP 12 11 10 09 08 07 06 05 04

To our husbands, David and Jack,
and our sons, Jeff, Stephen, Ian and Craig.
And to our mothers, both of whom were career
women — caring teachers by profession. By example,
they instilled in us the important values of honesty,
integrity and a strong desire to challenge ourselves
to continue to grow in our lifelong search for
knowledge. Without them, our friendship
would never have developed and this book
would never have been written.

Contents

Acknowledgments

THE AROMA FROM THE TEST KITCHEN permeates the neighborhood. Chocolate, cinnamon, apple, cheese and herbs furnish the appetizing fragrances of these tasty loaves.

Our test kitchen counters have been lined with over 30 bread machines — kneading, mixing, beeping and baking from early morning until late at night — testing and re-testing until the loaves were perfect. Each loaf was baked, weighed and sliced in several places — and, yes, tasted. Thank you to all the manufacturers — Philips Electronics, Proctor-Silex, Regal, Sunbeam/Oster, Toastmaster, West Bend, Black & Decker, Philips Norelco and Zojirushi — who supplied the machines used in testing. To our lifeline at Philips Electronics, Jean Hill, a special thanks for your continuing support and assistance.

We would also like to thank the individuals and companies who kindly supplied product to the test kitchen. For yeast and flour, thanks to Molly Pocklington-Thompson, Nadya Antoniades, Nathalie Radepont and Jim Kopp of fermipan® yeast from Lallemand Inc., Monique Croteau of Five Roses and Jim Rogers of Robin Hood Multifoods. To Bruce Wright of The Brewing Experience, thank you for providing malt syrup. And to Brian Creighton of Myer's Bulk Foods, our appreciation for filling our orders and serving as an ongoing source of product information. To Linda Williams and staff of New Horizons Foods, thank you for all your help. A special thanks goes to Carol Coulter, our favorite celiac, for her assistance with the gluten-free recipes.

We have always believed that photography is an important part of cookbooks. And we have once again been fortunate to work with a very talented group of people who make our breads look so appealing: Mark Shapiro, of Mark Shapiro Photography; food stylist Kate Bush; art director Sharon Matthews; and prop stylist Charlene Erricson. Thank you to all for your untiring efforts and ability to work miracles.

Special thanks go to our publisher, Bob Dees, and the staff of Robert Rose Inc. Also to editor Sue Sumeraj and the staff of PageWave Graphics for working through all the intricacies of editorial, design, layout and production.

Last but by no means least, we want to thank the people who are always there for us (even when we're not writing cookbooks) — our husbands, for their support, words of wisdom and unbiased (of course) taste testing. A special thank you to our sons and all the members of our extended families for the assistance they have supplied with their individual expertise.

Just ask us — are we tired of baking bread? The fragrance of baked bread is still warming to our hearts. We hope you have as many enjoyable hours baking the recipes from our cookbook as we have had developing them for you.

Preface

250 Best Canadian Bread Machine Recipes has been written for you, the person who cherishes homemade bread but can't remember life before your bread machine. We, too, can't get along without ours. First and most important, writing this cookbook has allowed two very good friends the opportunity to work together, in a business, doing work we love. We both enjoy the creativity of baking and the challenge of recipe development, and of course we love to eat.

Both professional home economists, we have university degrees in our field of study. Donna started Quality Professional Services in 1992 to develop recipes for small electrical appliances. Black & Decker was QPS's first customer. Recipes for the U.S. and Canadian markets were developed for Black & Decker's bread machines. Heather became a partner in 1994. Philips Electronics Ltd. asked QPS to develop recipes for the manuals of their two new horizontal bread machines. What a challenge! These machines have many new features and cycles including: Cake, Jam, Quick Bread, Rapid One-Hour Basic, Rapid Whole Wheat and Pasta. They bake two or three sizes of loaves with a choice of three crust colors.

As the home economists for Philips Electronics Ltd., and as the test kitchen experts for fermipan® yeast from Lallemand Inc., we speak with many of you while managing the call center and answering toll-free customer service calls. We thoroughly enjoy helping answer your questions. We love the challenge of not knowing what difficulty or what interesting bit of information the next caller may have to offer. As spokespersons for Robin Hood Multifood's bread flours, we have had the opportunity to promote bread machine baking on TV.

We also published a bimonthly 12-page newsletter for bread machine owners — called *The Bread Basket* — which featured new recipes, bread machine reviews and lots of tips and techniques. Our newsletter subscribers told us they could never get enough bread machine recipes. And we often got and continue to get requests for particular flavor combinations that come from recipes belonging to our readers' mothers or grandmothers. Many have special memories attached to holidays and family celebrations. We have adapted these to the bread machine and have included many of these requests in the first chapter of this book.

Our training and professional values are tested daily as we attempt to satisfy and protect our customers and you, our readers. On one hand, we have the manufacturers for whom we do recipe development; on the other, we have you, the consumer, for whom we try to do our best by sharing our knowledge and expertise. Practicality is the keynote of our work.

We can assure you that all the recipes in this cookbook have been tested and re-tested to meet the highest standards of quality and appeal. Well over 2,000 pounds of flour, 72 tins of yeast, gallons of honey, pounds of cracked wheat, etc. went into testing these recipes. Each and every dough was measured, cut, re-measured; every rising timed and re-timed. The oven temperatures were checked, the baked dough tapped on the bottom, sides and top. We want to provide you the best possible recipes to guarantee your success and enjoyment using your bread machine.

We hope you'll enjoy this wonderful collection of recipes. We've created them just for you — our fellow bread machine bakers.

Donna and Heather

Introduction

ABOUT THE RECIPES

There are many challenges in developing bread machine recipes. And one of the greatest is keeping up with changes in bread machines themselves. Originally, bread machines were of the "vertical" type, producing a tall loaf with a square slice. Today, the majority of machines sold are horizontal-style, producing a loaf that has a round top and looks like a traditional slice. In addition, some models bake hotter than others, some knead longer, some preheat before mixing and some have longer rising periods. Today's bread machines also have numerous new cycles, several crust settings and make more than one size of loaf. Some bake one size better than another.

Since the same recipe can look quite different in these various types of machine, we have tested each recipe in this book using a minimum of three different brands and models of both horizontal- and vertical-style. The recipe is then adjusted and retested until it produces the best possible loaf in all three machines.

As you begin to use our cookbook and to choose recipes, remember to read our helpful hints and useful practical tips found in each chapter. Now, all that remains for you is just to bake bread, taste it with enthusiasm and enjoy your handiwork. Happy bread baking, everyone!

Recipe Selection

The selection of recipes includes a mix ranging from old family favorites, often referred to as comfort foods, to some of the newest trends. Some are just the old standbys, but with a new twist. Whether new or old, all have been modified for the bread machine.

Every recipe provides both the imperial and metric volume measures. It doesn't matter which you use, just choose one and be consistent. It is never recommended to mix and match types of measuring equipment. The recipes are not conversions but are developed for the type of measuring you feel comfortable using. It is most important that you measure accurately.

Approximately half the recipes begin with the dough cycle, followed by forming, rising and baking. We have provided as much choice as possible with these. We don't like to make a recipe into one particular shape and don't feel that you need to either. Make your choices and enjoy the chance for lots of variety. Let your creativity shine through, and very soon you will feel comfortable enough to experiment and create shapes of your own. There is no better stress reliever than rolling up your sleeves, getting elbow deep in flour and working with a shaped dough.

Adjusting the Recipes

About the whole question of checking and adjusting the dough ball — we thought we'd like to give you our philosophy about this subject. We develop recipes so that the guesswork is taken out of baking bread with your bread machine. We do not believe there is a need for you to guess whether the dough is too stiff or too sticky. Sweet and rye breads have stickier dough balls than basic whites, just as oatmeal and pumpernickel loaves are denser than basic whites. Sweet bread dough must be softer than most bread dough or dried or candied fruit won't mix in, but will just sit on the outside and burn. Recipes containing oatmeal are thinner in the beginning, but thicken during kneading, resulting in fine-textured loaves.

However, given the variances between different types of machines (and your individual preferences), you may wish to adjust the recipe. We recommend that you first try the recipe as given. If the loaf is a bit compact and short, increase the yeast by $1/4$ to $1/2$ tsp (1 to 2 mL). On the other hand, if it mushrooms over the edges of the baking pan and hits the top, increase the flour slightly and decrease the yeast by $1/4$ to $1/2$ tsp (1 to 2 mL).

A friend of ours once complained that all breads from her bread machine were too much alike. You won't say that if you follow our recipes! Each recipe is developed to have a texture and flavor of its own. For example, the *Hawaiian Sunrise* (see recipe, page 296), is similar to an angel food cake in its lightness and fluffiness, while the *Swiss Rye* (see recipe, page 90) is heavier, with a fine texture. Remember, all you really need to do is measure accurately, press the button and return when signaled. Relax! Leave the recipe development to us!

Loaf Size

The recipes for loaves in this cookbook were developed in two sizes: 1.5 lb (750 g) and 2 lb (1 kg). Today there are many extra-large horizontal and vertical 2 lb (1 kg) bread machine models on the market. We have marked "extra large" beside loaves that will bake to the top of these baking pans. We strongly recommend you consult the chart below and follow the directions to determine which size of recipe will bake the best loaf in your particular model of bread machine. If your baking pan capacity is less than 12 cups (3 L), bake the smaller recipe size. These recipes work well in some of the new horizontal two-paddle machines, which are advertised by the manufacturers as 2.5 lb (1.25 kg) machines.

Bread Machine Baking Pan Size

Determine the volume of your baking pan by filling it with water, using a measuring cup. Consult the chart below to verify the size of recipe to use.

Bread Machine Sizes and Capacities

Loaf size	Weight	Capacity of baking pan
Medium	1.5 lb (750 g)	6 to 9 cups (1.5 to 2.25 L)
Large	2 lb (1 kg)	9 to 12 cups (2.25 to 3 L)
Extra large	2.5 lb (1.25 kg)	12 to 16 cups (3 to 4 L)

Temperature of Ingredients

The success of bread machine baking often depends on having ingredients at the right temperature. Loaves rise higher, with a lighter texture, if milk, vegetable juices and fruit juices are at room temperature. (To warm approximately 1 cup/250 mL liquid to room temperature, microwave on High for 1 minute.) Mixtures such as pumpkin, yams, squash, applesauce, pears and mashed banana should be at room temperature before using. Use eggs straight from the refrigerator unless otherwise specified in the recipe. Cream cheese and butter should be softened.

Testing for Doneness

There are two methods. The most common is to tap on the bottom — if the sound is hollow, the bread is baked. If you have an instant-read thermometer, insert into bread at least 2 inches (5 cm). The thermometer should register 190°F (93°C).

Hints for Successful Bread Machine Baking

1. Measure all the ingredients accurately.
2. Remove the baking pan from the bread machine when measuring and adding recipe ingredients; do not measure over the bread pan.
3. Follow your bread machine manufacturer's recommended order of adding recipe ingredients.
4. Consult your operating manual for the best ingredient temperature.
5. Keep dried fruits, grains and cereals away from the liquid in the pan.
6. Use the type of yeast specified in the recipe.
7. Make a well in the top of the flour for the yeast. It should not touch the liquid.
8. Keep cinnamon and garlic away from the yeast as they inhibit the rising.
9. Measure the fruit and nuts for the "add ingredient" signal and place them beside the bread machine before starting the machine.
10. Do not use the timer for recipes containing eggs, fresh milk, cheese and other perishables.

THE BREAD MACHINE PANTRY

Great bread depends on choosing the correct ingredients and measuring them accurately. Here's a guide to the most important ingredients you'll be using for the recipes in this book. Additional details can be found in the Ingredient Glossary (page 359).

Flour

Flour makes up the largest part of any yeast bread. It provides the gluten, a protein that forms the cell wall structure, trapping the gas bubbles and holding air, allowing the dough to rise. Only wheat and rye flours contain gluten.

Both all-purpose and bread flour can be used in Canada, as both contain enough gluten (protein) to bake excellent loaves. Do not use cake-and-pastry or self-rising blends to bake breads in your bread machine. Whether unbleached or bleached, all-purpose or bread flour will give the same baking results.

Most of the vitamins and minerals are found in the bran and germ. Enrichment is a process that adds back to the flour the vitamins and minerals removed during the refining process. The bran in whole wheat flour supplies the fiber found in whole wheat products. The small amount of fat found in the germ makes long-term storage in the freezer necessary. This prevents that fat from becoming rancid.

Both wheat and rye flours contain gluten, although rye flour has less, and must be used in combination with wheat flour in bread machine baking. Only small amounts of rye flour can be used. Be careful when working with rye flour, because the gluten in it is not very elastic and becomes sticky with too much kneading. It can be purchased in light, medium and dark varieties. Only the intensity of color of the finished product will vary. We do not recommend exceeding the amounts of rye flour given for any of the recipes in this book.

To preserve its "strength" (ability to rise), store all flour in an airtight container in a cool, dry place. Do not store flour in the refrigerator, where it can pick up moisture. Flour should be frozen for storage of longer than 6 months. Allow the flour to return to room temperature before using.

Liquids

The liquids you use in these recipes can include water, milk, and fruit and vegetable juices. Water tends to yield a crisper crust, while milk supplies some fat to bake a softer, more tender loaf.

Either fluid milk or powdered milk in combination with water can be used in bread machines. Use whatever type of fluid milk you prefer: homogenized, 2%, 1%, low-fat or skim. When using the timer on your machine, use skim milk powder or buttermilk powder. In recipes where you won't be using the timer, if powdered milk is specified you can use fluid milk to replace the water and omit the powder. Consult the manufacturer's manual for the temperature of the milk to add to your bread machine. We find that unless there are a lot of cold ingredients in the recipe, cold milk straight from the refrigerator can be used.

Fruit juice will help intensify flavor and color. Purchase unsweetened fruit juices for consistent results. The amount of sugar and salt varies in juices. Read the label to be sure the product you purchase is a fruit juice and not a "fruit drink." We recommend using the amount of each juice stated in the recipe.

Salt

While we have used only small amounts of salt in our recipes, the salt is necessary, since it controls the yeast's activity, and prevents the loaf from over-rising and collapsing. Breads made without salt are very bland and over-risen.

Yeast

Yeast converts the carbohydrates in flour and sugar to produce the carbon dioxide gas that causes dough to rise. The recipes in this cookbook were developed using bread machine yeast. We always recommend using the type of yeast called for in the recipe. Both bread machine and instant yeast are very active strains of yeast that can be added directly to the bread machine without the need for pre-activating.

The expiry date on the package indicates that it should be opened before that date and used within a 2-month period. Store a 2- to 3-month supply of yeast in an airtight container in the refrigerator. For long-term storage, yeast should be kept in an airtight container in the freezer. Do not transfer yeast from one container to another; exposing it to air can shorten its life.

Perform this test for freshness if you suspect that the yeast has become less active: Dissolve 1 tsp (5 mL) sugar in $1/2$ cup (125 mL) lukewarm water. Add 2 tsp (10 mL) yeast and stir gently. In 10 minutes, the mixture should have a strong yeasty smell and be foamy. If it doesn't, the yeast is too old — time to buy fresh yeast!

The amount of yeast used in large- and small-loaf versions of each recipe is specific to that recipe; it is not simply factored up or down according to size. In fact, for some recipes, the amount of yeast in the 2 lb (1 kg) version is the same as (or even smaller than) the amount of yeast used in the 1.5 lb (750 g) version.

Sugars

Sugar provides food for the yeast and flavor to the dough. Granulated sugar, packed brown sugar, honey, maple syrup, corn syrup and molasses can be used interchangeably. Results will vary slightly in color, flavor and texture. Aspartame-based sugar substitutes can be used, but not those based on saccharin. Substitute equal amounts for the sugar in the recipe. Loaves are lighter in color than when sugar is used.

Fats

Fat gives the crust its tenderness and the loaf its softness. It also helps to retain moisture, which keeps the loaf from going stale too quickly. The type of fat used is a matter of preference and can include shortening, margarine, butter or vegetable oil. (Your choice may have some effect on the loaf, however.) Do not use low-calorie margarine since its high water content will affect the size and texture of the loaf.

Cheese and egg yolk contribute to the fat in some recipes. Do not use recipes containing eggs or cheese with the timer. Use large eggs directly from the refrigerator. When measuring shredded cheese, do not pack. Weight is a more accurate measure than volume. If desired, small cubes of cheese can replace shredded, since cheese melts during baking.

Seeds, Nuts and Grains

These are added to supply flavor and body to the breads while adding fiber, vitamins and minerals. This category includes cereals such as Red River, 7-grain, 12-grain, cracked wheat, bulgur and cornmeal, in addition to seeds, nuts and dried fruits.

To prevent the dried fruit from breaking up or puréeing, add at the "add ingredient" signal or at least 5 minutes before the end of the last knead.

Other Flavoring Agents

Herbs and spices, dried fruits, garlic, onions and chocolate add to the flavor of the recipes. This group includes two enemies of yeast: cinnamon and garlic. Care must be taken to keep these ingredients from touching the yeast. Do not add extra amounts of either cinnamon or garlic. Resulting loaves will be short, heavy and very dense.

By Request

We frequently hear from readers with ideas for new and interesting flavor combinations — often based on old, traditional bread recipes passed down from mothers and grandmothers. We've incorporated some of these ideas here. Perhaps you'll find a new family favorite of your own.

Tips for Terrific Loaves

- Measure accurately. The bread machine is unforgiving!
- For a more tender loaf, use homogenized or 2% milk, or cultured buttermilk, instead of water and skim milk powder or buttermilk powder. Just add an amount equal to the water called for in the recipe.
- If using buttermilk powder, it should be added after the flour. Adding it directly to the water will cause lumps.
- Most loaves can be baked using the timer. Exceptions are those containing dairy products and other perishables such as eggs and meats.
- Use large-size eggs, cold from the refrigerator.
- Butter should be at room temperature and added in small dollops.
- Where cinnamon or garlic is used in a recipe, do not exceed the amount specified. These ingredients can inhibit the action of the yeast.
- For recipes that call for milk and large quantities of fruits and vegetables (such as sweet potatoes and applesauce) these ingredients should be warmed to room temperature before adding to the baking pan.

Old-Fashioned Goodness Cracked Wheat Bread

Here's an old favorite, updated and adapted for your bread machine.

Tips

Substitute $3^{1}/_{4}$ cups (800 mL) wheat blend flour for the whole wheat flour and cracked wheat in the smaller loaf and $3^{3}/_{4}$ cups (925 mL) in the larger loaf. Select **Basic Cycle**.

Keep cracked wheat from coming into contact with the water when you bake this loaf. Cracked wheat quickly absorbs water, resulting in a shorter and heavier loaf.

Variation

Substituting an equal amount of bulgur for the cracked wheat results in a nuttier flavor and rougher texture.

1.5 LB (750 G)		
$1^{1}/_{3}$ cups	water	325 mL
$^{1}/_{4}$ cup	skim milk powder	50 mL
$1^{1}/_{4}$ tsp	salt	5 mL
1 tbsp	liquid honey	15 mL
2 tbsp	shortening or vegetable oil	25 mL
$2^{3}/_{4}$ cups	whole wheat flour	700 mL
$^{1}/_{2}$ cup	cracked wheat	125 mL
$^{3}/_{4}$ tsp	bread machine yeast	4 mL

2 LB (1 KG)		
$1^{1}/_{2}$ cups	water	375 mL
$^{1}/_{4}$ cup	skim milk powder	50 mL
$1^{1}/_{2}$ tsp	salt	7 mL
2 tbsp	liquid honey	25 mL
2 tbsp	shortening or vegetable oil	25 mL
3 cups	whole wheat flour	750 mL
$^{3}/_{4}$ cup	cracked wheat	175 mL
$1^{1}/_{4}$ tsp	bread machine yeast	5 mL

1. Measure ingredients into baking pan in the order recommended by the manufacturer. Insert pan into the oven chamber.
2. Select **Whole Wheat Cycle**.

Malted Rye Bread

Britain's Hovis bread with a modern twist! Enjoy with Stilton cheese and red or black grapes.

Tips

Purchase malt syrup at a "brew your own" facility.

If your machine has a **Rapid Whole Wheat Cycle,** you can use it to bake either recipe; just increase the yeast by ³/₄ tsp (4 mL).

Yes, you're reading it right: The 1.5 lb (750 g) recipe contains the *same* amount of yeast as the 2 lb (1 kg).

Variation

Add ¹/₃ to ¹/₂ cup (75 to 125 mL) raisins to increase sweetness naturally.

1.5 LB (750 G)

1 cup	water	250 mL
¹/₄ cup	skim milk powder	50 mL
1 ¹/₄ tsp	salt	6 mL
¹/₄ cup	malt syrup	50 mL
2 tbsp	molasses	25 mL
2 tbsp	shortening or vegetable oil	25 mL
1 ¹/₂ cups	whole wheat flour	375 mL
1 cup	all-purpose flour or bread flour	250 mL
¹/₂ cup	rye flour	125 mL
1 ¹/₂ tsp	bread machine yeast	7 mL

2 LB (1 KG)

1 ¹/₃ cups	water	325 mL
¹/₃ cup	skim milk powder	75 mL
1 ¹/₂ tsp	salt	7 mL
¹/₄ cup	malt syrup	50 mL
3 tbsp	molasses	45 mL
2 tbsp	shortening or vegetable oil	25 mL
2 cups	whole wheat flour	500 mL
1 ¹/₂ cups	all-purpose flour or bread flour	375 mL
¹/₂ cup	rye flour	125 mL
1 ¹/₂ tsp	bread machine yeast	7 mL

1. Measure ingredients into baking pan in the order recommended by the manufacturer. Insert pan into the oven chamber.
2. Select **Whole Wheat Cycle.**

Raisin Malt Bread

A traditional English favorite, this rich, dark-brown loaf is lightly sweetened with malt powder.

Tips

The added malt will keep the loaf fresh longer.

Store malt powder in an airtight container; it lumps with a small amount of moisture. Sift before adding, if necessary.

Yes, you're reading it right: The 1.5 lb (750 g) recipe contains the *same* amount of yeast as the 2 lb (1 kg).

Variation

Prepare using the **Dough Cycle**, then bake in coffee tins for loaves with the traditional ridged edges.

1.5 LB (750 G)

1 1/4 cups	water	300 mL
1/4 cup	skim milk powder	50 mL
1 1/2 tsp	salt	7 mL
2 tbsp	molasses	25 mL
2 tbsp	shortening or vegetable oil	25 mL
2 cups	whole wheat flour	500 mL
1 1/4 cups	all-purpose flour or bread flour	300 mL
1/4 cup	malt powder	50 mL
1 1/2 tsp	bread machine yeast	7 mL
1/2 cup	raisins	125 mL

2 LB (1 KG)

1 1/2 cups	water	375 mL
1/4 cup	skim milk powder	50 mL
1 1/2 tsp	salt	7 mL
2 tbsp	molasses	25 mL
2 tbsp	shortening or vegetable oil	25 mL
2 2/3 cups	whole wheat flour	650 mL
1 1/2 cups	all-purpose flour or bread flour	375 mL
1/3 cup	malt powder	75 mL
1 1/2 tsp	bread machine yeast	7 mL
2/3 cup	raisins	150 mL

1. Measure all ingredients *except the raisins* into baking pan in the order recommended by the manufacturer. Insert pan into the oven chamber.

2. Select **Basic** or **Whole Wheat Cycle**.

3. Add raisins at the "add ingredient" signal.

Tried

Oatmeal Raisin Bread

Oats make this loaf high in fiber — higher than an ordinary sweet raisin bread.

Tip

Add oat bran or cooked whole oat kernels for an "oatier" flavor.

Variation

Increase the fiber by adding 2 tbsp (25 mL) oat bran. The top may vary slightly, but the loaf will be delicious.

1.5 LB (750 G)

1 1/4 cups	water	300 mL
1 1/4 tsp	salt	6 mL
2 tbsp	granulated sugar	25 mL
2 tbsp	shortening or vegetable oil	25 mL
3 cups	all-purpose flour or bread flour	750 mL
1/3 cup	quick-cooking oats	75 mL
1/2 cup	buttermilk powder	125 mL
1 1/4 tsp	bread machine yeast	6 mL
1 cup	raisins	250 mL

2 LB (1 KG)

1 1/3 cups	water	325 mL
1 1/2 tsp	salt	7 mL
3 tbsp	granulated sugar	40 mL
3 tbsp	shortening or vegetable oil	40 mL
3 cups	all-purpose flour or bread flour	750 mL
1/2 cup	quick-cooking oats	125 mL
1/2 cup	buttermilk powder	125 mL
1 1/2 tsp	bread machine yeast	7 mL
1 1/3 cups	raisins	325 mL

1. Measure all ingredients _except raisins_ into baking pan in the order recommended by the manufacturer. Insert pan into the oven chamber.
2. Select **Basic Cycle** or **Sweet Cycle**.
3. Add raisins at the "add ingredient" signal.

Asiago Herb Loaf (page 47)

Overleaf: (from left) Irish Freckle Bread (page 35), Christine's Fruited Pumpernickel (page 42), Brown Seed Bread (page 102) and Pumpernickel Turban (page 232)

Sally Lunn Bread

Here's an updated version of Grandma's favorite. This rich butter-and-egg bread is traditionally made in a ring mold and served hot from the oven.

Tips

Use large eggs straight from the refrigerator for bread machine recipes. Warm the milk to room temperature before adding.

Recipes containing eggs, milk and butter should not be baked using the timer.

Yes, you're reading it right: The 1.5 lb (750 g) recipe contains *more* yeast than the 2 lb (1 kg).

Variation

Substitute ⅓ cup (75 mL) buttermilk powder and 1 cup (250 mL) water for every cup of milk required in the recipe.

1.5 LB (750 G)		
1 cup	milk (room temperature)	250 mL
1	egg	1
¾ tsp	salt	3 mL
3 tbsp	granulated sugar	45 mL
2 tbsp	butter	25 mL
3¼ cups	all-purpose flour or bread flour	800 mL
1 tsp	bread machine yeast	5 mL

2 LB (1 KG) • extra large		
1¼ cups	milk (room temperature)	300 mL
1	egg	1
1¼ tsp	salt	6 mL
¼ cup	granulated sugar	50 mL
3 tbsp	butter	45 mL
3½ cups	all-purpose flour or bread flour	875 mL
¾ tsp	bread machine yeast	4 mL

1. Measure ingredients into baking pan in the order recommended by the manufacturer. Insert pan into the oven chamber.
2. Select **Sweet Cycle**.

Chunky Chili Cornbread (page 51)

Spelt Bread

Tips

Although spelt contains gluten, it is tolerated by many "wheat sensitive" people.

This recipe is based on using light spelt flour. If you want to use the dark variety, increase yeast by ¼ tsp (1 mL). The loaf is shorter and finer textured.

Yes, you're reading it right: The 1.5 lb (750 g) recipe contains *more* yeast than the 2 lb (1 kg).

Variation

For added texture and flavor, add ½ cup (125 mL) of flaxseeds or toasted almonds.

1.5 LB (750 G)		
½ cup	water	125 mL
½ cup	unsweetened apple juice	125 mL
2	eggs	2
1½ tsp	salt	7 mL
2 tbsp	packed brown sugar	25 mL
1 tbsp	vegetable oil	15 mL
3 cups	light spelt flour (see Tip, at left)	750 mL
⅓ cup	cornmeal	75 mL
1¼ tsp	bread machine yeast	6 mL

2 LB (1 KG)		
⅔ cup	water	150 mL
⅔ cup	unsweetened apple juice	150 mL
2	eggs	2
1¾ tsp	salt	8 mL
3 tbsp	packed brown sugar	45 mL
2 tbsp	vegetable oil	25 mL
4 cups	light spelt flour (see Tip, at left)	1000 mL
½ cup	cornmeal	125 mL
¾ tsp	bread machine yeast	4 mL

1. Measure ingredients into baking pan in the order recommended by the manufacturer. Insert pan into the oven chamber.
2. Select **Basic Cycle.**

Maritime Brown Bread

What would Saturday night be on the east coast of North America without molasses-flavored baked beans and brown bread? Try our updated version for your bread machine.

Tip

Store molasses in the refrigerator. Microwave a few seconds before using for easier measuring.

Variation

Another regional treasure, maple syrup, can be substituted for the molasses to provide sweetness in either the beans or the brown bread. Or use a combination of both.

1.5 LB (750 G)		
1 1/4 cups	water	300 mL
1/4 cup	skim milk powder	50 mL
1 1/4 tsp	salt	6 mL
2 tbsp	packed brown sugar	25 mL
1 tbsp	molasses	15 mL
2 tbsp	shortening or vegetable oil	25 mL
2 cups	whole wheat flour	500 mL
1 cup	all-purpose flour or bread flour	250 mL
1 tsp	bread machine yeast	5 mL

2 LB (1 KG)		
1 1/2 cups	water	375 mL
1/4 cup	skim milk powder	50 mL
1 1/2 tsp	salt	7 mL
1/4 cup	packed brown sugar	50 mL
2 tbsp	molasses	25 mL
2 tbsp	shortening or vegetable oil	25 mL
2 1/2 cups	whole wheat flour	625 mL
1 1/2 cups	all-purpose flour or bread flour	375 mL
1 1/4 tsp	bread machine yeast	6 mL

1. Measure ingredients into baking pan in the order recommended by the manufacturer. Insert pan into the oven chamber.

2. Select **Whole Wheat Cycle**.

New England Anadama Bread

Tip

Before measuring the molasses, dip the measuring spoon into hot water.

Variation

This loaf has a strong molasses flavor. For a milder flavor, substitute 1 tbsp (15 mL) brown sugar for 1 tbsp (15 mL) of the molasses.

1.5 LB (750 G)		
1 1/4 cups	water	300 mL
1/4 cup	skim milk powder	50 mL
1 tsp	salt	5 mL
3 tbsp	molasses	40 mL
2 tbsp	shortening or vegetable oil	25 mL
3 cups	all-purpose flour or bread flour	750 mL
1/3 cup	cornmeal	75 mL
1 1/4 tsp	bread machine yeast	6 mL

2 LB (1 KG)		
1 1/2 cups	water	375 mL
1/4 cup	skim milk powder	50 mL
1 1/2 tsp	salt	7 mL
1/4 cup	molasses	50 mL
2 tbsp	shortening or vegetable oil	25 mL
3 1/2 cups	all-purpose flour or bread flour	875 mL
1/2 cup	cornmeal	125 mL
1 1/2 tsp	bread machine yeast	7 mL

1. Measure ingredients into baking pan in the order recommended by the manufacturer. Insert pan into the oven chamber.

2. Select **Basic Cycle**.

Using the Rapid One-Hour and Seventy-Minute Basic Cycles

Yeast bread normally requires 3 to 4 hours to produce a soft, even-textured loaf. The new "Rapid Cycles" available on many bread machines today allow you to accelerate the process.

Preparing bread in less time means decreasing the kneading and proofing times, as well as increasing the proofing and baking temperatures. As a result, the loaf is shorter and denser. The loaf may have a thicker, smoother crust with a lengthwise crack on the top. The texture may be similar to a pound cake — uneven, with some large holes.

For successful rapid baking, follow these helpful suggestions:

- Heat the water to 125°F (55°C).

- Warm the eggs to room temperature by covering with warm (not hot) water for up to 5 minutes.

- Have all remaining ingredients at room temperature.

- As soon as you start the bread machine, scrape the sides and bottom of the bread pan with a rubber or plastic spatula. Continue to scrape until all the dry ingredients are mixed in.

- Slash the top crust once it has started to bake. There should be approximately 40 minutes (display window reads 0:40) left on the program. This allows any one-hour loaf to rise higher, resulting in an improved interior texture and crust.

San Francisco Firehouse Bread

Tip

Use triple the amount of fresh herbs for dried. Wash and dry well before snipping with kitchen shears.

Yes, you're reading it right: The 1.5 lb (750 g) recipe contains *more* yeast than the 2 lb (1 kg).

Variation

Substitute different herbs — try summer savory, purple basil and a variegated thyme.

1.5 LB (750 G)		
1 cup	evaporated milk	250 mL
1/2 cup	water	125 mL
1 1/4 tsp	salt	6 mL
3 tbsp	granulated sugar	45 mL
2 tbsp	vegetable oil	25 mL
2 cups	whole wheat flour	500 mL
1 cup	all-purpose flour or bread flour	250 mL
1/3 cup	cornmeal	75 mL
2 tbsp	minced dried onion	25 mL
1 tbsp	dried parsley	15 mL
1 1/4 tsp	dried rubbed sage	6 mL
1 tsp	dried dillweed	5 mL
1 1/2 tsp	bread machine yeast	7 mL

2 LB (1 KG)		
1	can (13 oz/385 mL) evaporated milk	1
3/4 cup	water	175 mL
1 1/2 tsp	salt	7 mL
1/4 cup	granulated sugar	50 mL
3 tbsp	vegetable oil	45 mL
2 1/4 cups	whole wheat flour	550 mL
1 1/2 cups	all-purpose flour or bread flour	375 mL
1/2 cup	cornmeal	125 mL
3 tbsp	minced dried onion	45 mL
1 tbsp	dried parsley	15 mL
1 3/4 tsp	dried rubbed sage	8 mL
1 1/4 tsp	dried dillweed	6 mL
1 tsp	bread machine yeast	5 mL

1. Measure ingredients into baking pan in the order recommended by the manufacturer. Insert pan into the oven chamber.

2. Select **Whole Wheat Cycle**.

The Sweet Cycle

The **Sweet** or **Fruit/Nut Cycle** has a lower baking temperature than the **Basic** or **Whole Wheat** cycles because loaves high in sugar and fat bake darker crusts than those high in grains or white flour. Included in this category are ingredients that add fat and sugar, such as cheese, eggs, roasted garlic, candied dried mixed peel and large amounts of molasses, honey or buttermilk powder. Recipes using soy flour and ground flaxseed also bake darker crusts.

If your bread machine doesn't have a **Sweet Cycle**, select the **Basic Cycle** and a light crust setting. Most Sweet cycles have an "add ingredient" signal that beeps 5 minutes before the end of the last long knead to indicate when to add the fruit or nuts. If your machine doesn't have this signal, look in the manual that came with your machine for the length of the kneading time and set a timer for 5 minutes before the end of it. Add the fruit at that time. If added too early, fruit will break up; if added too late, it will remain on the outside and burn.

The dough balls for sweet loaves are softer, so fruit will mix in — in fact, some doughs, such as that for *Italian Panettone* (see page 253), are almost soupy in texture. Don't adjust the dough ball by adding more flour or the large amounts of fruit will not mix in to distribute evenly. If some dry ingredients remain in the corners after the mixing and kneading stages, just mix them in with a rubber spatula when you add the fruit.

California Garlic with Sun-Dried Tomatoes

There's nothing timid about the flavor of this full-bodied bread. It's perfect with a bean casserole or summer soup.

Tips

For a richer tomato color, add the snipped sun-dried tomatoes to the water.

Use dry (not oil-packed) sun-dried tomatoes.

See the Techniques Glossary (page 369) for instructions on roasting garlic.

Yes, you're reading it right: The 1.5 lb (750 g) recipe contains the *same* amount of yeast as the 2 lb (1 kg).

Variation

For stronger garlic flavor, use fresh instead of roasted garlic.

1.5 LB (750 G)		
1 1/2 cups	tomato-vegetable juice (room temperature)	375 mL
1/3 cup	snipped sun-dried tomatoes	75 mL
3	cloves roasted garlic	3
1 1/2 tsp	salt	7 mL
2 tbsp	granulated sugar	25 mL
2 tbsp	olive oil	25 mL
3 1/2 cups	all-purpose flour or bread flour	875 mL
1 tbsp	dried basil	15 mL
1 1/2 tsp	bread machine yeast	7 mL

2 LB (1 KG)		
1 3/4 cups	tomato-vegetable juice (room temperature)	425 mL
1/2 cup	snipped sun-dried tomatoes	125 mL
4	cloves roasted garlic	4
1 3/4 tsp	salt	8 mL
3 tbsp	granulated sugar	45 mL
2 tbsp	olive oil	25 mL
4 cups	all-purpose flour or bread flour	1000 mL
2 tbsp	dried basil	25 mL
1 1/2 tsp	bread machine yeast	7 mL

1. Measure ingredients into baking pan in the order recommended by the manufacturer. Insert pan into the oven chamber.

2. Select **Basic Cycle**.

Tex-Mex Bread with Monterey Jack and Chilies

The unique blend of savory, smoke and spices make this loaf a perfect accompaniment to homemade stew on a cold winter's night.

Tips

Be sure to cook bacon until crisp, then drain on a paper towel.

Serve yogurt as an accompaniment to cool the palate.

Variation

To increase the heat of the loaf, add hot pepper sauce or crushed red chili peppers.

1.5 LB (750 G)		
1 cup	water	250 mL
¼ cup	chopped canned green chilies	50 mL
½ tsp	salt	2 mL
1 tbsp	granulated sugar	15 mL
3½ cups	all-purpose flour or bread flour	875 mL
½ cup	shredded Monterey Jack cheese	125 mL
4	slices crisp bacon, crumbled	4
¾ tsp	bread machine yeast	4 mL

2 LB (1 KG)		
1¼ cups	water	300 mL
⅓ cup	chopped canned green chilies	75 mL
1 tsp	salt	5 mL
1 tbsp	granulated sugar	15 mL
3¾ cups	all-purpose flour or bread flour	950 mL
½ cup	shredded Monterey Jack cheese	125 mL
6	slices crisp bacon, crumbled	6
1 tsp	bread machine yeast	5 mL

1. Measure ingredients into baking pan in the order recommended by the manufacturer. Insert pan into the oven chamber.
2. Select **Sweet Cycle**.

English Muffin Loaf

Enjoy the texture of an English muffin, but not the work of cutting and grilling the small rounds? Just bake this loaf and toast each slice.

Tip

This recipe bakes an extra-large loaf — try the 1.5 lb (750 g) recipe first.

Variation

Substitute 1 cup (250 mL) wheat blend flour for an equal amount of white flour.

1.5 LB (750 G)		
³⁄₄ cup	milk (room temperature)	175 mL
2	eggs	2
1 tsp	salt	5 mL
2 tbsp	granulated sugar	25 mL
2 tbsp	shortening or vegetable oil	25 mL
2¹⁄₂ cups	all-purpose flour or bread flour	625 mL
1¹⁄₄ tsp	bread machine yeast	6 mL

2 LB (1 KG) • extra large		
1 cup	milk (room temperature)	250 mL
2	eggs	2
1¹⁄₄ tsp	salt	6 mL
2 tbsp	granulated sugar	25 mL
2 tbsp	shortening or vegetable oil	25 mL
3 cups	all-purpose flour or bread flour	750 mL
1¹⁄₂ tsp	bread machine yeast	7 mL

1. Measure ingredients into baking pan in the order recommended by the manufacturer. Insert pan into the oven chamber.
2. Select **Basic Cycle**.

Irish Freckle Bread

1.5 LB (750 G)		
1 1/4 cups	water	300 mL
1 1/2 tsp	salt	7 mL
2 tbsp	granulated sugar	25 mL
2 tbsp	shortening or vegetable oil	25 mL
2 1/2 cups	all-purpose flour or bread flour	625 mL
1/3 cup	buttermilk powder	75 mL
1/4 tsp	baking soda	1 mL
2 tsp	caraway seeds	10 mL
1 3/4 tsp	bread machine yeast	8 mL
1/2 cup	raisins	125 mL

2 LB (1 KG)		
1 1/2 cups	water	375 mL
1 3/4 tsp	salt	8 mL
3 tbsp	granulated sugar	45 mL
2 tbsp	shortening or vegetable oil	25 mL
3 1/2 cups	all-purpose flour or bread flour	850 mL
1/2 cup	buttermilk powder	125 mL
1/4 tsp	baking soda	1 mL
1 tbsp	caraway seeds	15 mL
1 1/2 tsp	bread machine yeast	7 mL
3/4 cup	raisins	175 mL

1. Measure all ingredients *except raisins* into baking pan in the order recommended by the manufacturer. Insert pan into the oven chamber.
2. Select **Basic Cycle**.
3. Add raisins at the "add ingredient" signal.

Mediterranean Bread

This soft-textured loaf is packed with all the great flavors of Mediterranean cuisine: garlic, olives, feta cheese and oregano.

Tips

To save time, buy pitted, sliced Kalamata olives.

Be sure the feta cheese is well drained before crumbling.

Yes, you're reading it right: The 1.5 lb (750 g) recipe contains the *same* amount of yeast as the 2 lb (1 kg).

Variation

Substitute 3 tbsp (45 mL) fresh basil for the oregano.

1.5 LB (750 G)		
1 cup	water	250 mL
1/3 cup	crumbled feta cheese	75 mL
3	cloves garlic, minced	3
1 1/4 tsp	salt	6 mL
1 tbsp	liquid honey	15 mL
1 tbsp	olive oil	15 mL
3 1/2 cups	all-purpose flour or bread flour	875 mL
1/2 cup	sliced Kalamata olives	125 mL
2 tsp	dried oregano	10 mL
3/4 tsp	bread machine yeast	4 mL

2 LB (1 KG)		
1 1/4 cups	water	300 mL
1/2 cup	crumbled feta cheese	125 mL
4	cloves garlic, minced	4
1 1/2 tsp	salt	7 mL
1 tbsp	liquid honey	15 mL
2 tbsp	olive oil	25 mL
4 cups	all-purpose flour or bread flour	1000 mL
3/4 cup	sliced Kalamata olives	175 mL
1 tbsp	dried oregano	15 mL
3/4 tsp	bread machine yeast	4 mL

1. Measure ingredients into baking pan in the order recommended by the manufacturer. Insert pan into the oven chamber.
2. Select **Basic Cycle**.

Apple Yam Loaf

1.5 LB (750 G)		
¹⁄₂ cup	unsweetened apple juice	125 mL
¹⁄₂ cup	canned yams, well-drained and chopped	125 mL
1	medium apple, shredded or chopped	1
1¹⁄₄ tsp	salt	6 mL
2 tbsp	butter	25 mL
3¹⁄₂ cups	all-purpose flour or bread flour	875 mL
1¹⁄₄ tsp	bread machine yeast	7 mL

2 LB (1 KG) • extra large		
²⁄₃ cup	unsweetened apple juice	150 mL
²⁄₃ cup	canned yams, well-drained and chopped	150 mL
1	medium apple, shredded or chopped	1
1¹⁄₂ tsp	salt	7 mL
2 tbsp	butter	25 mL
3³⁄₄ cups	all-purpose flour or bread flour	925 mL
1¹⁄₂ tsp	bread machine yeast	7 mL

1. Measure ingredients into baking pan in the order recommended by the manufacturer. Insert pan into the oven chamber.
2. Select **Sweet Cycle**.

Cinnamon Apple Oat

The traditional flavor duo of apples and cinnamon combines here with heart–healthy oats and oat bran.

Tip

Use small- or medium-flaked, regular or quick-cooking oats, but not the "instant" variety.

Yes, you're reading it right: The 1.5 lb (750 g) recipe contains *more* yeast than the 2 lb (1 kg).

Variation

Substitute a shredded or chopped small apple for the unsweetened applesauce.

1.5 LB (750 G)

1/3 cup	water	75 mL
2/3 cup	unsweetened apple juice	150 mL
1/3 cup	unsweetened applesauce	75 mL
1 1/2 tsp	salt	7 mL
3 tbsp	liquid honey	45 mL
2 tbsp	shortening or vegetable oil	25 mL
2 3/4 cups	all-purpose flour or bread flour	675 mL
1/3 cup	quick-cooking oats	75 mL
1/4 cup	oat bran	50 mL
1 1/2 tsp	ground cinnamon	7 mL
2 tsp	bread machine yeast	10 mL

2 LB (1 KG) • extra large

1/2 cup	water	125 mL
3/4 cup	unsweetened apple juice	175 mL
1/2 cup	unsweetened applesauce	125 mL
1 1/2 tsp	salt	7 mL
1/4 cup	liquid honey	50 mL
2 tbsp	shortening or vegetable oil	25 mL
3 1/2 cups	all-purpose flour or bread flour	875 mL
1/2 cup	quick-cooking oats	125 mL
1/3 cup	oat bran	75 mL
2 tsp	ground cinnamon	10 mL
1 1/2 tsp	bread machine yeast	7 mL

1. Measure ingredients into baking pan in the order recommended by the manufacturer. Insert pan into the oven chamber.
2. Select **Basic Cycle**.

Whole Wheat Applesauce Loaf

1.5 LB (750 G)		
1 1/4 cups	unsweetened applesauce (room temperature)	300 mL
1	egg	1
1 1/2 tsp	salt	7 mL
2 tbsp	packed brown sugar	25 mL
1 tbsp	molasses	15 mL
2 tbsp	vegetable oil	25 mL
3 cups	whole wheat flour	750 mL
1 tsp	ground ginger	5 mL
1 1/2 tsp	bread machine yeast	7 mL
2/3 cup	raisins	150 mL

2 LB (1 KG)		
1 1/2 cups	unsweetened applesauce (room temperature)	375 mL
1	egg	1
1 1/2 tsp	salt	7 mL
3 tbsp	packed brown sugar	45 mL
1 tbsp	molasses	15 mL
3 tbsp	vegetable oil	45 mL
3 1/2 cups	whole wheat flour	875 mL
1 1/2 tsp	ground ginger	7 mL
1 1/2 tsp	bread machine yeast	7 mL
3/4 cup	raisins	175 mL

1. Measure all ingredients *except raisins* into baking pan in the order recommended by the manufacturer. Insert pan into the oven chamber.
2. Select **Whole Wheat Cycle**.
3. Add raisins at "add ingredient" signal. (See Tip, at left, if your machine does not have this signal on the **Whole Wheat Cycle**.)

Carrot Pineapple Bread

Your child won't eat veggies? Spread this slightly sweet bread with peanut butter. You'll be asked for seconds.

Tip

Use unsweetened pineapple tidbits packed in pineapple juice (not syrup). A 19-oz (540 mL) can contains approximately 2 cups (500 mL).

Yes, you're reading it right: The 1.5 lb (750 g) recipe contains *more* yeast than the 2 lb (1 kg).

Variation

For an extra burst of flavor, add 1 to 2 tsp (5 to 10 mL) orange zest.

1.5 LB (750 G)		
1 cup	shredded carrots	250 mL
$1/2$ cup	pineapple tidbits, juice reserved	125 mL
$1/2$ cup	pineapple juice (drained from tidbits)	125 mL
$1/4$ cup	skim milk powder	50 mL
$1 1/4$ tsp	salt	6 mL
3 tbsp	granulated sugar	45 mL
1 tbsp	vegetable oil	15 mL
3 cups	all purpose flour or bread flour	750 mL
2 tsp	bread machine yeast	10 mL

2 LB (1 KG) • extra large		
$1 1/4$ cups	shredded carrots	300 mL
$3/4$ cup	pineapple tidbits, juice reserved	175 mL
$1/2$ cup	pineapple juice (drained from tidbits)	125 mL
$1/3$ cup	skim milk powder	75 mL
$1 1/2$ tsp	salt	7 mL
$1/4$ cup	granulated sugar	50 mL
2 tbsp	vegetable oil	25 mL
4 cups	all purpose flour or bread flour	1000 mL
$1 3/4$ tsp	bread machine yeast	8 mL

1. Measure ingredients into baking pan in the order recommended by the manufacturer. Insert pan into the oven chamber.

2. Select **Basic Cycle**.

Sour Cherry Almond Loaf

Nuggets of dried sour cherries and slivered almonds give this loaf a festive appearance.

Tip

Toast the almonds on a baking sheet in a 350°F (180°C) oven for 10 minutes. Remove when lightly browned. The almonds will continue to darken as they cool.

Yes, you're reading it right: The 1.5 lb (750 g) recipe contains *more* yeast than the 2 lb (1 kg).

Variation

Other dried fruits — such as blueberries, cranberries, apples, raisins or apricots — may be used instead of cherries.

1.5 LB (750 G)		
1 1/4 cups	milk (room temperature)	300 mL
1/4 tsp	almond extract	1 mL
1	egg	1
1 1/2 tsp	salt	7 mL
1 tbsp	liquid honey	15 mL
1 tbsp	shortening or vegetable oil	15 mL
3 1/2 cups	all-purpose flour or bread flour	875 mL
1 1/2 tsp	bread machine yeast	7 mL
1/2 cup	dried sour red cherries	125 mL
1/2 cup	toasted slivered almonds	125 mL

2 LB (1 KG)		
1 1/3 cups	milk (room temperature)	325 mL
1/2 tsp	almond extract	2 mL
2	eggs	2
1 1/2 tsp	salt	7 mL
2 tbsp	liquid honey	25 mL
2 tbsp	shortening or vegetable oil	25 mL
3 3/4 cups	all-purpose flour or bread flour	950 mL
1 1/4 tsp	bread machine yeast	6 mL
2/3 cup	dried sour red cherries	150 mL
2/3 cup	toasted slivered almonds	150 mL

1. Measure all ingredients *except the sour cherries and toasted almonds* into baking pan in the order recommended by the manufacturer. Insert pan into the oven chamber.
2. Select **Sweet Cycle**.
3. Add the cherries and almonds at the "add ingredient" signal.

Christine's Fruited Pumpernickel

This rich, moist, black bread is a favorite of our 93-year-old, German-born neighbor, Christine Feenstra. With the sweetness of dates and apricots, it's perfect with fresh fruit and cheese for lunch.

Tip

If your machine does not have an "add ingredient" signal on the **Whole Wheat Cycle**, add the dates and dried apricots after the flour.

Variation

Substitute chopped prunes or figs for the dates and dried apples for the apricots.

1.5 LB (750 G)		
1 1/4 cups	water	300 mL
1 tbsp	vinegar	15 mL
1 1/4 tsp	salt	6 mL
1 tbsp	molasses	15 mL
1 tbsp	packed brown sugar	15 mL
2 tbsp	shortening or vegetable oil	25 mL
2 1/2 cups	all-purpose flour or bread flour	625 mL
1/2 cup	rye flour	125 mL
2 tsp	unsweetened cocoa powder	10 mL
2 tsp	instant coffee granules	10 mL
1/2 tsp	ground ginger	2 mL
1 1/2 tsp	bread machine yeast	7 mL
1/3 cup	quartered dried apricots	75 mL
1/3 cup	whole pitted dates	75 mL

2 LB (1 KG)		
1 1/2 cups	water	375 mL
2 tbsp	vinegar	25 mL
1 1/2 tsp	salt	7 mL
2 tbsp	molasses	25 mL
1 tbsp	packed brown sugar	15 mL
3 tbsp	shortening or vegetable oil	45 mL
3 cups	all-purpose flour or bread flour	750 mL
3/4 cup	rye flour	175 mL
1 tbsp	unsweetened cocoa powder	15 mL
1 tbsp	instant coffee granules	15 mL
1 tsp	ground ginger	5 mL
1 3/4 tsp	bread machine yeast	8 mL
1/2 cup	quartered dried apricots	125 mL
1/2 cup	whole pitted dates	125 mL

1. Measure all ingredients *except apricots and dates* into baking pan in the order recommended by the manufacturer. Insert pan into the oven chamber.
2. Select **Whole Wheat Cycle**.
3. Add the apricots and dates at the "add ingredient" signal.

Using the Timer

Imagine waking up to the smell of fresh-baked bread or returning home after a hard day to the enticing aroma of hot bread. With the use of the timer, you can! Most bread machines available today allow you to delay the start of the cycle.

Avoid recipes that use perishable foods stored in the refrigerator such as fluid milk, eggs, butter, cheese, yogurt, sour cream or meats. Substitute skim milk or buttermilk powder for the fresh fluid products. No need to adjust the liquid. Add skim milk powder with the liquids, but add buttermilk powder with the dry ingredients — it lumps if added with the liquids.

Avoid the "add ingredient" signal. Instead, use the whole fruit or nut, rather than chopped, and measure it on top of the flour. Dates, walnuts, pecans, dried blueberries and dried cranberries are better choices than raisins and currants.

Make a well in the flour and measure the yeast into the well to ensure it doesn't get wet until the mixing begins. Spread the flour into the corners of the baking pan before measuring in multigrain cereal, cracked wheat, buttermilk powder, bulgur, wheat or oat bran, oatmeal, fruit or vegetables. These should not become moist before the bread machine starts to mix and knead, or the loaf will be short and heavy.

For more information, consult your manual for the manufacturer's instructions.

Cheesy Potato Loaf

Tip

For cheese
weight/volume
equivalents, see
Ingredient Glossary
(page 360).

Variation

Substitute Monterey
Jack, Swiss, Parmesan,
Romano or a mixture
of these cheeses for
the Cheddar.

1.5 LB (750 G)		
1$\frac{1}{3}$ cups	water	325 mL
$\frac{1}{4}$ cup	skim milk powder	50 mL
1$\frac{1}{4}$ tsp	salt	6 mL
2 tbsp	granulated sugar	25 mL
2$\frac{3}{4}$ cups	all-purpose flour or bread flour	675 mL
$\frac{1}{3}$ cup	instant potato flakes	75 mL
$\frac{3}{4}$ cup	shredded old Cheddar cheese	175 mL
$\frac{1}{4}$ tsp	dry mustard powder	1 mL
1 tsp	bread machine yeast	5 mL

2 LB (1 KG)		
1$\frac{2}{3}$ cups	water	400 mL
$\frac{1}{3}$ cup	skim milk powder	75 mL
1$\frac{1}{2}$ tsp	salt	7 mL
3 tbsp	granulated sugar	45 mL
3$\frac{1}{4}$ cups	all-purpose flour or bread flour	800 mL
$\frac{1}{2}$ cup	instant potato flakes	125 mL
1 cup	shredded old Cheddar cheese	250 mL
$\frac{1}{2}$ tsp	dry mustard powder	2 mL
1$\frac{1}{4}$ tsp	bread machine yeast	6 mL

1. Measure ingredients into baking pan in the order recommended by the manufacturer. Insert pan into the oven chamber.

2. Select **Basic Cycle**.

Cheddar Beer Bread

Is there a cheese lover who doesn't enjoy the combination of cheese and beer? What a perfect loaf!

Tip

Add 1/4 tsp (1 mL) dry mustard powder to sharpen the cheese flavor.

Variation

Replace beer with an equal amount of water or "lite" beer.

1.5 LB (750 G)		
1 1/4 cups	beer	300 mL
1 1/4 tsp	salt	6 mL
2 tbsp	granulated sugar	25 mL
3 cups	all-purpose flour or bread flour	750 mL
1/3 cup	buttermilk powder	75 mL
1/2 cup	shredded old Cheddar cheese	125 mL
2 tbsp	grated Parmesan cheese	25 mL
1 1/4 tsp	bread machine yeast	6 mL

2 LB (1 KG)		
1 1/2 cups	beer	375 mL
1 1/2 tsp	salt	7 mL
2 tbsp	granulated sugar	25 mL
3 1/2 cups	all-purpose flour or bread flour	950 mL
1/2 cup	buttermilk powder	125 mL
3/4 cup	shredded old Cheddar cheese	175 mL
1/4 cup	grated Parmesan cheese	50 mL
1 1/2 tsp	bread machine yeast	7 mL

1. Measure ingredients into baking pan in the order recommended by the manufacturer. Insert pan into the oven chamber.
2. Select **Sweet Cycle**.

Jalapeño Cheese Bread

1.5 LB (750 G)

1 1/4 cups	water	300 mL
1/2 tsp	hot pepper sauce	2 mL
1/4 cup	skim milk powder	50 mL
1 1/2 tsp	salt	7 mL
1 tbsp	granulated sugar	15 mL
3 1/4 cups	all-purpose flour or bread flour	800 mL
3/4 cup	cornmeal	175 mL
2 tsp	crushed dried jalapeño peppers	10 mL
1/2 cup	shredded old Cheddar cheese	125 mL
1 1/4 tsp	bread machine yeast	6 mL

2 LB (1 KG)

1 1/3 cups	water	325 mL
1 tsp	hot pepper sauce	5 mL
1/4 cup	skim milk powder	50 mL
1 1/2 tsp	salt	7 mL
2 tbsp	granulated sugar	25 mL
3 1/2 cups	all-purpose flour or bread flour	875 mL
1 cup	cornmeal	250 mL
1 tbsp	crushed dried jalapeño peppers	15 mL
2/3 cup	shredded old Cheddar cheese	150 mL
1 1/2 tsp	bread machine yeast	7 mL

1. Measure ingredients into baking pan in the order recommended by the manufacturer. Insert pan into the oven chamber.
2. Select **Sweet Cycle**.

Asiago Herb Loaf

The sweet aroma of this loaf baking will have you counting the minutes until you can slice it.

Tips

In all recipes calling for cheese, cut it into chunks or shred it. Chunks will melt during baking.

If you have leftovers, this loaf makes the tastiest croutons. Sprinkle over a green or Caesar salad.

1.5 LB (750 G)		
1 cup	water	250 mL
3/4 tsp	salt	4 mL
1 tbsp	granulated sugar	15 mL
3 cups	all-purpose flour or bread flour	750 mL
1/2 cup	Asiago cheese	125 mL
1 tsp	dried basil	5 mL
1 tsp	fennel seeds	5 mL
1 tsp	dried oregano	5 mL
1 1/4 tsp	bread machine yeast	6 mL

2 LB (1 KG)		
1 1/3 cups	water	325 mL
1 tsp	salt	5 mL
1 tbsp	granulated sugar	15 mL
4 cups	all-purpose flour or bread flour	1000 mL
3/4 cup	Asiago cheese	175 mL
1 1/2 tsp	dried basil	7 mL
1 1/2 tsp	fennel seeds	7 mL
1 1/2 tsp	dried oregano	7 mL
1 1/2 tsp	bread machine yeast	7 mL

1. Measure ingredients into baking pan in the order recommended by the manufacturer. Insert pan into the oven chamber.
2. Select **Sweet Cycle**.

Rosemary Caesar Bread

The robust flavor of fresh rosemary combined with the deep red of the tomato–vegetable juice will bring compliments every time.

Tips

Large amounts of liquids, such as tomato-vegetable juice, should be warmed to room temperature for higher, more open-textured loaves.

Use dry, not oil-packed, sun-dried tomatoes.

To soften sun-dried tomatoes, pour boiling water over them and let them soak for 10 minutes. Drain well and pat dry with a paper towel.

Variation

Substitute 1 to 2 tbsp (15 to 25 mL) garlic powder for the fresh rosemary. An equal amount of tomato juice can be substituted for the tomato-vegetable juice.

1.5 LB (750 G)		
1 1/4 cups	tomato-vegetable juice	300 mL
1 tbsp	granulated sugar	15 mL
1 tbsp	olive oil	15 mL
3 1/4 cups	all-purpose flour or bread flour	800 mL
1/3 cup	snipped sun-dried tomatoes	75 mL
1/4 cup	snipped fresh rosemary	50 mL
1/4 tsp	paprika	1 mL
1 1/4 tsp	bread machine yeast	6 mL

2 LB (1 KG)		
1 1/2 cups	tomato-vegetable juice	375 mL
2 tbsp	granulated sugar	25 mL
2 tbsp	olive oil	25 mL
3 1/2 cups	all-purpose flour or bread flour	875 mL
1/2 cup	snipped sun-dried tomatoes	125 mL
1/3 cup	snipped fresh rosemary	75 mL
1/2 tsp	paprika	3 mL
1 1/2 tsp	bread machine yeast	8 mL

1. Measure ingredients into baking pan in the order recommended by the manufacturer. Insert pan into the oven chamber.
2. Select **Basic Cycle**.

Carrot Lovers'
Poppy Seed Bread (page 74)

Pesto Loaf

Tips

For an authentic, zesty flavor, use Reggiano Parmesan. It costs more, but it's worth it.

Pesto sauce is made from basil and pine nuts. It is widely available in supermarkets.

Yes, you're reading it right: The 1.5 lb (750 g) recipe contains *more* yeast than the 2 lb (1 kg).

Variations

Add ⅓ to ½ cup (75 to 125 mL) pine nuts for an added crunch.

Use a combination of cheeses, such as Parmesan and Emmental. Keep the total volume of cheese the same.

Wild Rice and Cranberry Loaf (page 94)

1.5 LB (750 G)		
1¼ cups	water	300 mL
¼ cup	skim milk powder	50 mL
1½ tsp	salt	7 mL
2 tbsp	granulated sugar	25 mL
2 tbsp	pesto sauce	25 mL
3¾ cups	all-purpose flour or bread flour	925 mL
½ cup	grated Parmesan cheese	125 mL
1¾ tsp	bread machine yeast	8 mL

2 LB (1 KG) • extra large		
1½ cups	water	375 mL
⅓ cup	skim milk powder	75 mL
1¾ tsp	salt	8 mL
3 tbsp	granulated sugar	45 mL
3 tbsp	pesto sauce	45 mL
4¼ cups	all-purpose flour or bread flour	1050 mL
¾ cup	grated Parmesan cheese	175 mL
1½ tsp	bread machine yeast	7 mL

1. Measure ingredients into baking pan in the order recommended by the manufacturer. Insert pan into the oven chamber.
2. Select **French Cycle** or **Basic Cycle**.

Roasted Garlic Bread

Cloves of fresh garlic, roasted in the oven, give a sweet, mild garlic aroma and flavor to this loaf.

Tips

Use 2 drops of olive oil for each bulb when roasting garlic. Extra oil will cause the loaf to be short and dense. (To roast garlic, see Techniques Glossary, page 369).

Avoid the temptation to add more garlic, as it inhibits the yeast. Too much garlic and the loaf will be short and heavy.

Yes, you're reading it right: The 1.5 lb (750 g) recipe contains the *same* amount of yeast as the 2 lb (1 kg).

Variation

For a stronger, more prominent garlic flavor, serve toasted or warmed with either garlic butter or a garlic-flavored spread.

1.5 LB (750 G)

1 1/4 cups	water	300 mL
1/4 cup	skim milk powder	50 mL
1 tsp	salt	5 mL
2 tbsp	liquid honey	25 mL
2 tbsp	olive oil	25 mL
4	cloves roasted garlic	4
3 1/4 cups	all-purpose flour or bread flour	800 mL
3/4 tsp	bread machine yeast	4 mL

2 LB (1 KG)

1 1/2 cups	water	375 mL
1/4 cup	skim milk powder	50 mL
1 1/2 tsp	salt	8 mL
3 tbsp	liquid honey	45 mL
2 tbsp	olive oil	25 mL
6	cloves roasted garlic	6
3 3/4 cups	all-purpose flour or bread flour	950 mL
3/4 tsp	bread machine yeast	4 mL

1. Measure ingredients into baking pan in the order recommended by the manufacturer. Insert pan into the oven chamber.
2. Select **Sweet Cycle**.

Chunky Chili Cornbread

Summer brings juicy sweet ears of fresh corn to the farmers' market, but this loaf can be a year-round treasure.

Tips

Thaw the frozen corn kernels completely and drain well before adding.

The 2 lb (1 kg) recipe makes an extra large loaf. It can be baked in a 2.5 lb (1.25 kg) machine. If you have a smaller bread pan, prepare the 1.5 lb (750 g) recipe. (See chart, page 14.)

Variation

Replace frozen corn with leftover cooked corn sliced from the cob.

1.5 LB (750 G)		
1 1/4 cups	water	300 mL
1	egg	1
1/4 cup	skim milk powder	50 mL
1 tsp	salt	5 mL
2 tbsp	granulated sugar	25 mL
2 tbsp	shortening or vegetable oil	25 mL
3 cups	all-purpose flour or bread flour	750 mL
1/3 cup	cornmeal	75 mL
2/3 cup	thawed frozen corn kernels, well drained	150 mL
1 1/2 tsp	crushed red chili peppers	7 mL
1 tsp	bread machine yeast	5 mL

2 LB (1 KG) • extra large		
1 1/3 cups	water	325 mL
1	egg	1
1/4 cup	skim milk powder	50 mL
1 tsp	salt	5 mL
2 tbsp	granulated sugar	25 mL
2 tbsp	shortening or vegetable oil	25 mL
3 2/3 cups	all-purpose flour or bread flour	900 mL
2/3 cup	cornmeal	150 mL
3/4 cup	thawed frozen corn kernels, well drained	175 mL
2 tsp	crushed red chili peppers	10 mL
1 1/2 tsp	bread machine yeast	7 mL

1. Measure ingredients into baking pan in the order recommended by the manufacturer. Insert pan into the oven chamber.
2. Select **Basic Cycle**.

Green Peppercorn Mustard Rye

Tip

Do not substitute "Dijonnaise" for the Dijon mustard. It is a completely different product — and too high in fat.

Variation

Substitute an equal amount of tarragon mustard for the coarsely ground green peppercorn mustard.

1.5 LB (750 G)		
1 1/4 cups	water	300 mL
1/4 cup	green peppercorn mustard or Dijon mustard	50 mL
1/4 cup	skim milk powder	50 mL
1/2 tsp	salt	2 mL
1 tbsp	packed brown sugar	15 mL
2 tbsp	olive oil	25 mL
3/4 cup	whole wheat flour	175 mL
2 cups	all-purpose flour or bread flour	500 mL
2/3 cup	rye flour	150 mL
2 tsp	dill seeds	10 mL
1 1/4 tsp	bread machine yeast	6 mL

2 LB (1 KG)		
1 1/3 cups	water	325 mL
1/3 cup	green peppercorn mustard or Dijon mustard	75 mL
1/4 cup	skim milk powder	50 mL
3/4 tsp	salt	3 mL
2 tbsp	packed brown sugar	25 mL
2 tbsp	olive oil	25 mL
1 cup	whole wheat flour	250 mL
2 cups	all-purpose flour or bread flour	500 mL
3/4 cup	rye flour	200 mL
1 tbsp	dill seeds	15 mL
1 3/4 tsp	bread machine yeast	8 mL

1. Measure ingredients into baking pan in the order recommended by the manufacturer. Insert pan into the oven chamber.
2. Select **Whole Wheat Cycle**.

Honey Dijon with Bits of Bacon

A hint of sweet mustard contrasts with the savory, smoky bacon to give this loaf a unique flavor.

Tip

Cook the bacon in the microwave for a crisper texture. Drain it well on paper towels.

Yes, you're reading it right: The 1.5 lb (750 g) recipe contains the *same* amount of yeast as the 2 lb (1 kg).

Variation

Prepared mustard may be substituted for honey Dijon.

1.5 LB (750 G)		
1 1/4 cups	water	300 mL
2 tbsp	honey Dijon mustard	25 mL
1/4 cup	skim milk powder	50 mL
1 tsp	salt	5 mL
2 tbsp	liquid honey	25 mL
1 tbsp	shortening or vegetable oil	15 mL
3 cups	all-purpose flour or bread flour	750 mL
3	slices crisp bacon	3
3/4 tsp	bread machine yeast	3 mL

2 LB (1 KG) • extra large		
1 1/2 cups	water	375 mL
1/4 cup	honey Dijon mustard	50 mL
1/4 cup	skim milk powder	50 mL
1 1/4 tsp	salt	6 mL
2 tbsp	liquid honey	25 mL
1 tbsp	shortening or vegetable oil	15 mL
3 1/2 cups	all-purpose flour or bread flour	875 mL
4	slices crisp bacon	4
3/4 tsp	bread machine yeast	4 mL

1. Measure ingredients into baking pan in the order recommended by the manufacturer. Insert pan into the oven chamber.
2. Select **Sweet Cycle**.

Quick Poultry-Stuffing Loaf

*All the seasonings you
need are right in this
bread. No need to add
extra when preparing
the stuffing.*

Tip
The 1.5 lb (750 g)
loaf can be baked on
a **Rapid One-Hour
Basic Cycle**. The 2 lb
(1 kg) loaf is too large
to bake completely in
this shorter length
of time.

*Yes, you're reading it
right:* The 1.5 lb
(750 g) recipe contains
the *same* amount of
yeast as the 2 lb (1 kg).

Variation
To make croutons, cut
the bread into 1-inch
(2.5 cm) cubes, bake
and toss with a bowl
of crisp greens.

1 5 LB (750 G)		
1 1/4 cups	water	300 mL
1/4 cup	skim milk powder	50 mL
1 1/4 tsp	salt	6 mL
2 tbsp	granulated sugar	25 mL
2 tbsp	shortening or vegetable oil	25 mL
2 3/4 cups	all-purpose flour or bread flour	675 mL
2 tbsp	minced dried onion	25 mL
1 tbsp	dried parsley	15 mL
1 tbsp	dried rubbed sage	15 mL
1 tbsp	dried savory	15 mL
1 tsp	celery seeds	5 mL
1 tbsp	bread machine yeast	15 mL

2 LB (1 KG)		
1 1/3 cups	water	325 mL
1/3 cup	skim milk powder	75 mL
1 1/2 tsp	salt	7 mL
3 tbsp	granulated sugar	45 mL
2 tbsp	shortening or vegetable oil	25 mL
3 cups	all-purpose flour or bread flour	750 mL
3 tbsp	minced dried onion	45 mL
2 tbsp	dried parsley	25 mL
2 tbsp	dried rubbed sage	25 mL
2 tbsp	dried savory	25 mL
1 1/2 tsp	celery seeds	7 mL
1 tbsp	bread machine yeast	15 mL

1. Measure ingredients into baking pan in the order recommended by the manufacturer. Insert pan into the oven chamber.

2. Select **Rapid Two-Hour Basic Cycle**.

Everyone loves the soft texture of potato bread. This one includes the garnish in the loaf.

Tip

One medium potato yields approximately ³⁄₄ cup (175 mL) when baked and mashed. Do not add butter or salt when mashing.

Yes, you're reading it right: The 1.5 lb (750 g) recipe contains the *same* amount of yeast as the 2 lb (1 kg).

Variation

Substitute dried or fresh chives for the parsley, and ham for the bacon.

Twice-Baked Potato Bread

1.5 LB (750 G)		
1¹⁄₄ cups	water	300 mL
¹⁄₄ cup	skim milk powder	50 mL
1 tsp	salt	5 mL
3 tbsp	granulated sugar	45 mL
2³⁄₄ cups	all-purpose flour or bread flour	675 mL
³⁄₄ cup	mashed baked potato	175 mL
³⁄₄ cup	shredded old Cheddar cheese	175 mL
2 tbsp	snipped fresh parsley	25 mL
¹⁄₄ tsp	dry mustard	1 mL
4	slices crisp bacon, crumbled	4
³⁄₄ tsp	bread machine yeast	4 mL

2 LB (1 KG)		
1¹⁄₂ cups	water	375 mL
¹⁄₃ cup	skim milk powder	75 mL
1¹⁄₄ tsp	salt	6 mL
¹⁄₄ cup	granulated sugar	50 mL
3¹⁄₄ cups	all-purpose flour or bread flour	800 mL
1 cup	mashed baked potato	250 mL
1 cup	shredded old Cheddar cheese	250 mL
3 tbsp	snipped fresh parsley	45 mL
¹⁄₂ tsp	dry mustard	2 mL
6	slices crisp bacon, crumbled	6
³⁄₄ tsp	bread machine yeast	4 mL

1. Measure ingredients into baking pan in the order recommended by the manufacturer. Insert pan into the oven chamber.

2. Select **Basic Cycle**.

Mushroom Leek Bread

Looking for the perfect bread to serve with a summer salad? Look no further. This one's a crowd pleaser!

Tip

No need to wait for the sautéed mushrooms and leeks to cool. Add them immediately to the water in baking pan.

Variation

According to Donna's sister, Marilyn, this is the best loaf to cube or crumble for stuffing a boneless pork loin roast.

1.5 LB (750 G)		
2 tbsp	butter	25 mL
1 1/2 cups	sliced mushrooms	375 mL
1/2 cup	sliced leeks	125 mL
1 tsp	dried thyme	5 mL
1 1/4 cups	water	300 mL
1 1/4 tsp	salt	6 mL
1 tbsp	liquid honey	15 mL
1 cup	whole wheat flour	250 mL
2 1/4 cups	all-purpose flour or bread flour	550 mL
3/4 tsp	bread machine yeast	4 mL

2 LB (1 KG)		
2 tbsp	butter	25 mL
2 cups	sliced mushrooms	500 mL
3/4 cup	sliced leeks	175 mL
1 1/2 tsp	dried thyme	7 mL
1 1/3 cups	water	325 mL
1 1/2 tsp	salt	7 mL
2 tbsp	liquid honey	25 mL
1 1/4 cups	whole wheat flour	300 mL
3 cups	all-purpose flour or bread flour	750 mL
1 tsp	bread machine yeast	5 mL

1. In a saucepan, heat butter over medium-high heat. Add mushrooms, leeks and thyme; sauté just until tender. Immediately place in baking pan.

2. Measure remaining ingredients into baking pan in the order recommended by the manufacturer. Insert pan into the oven chamber.

3. Select **Basic Cycle**.

Lower-Fat
and Flavorful

Canada's Guidelines for Healthy Eating *recommends that we choose lower-fat foods more often. Bake these delicious breads containing little or no added fat.*

Flavor Enhancers for Lower-Fat Breads

Add any one of the following. Do not exceed the amounts suggested.

1/4 cup	minced dried onion	50 mL
1/4 cup	snipped sun-dried tomatoes (not oil-packed)	50 mL
1/4 cup	snipped fresh herbs such as parsley, basil, chives	50 mL
2 tbsp	orange zest	25 mL
2 tbsp	unsweetened applesauce	25 mL
2 tbsp	mashed overripe banana	25 mL
2 tbsp	shredded carrot	25 mL
2 tsp	lemon zest	10 mL
2 tsp	freshly squeezed lemon juice	10 mL

Buttermilk White Bread

The texture and flavor of this loaf reminds us of days gone by when Grandma baked her recipe for white bread.

Tip

Add the buttermilk powder after the flour. It clumps when added with the liquids.

Variation

If buttermilk powder is unavailable, substitute $1/4$ cup (50 mL) skim milk powder in either the 1.5 lb or 2 lb recipe.

1.5 LB (750 G)		
$1^1/_4$ cups	water	325 mL
$1^1/_4$ tsp	salt	6 mL
1 tbsp	granulated sugar	15 mL
1 tbsp	shortening or vegetable oil	15 mL
$3^1/_2$ cups	all-purpose flour or bread flour	875 mL
$^1/_3$ cup	buttermilk powder	75 mL
1 tsp	bread machine yeast	5 mL

2 LB (1 KG) • extra large		
$1^1/_2$ cups	water	375 mL
$1^1/_2$ tsp	salt	7 mL
2 tbsp	granulated sugar	25 mL
2 tbsp	shortening or vegetable oil	25 mL
$3^3/_4$ cups	all-purpose flour or bread flour	925 mL
$^1/_2$ cup	buttermilk powder	125 mL
$1^1/_4$ tsp	bread machine yeast	6 mL

1. Measure ingredients into baking pan in the order recommended by the manufacturer. Insert pan into the oven chamber.

2. Select **Basic Cycle**.

Buttermilk Cracked Wheat Loaf

A bit of tang, a soft texture and a nutty crunch — all rolled into one.

Tip

Despite its name, buttermilk is actually low in fat. It also adds tenderness to the crumb of this bread.

Variation

Substitute an equal amount of buttermilk for the water and omit the buttermilk powder.

1.5 LB (750 G)		
1¼ cups	water	300 mL
1¼ tsp	salt	6 mL
2 tbsp	liquid honey	25 mL
1 tbsp	shortening or vegetable oil	15 mL
1½ cups	whole wheat flour	375 mL
1¼ cups	all-purpose flour or bread flour	300 mL
¾ cup	cracked wheat	175 mL
⅓ cup	buttermilk powder	75 mL
1¼ tsp	bread machine yeast	6 mL

2 LB (1 KG) • extra large		
1½ cups	water	375 mL
1½ tsp	salt	7 mL
2 tbsp	liquid honey	25 mL
2 tbsp	shortening or vegetable oil	25 mL
1½ cups	whole wheat flour	375 mL
2 cups	all-purpose flour or bread flour	500 mL
¾ cup	cracked wheat	175 mL
½ cup	buttermilk powder	125 mL
1½ tsp	bread machine yeast	7 mL

1. Measure ingredients into baking pan in the order recommended by the manufacturer. Insert pan into the oven chamber.
2. Select **Whole Wheat Cycle**.

Seven-Grain Goodness Bread

Tips

Add applesauce and apple juice at room temperature for a lighter textured, higher loaf.

Store grains in an airtight container in the refrigerator or freezer and only purchase an amount you can use within 3 months.

Variation

Substitute 3-, 5-, 9- or 12-grain cereals.

1.5 LB (750 G)		
1 cup	unsweetened apple juice	250 mL
1/3 cup	unsweetened applesauce	75 mL
1 1/4 tsp	salt	6 mL
2 tbsp	liquid honey	25 mL
1 tbsp	shortening or vegetable oil	15 mL
1 cup	whole wheat flour	250 mL
2 cups	all-purpose flour or bread flour	500 mL
1/2 cup	7-grain cereal	125 mL
1/3 cup	buttermilk powder	75 mL
1 1/2 tsp	bread machine yeast	7 mL

2 LB (1 KG)		
1 1/4 cups	unsweetened apple juice	300 mL
1/2 cup	unsweetened applesauce	125 mL
1 1/2 tsp	salt	7 mL
2 tbsp	liquid honey	25 mL
1 tbsp	shortening or vegetable oil	15 mL
1 1/2 cups	whole wheat flour	375 mL
2 cups	all-purpose flour or bread flour	500 mL
3/4 cup	7-grain cereal	175 mL
1/2 cup	buttermilk powder	125 mL
1 3/4 tsp	bread machine yeast	8 mL

1. Measure ingredients into baking pan in the order recommended by the manufacturer. Insert pan into the oven chamber.
2. Select **Whole Wheat Cycle**.

French Bread

Enjoy the crisp crust and traditional texture of French bread for your dinner. No need to fuss with shaping it into a stick.

Tips

If your bread machine doesn't have a **French Cycle**, bake on the **Basic Cycle** with a dark crust setting.

When finished baking, remove immediately and serve the same day. Store in a paper bag, not plastic, to retain a crisp crust.

Yes, you're reading it right: The 1.5 lb (750 g) recipe contains the *same* amount of yeast as the 2 lb (1 kg).

Variation

Add 2 tbsp (25 mL) dried onion flakes for a French Onion Bread.

1.5 LB (750 G)		
1$\frac{1}{3}$ cups	water	325 mL
1$\frac{1}{2}$ tsp	salt	7 mL
1 tbsp	granulated sugar	15 mL
3$\frac{2}{3}$ cups	all-purpose flour or bread flour	825 mL
1$\frac{1}{4}$ tsp	bread machine yeast	6 mL

2 LB (1 KG) • extra large		
1$\frac{1}{2}$ cups	water	350 mL
1$\frac{1}{2}$ tsp	salt	7 mL
2 tbsp	granulated sugar	25 mL
4 cups	all-purpose flour or bread flour	950 mL
1$\frac{1}{4}$ tsp	bread machine yeast	6 mL

1. Measure ingredients into baking pan in the order recommended by the manufacturer. Insert pan into the oven chamber.
2. Select **French Cycle**.

Italian Herb Bread

The fragrant aroma of this loaf makes waiting to eat extremely difficult. Serve this zesty herb bread with any course — soup, salad or entrée.

Tip

Wash and dry the fresh herbs thoroughly before snipping with scissors. Pack firmly to measure.

Variation

Croutons made from this loaf complement any salad. Cut leftover bread into 1/2-inch (1 cm) cubes, toss with melted butter and toast until crisp and lightly browned.

1.5 LB (750 G)

1 1/4 cups	water	300 mL
1/4 cup	skim milk powder	50 mL
1 tsp	salt	5 mL
1 tbsp	granulated sugar	15 mL
1 tbsp	shortening or vegetable oil	15 mL
3 1/3 cups	all-purpose flour or bread flour	825 mL
1/4 cup	snipped fresh parsley	50 mL
1 tsp	dried basil	5 mL
1 tsp	dried marjoram	5 mL
1 tsp	dried thyme	5 mL
1 tsp	bread machine yeast	5 mL

2 LB (1 KG) • extra large

1 1/2 cups	water	350 mL
1/4 cup	skim milk powder	50 mL
1 1/2 tsp	salt	7 mL
2 tbsp	granulated sugar	25 mL
2 tbsp	shortening or vegetable oil	25 mL
4 cups	all-purpose flour or bread flour	1000 mL
1/3 cup	snipped fresh parsley	75 mL
1 1/4 tsp	dried basil	6 mL
1 1/4 tsp	dried marjoram	6 mL
1 1/4 tsp	dried thyme	6 mL
1 1/4 tsp	bread machine yeast	6 mL

1. Measure ingredients into baking pan in the order recommended by the manufacturer. Insert pan into the oven chamber.

2. Select **Basic Cycle**.

Quick Honey Flaxseed Bread

*This recipe can be made using either the **Rapid Two-Hour Basic Cycle** (this page) or the **Rapid One-Hour Basic Cycle** (facing page).*

Tips

There's no added fat in this recipe! The ground flaxseed keeps this bread moist.

Other recipes with no added fat include *Twelve-Grain Rolls* (see recipe, page 198), *Spinach Pitas* (see recipe, page 151) and *Sourdough Baguettes* (see recipe, page 183).

For instructions on grinding flaxseeds, see Techniques Glossary, page 368.

Yes, you're reading it right: The 1.5 lb (750 g) recipe contains the *same* amount of yeast as the 2 lb (1 kg).

1.5 LB (750 G)		
1¼ cups	water	300 mL
¼ cup	skim milk powder	50 mL
1¼ tsp	salt	6 mL
¼ cup	liquid honey	50 mL
3 cups	all-purpose flour or bread flour	750 mL
¾ cup	ground flaxseed	175 mL
2¼ tsp	bread machine yeast	11 mL

2 LB (1 KG)		
1⅔ cups	water	400 mL
⅓ cup	skim milk powder	75 mL
1½ tsp	salt	7 mL
¼ cup	liquid honey	50 mL
3¾ cups	all-purpose flour or bread flour	925 mL
1 cup	ground flaxseed	250 mL
2¼ tsp	bread machine yeast	11 mL

1. Measure ingredients into baking pan in the order recommended by the manufacturer. Insert pan into the oven chamber.
2. Select **Rapid Two-Hour Basic Cycle**.

See page 29 for
suggestions on using
the rapid one-hour
and seventy-minute
basic cycles.

For more information
on flaxseed, see
page 109.

RAPID ONE-HOUR BASIC RECIPE

1 ¼ cups	water (warmed to 125°F/55°C)	300 mL
¼ cup	skim milk powder	50 mL
1 ¼ tsp	salt	6 mL
¼ cup	liquid honey	50 mL
2 ¾ cups	all-purpose flour or bread flour	675 mL
½ cup	ground flaxseed	125 mL
2 tbsp	bread machine yeast	25 mL

1. Measure ingredients into baking pan in the order recommended by the manufacturer. Insert pan into the oven chamber.

2. Select **Rapid One-Hour Basic Cycle**.

3. When 40 minutes remain on the bread machine display window, take a lame or sharp knife and quickly slash the top diagonally.

Apple Cinnamon Sticky Buns

Tip

Choose Granny Smith or another quality baking apple for the filling.

Variations

Try this Cranberry-Orange Filling: Mix together 2 cups (500 mL) whole cranberry sauce and 1 tbsp (15 mL) orange zest.

Substitute raspberries for half the apples in the filling.

● *Two 8-inch (2 L) square baking pans, lightly greased*

¹/₂ cup	unsweetened applesauce	125 mL
¹/₂ cup	grated apple	125 mL
2	egg whites	2
¹/₂ tsp	salt	2 mL
3 tbsp	granulated sugar	45 mL
1 tbsp	shortening or vegetable oil	15 mL
1 cup	whole wheat flour	250 mL
2 cups	all-purpose flour or bread flour	500 mL
2 tsp	bread machine yeast	10 mL

APPLE CINNAMON FILLING

3 cups	coarsely chopped apples	750 mL
1 cup	raisins	250 mL
¹/₄ cup	liquid honey	50 mL
2 tsp	ground cinnamon	10 mL
1 tsp	ground nutmeg	5 mL

1. Measure ingredients into baking pan in the order recommended by the manufacturer. Insert pan into the oven chamber. Select **Dough Cycle**.

2. *Meanwhile, prepare the filling:* Gently combine the filling ingredients; set aside.

3. Remove prepared dough to a lightly floured board; cover with a large bowl and let rest for 10 to 15 minutes. Divide the dough in half. Roll out each into a 12- by 9-inch (30 by 23 cm) rectangle.

4. Spread half of the filling to within $1/2$ inch (1 cm) of the edges. Beginning at a long side, roll up jellyroll style. Pinch to seal the seam. Cut into 9 equal slices. Place cut-side up in prepared pan. Repeat with remaining half of the dough.

5. Cover pans and let dough rise in a warm, draft-free place for 30 to 45 minutes, or until doubled in volume. Meanwhile, preheat oven to 350°F (180°C).

6. Bake in preheated oven for 30 to 35 minutes, or until the buns sound hollow when tapped on the bottom. If necessary, cover loosely with foil for the last 10 to 15 minutes to prevent over-browning. Invert the buns onto a serving plate; carefully remove the pan.

Lowering the Fat
Without Losing the Flavor

- Substitute lower-fat cheeses, adding a dash of dry mustard in cheese breads.
- Replace sour cream with lower-fat yogurt.
- Use 2 egg whites instead of a whole egg.
- Substitute raisins, dried apricots, figs or dates for nuts and seeds.
- Replace 1 cup (250 mL) whole milk with $1/3$ cup (75 mL) buttermilk powder and 1 cup (250 mL) water.
- Spray baking pans with nonstick cooking spray instead of greasing with shortening, butter or margarine.
- Replace up to $1/4$ cup (50 mL) fat with an equal amount of unsweetened applesauce.
- Top bread slices with jam or lower-fat spreads instead of butter or margarine.

Cottage Cheese Dill Bread

In this light loaf, cottage cheese (naturally low in fat) replaces some of the fat in a traditional white bread.

Tip

Choose a creamy or small-curd cottage cheese for smoother blending. Read the label to select and identify the fat content of the cottage cheese you prefer.

Yes, you're reading it right: The 1.5 lb (750 g) recipe contains *more* yeast than the 2 lb (1 kg).

Variation

Substitute dill seeds for the fresh dill.

1.5 LB (750 G)		
1 1/4 cups	water	300 mL
1/3 cup	lower-fat cottage cheese	75 mL
1 1/4 tsp	salt	6 mL
1 tbsp	granulated sugar	15 mL
1 tbsp	shortening or vegetable oil	15 mL
3 1/2 cups	all-purpose flour or bread flour	875 mL
1 tbsp	snipped fresh dill	15 mL
1 1/2 tsp	bread machine yeast	7 mL

2 LB (1 KG) • extra large		
1 1/3 cups	water	325 mL
1/2 cup	lower-fat cottage cheese	125 mL
1 1/2 tsp	salt	7 mL
2 tbsp	granulated sugar	25 mL
2 tbsp	shortening or vegetable oil	25 mL
3 3/4 cups	all-purpose flour or bread flour	925 mL
2 tbsp	snipped fresh dill	25 mL
1 1/4 tsp	bread machine yeast	6 mL

1. Measure ingredients into baking pan in the order recommended by the manufacturer. Insert pan into the oven chamber.
2. Select **Basic Cycle**.

Yummy Yogurt Dill Loaf

Tried

1.5 LB (750 G)		
¼ cup	water	50 mL
1 cup	lower-fat yogurt	250 mL
2	egg whites	2
1½ tsp	salt	7 mL
3 tbsp	granulated sugar	45 mL
1 tbsp	vegetable oil	15 mL
3⅓ cups	all-purpose flour or bread flour	825 mL
2 tbsp	minced dried onion	25 mL
1 tbsp	dried dillweed	15 mL
1½ tsp	bread machine yeast	7 mL

2 LB (1 KG) • extra large		
¼ cup	water	50 mL
1¼ cups	lower-fat yogurt	300 mL
3	egg whites	3
1½ tsp	salt	7 mL
3 tbsp	granulated sugar	45 mL
1 tbsp	vegetable oil	15 mL
3½ cups	all-purpose flour or bread flour	875 mL
3 tbsp	minced dried onion	45 mL
1 tbsp	dried dillweed	15 mL
1½ tsp	bread machine yeast	7 mL

1. Measure ingredients into baking pan in the order recommended by the manufacturer. Insert pan into the oven chamber.
2. Select **Basic Cycle**.

Potato Chive Bread

This mild-flavored, even-textured loaf has been a baker's favorite for generations.

Tip

Use 2 tbsp (25 mL) dried chives for $^1/_3$ cup (75 mL) fresh and $^1/_4$ cup (50 mL) dried chives for $^2/_3$ cup (150 mL) fresh.

Yes, you're reading it right: The 1.5 lb (750 g) recipe contains the *same* amount of yeast as the 2 lb (1 kg).

Variation

Substitute mashed potatoes for the potato flakes. Do not add milk or butter when mashing the potatoes. Decrease the water by 2 tbsp (25 mL).

1.5 LB (750 G)

1$^1/_3$ cups	water	325 mL
$^1/_4$ cup	skim milk powder	50 mL
1$^1/_4$ tsp	salt	6 mL
1 tbsp	granulated sugar	15 mL
1 tbsp	vegetable oil	15 mL
3$^1/_4$ cups	all-purpose flour or bread flour	800 mL
$^1/_3$ cup	instant potato flakes	75 mL
$^1/_4$ cup	snipped fresh parsley	50 mL
$^1/_3$ cup	snipped fresh chives	75 mL
2 tsp	bread machine yeast	10 mL

2 LB (1 KG)

1$^1/_2$ cups	water	375 mL
$^1/_4$ cup	skim milk powder	50 mL
1$^1/_2$ tsp	salt	7 mL
2 tbsp	granulated sugar	25 mL
1 tbsp	vegetable oil	15 mL
3$^1/_4$ cups	all-purpose flour or bread flour	800 mL
$^1/_2$ cup	instant potato flakes	125 mL
$^1/_3$ cup	snipped fresh parsley	75 mL
$^2/_3$ cup	snipped fresh chives	150 mL
2 tsp	bread machine yeast	10 mL

1. Measure ingredients into baking pan in the order recommended by the manufacturer. Insert pan into the oven chamber.
2. Select **Rapid Two-Hour Basic Cycle.**

Vegetable Tarragon Wheat Bread

Fresh tarragon gives this loaf its sweet flavor.

Tips

If fresh tarragon is unavailable, use 2 to 3 tsp (10 to 15 mL) dried tarragon leaves.

Use an individual serving size of instant vegetable soup mix.

Yes, you're reading it right: The 1.5 lb (750 g) recipe contains the *same* amount of yeast as the 2 lb (1 kg).

Variation

Substitute basil for the tarragon. It makes an equally delicious loaf. For a more subtle flavor, use dill or parsley.

1.5 LB (750 G)		
1 cup	water	250 mL
$1/4$ tsp	orange extract	1 mL
$1/4$ cup	skim milk powder	50 mL
$1 1/4$ tsp	salt	6 mL
2 tbsp	liquid honey	25 mL
1 tbsp	vegetable oil	15 mL
1 cup	whole wheat flour	250 mL
$1 3/4$ cups	all-purpose flour or bread flour	425 mL
$1/2$ cup	cracked wheat	125 mL
$3/4$ cup	shredded carrots	175 mL
2 tbsp	vegetable soup mix	25 mL
2 tbsp	fresh tarragon	25 mL
2 tsp	orange zest	10 mL
$1 1/2$ tsp	bread machine yeast	7 mL

2 LB (1 KG)		
$1 1/3$ cups	water	325 mL
$1/4$ tsp	orange extract	1 mL
$1/4$ cup	skim milk powder	50 mL
$1 1/4$ tsp	salt	6 mL
2 tbsp	liquid honey	25 mL
1 tbsp	vegetable oil	15 mL
$1 1/4$ cups	whole wheat flour	300 mL
$2 1/4$ cups	all-purpose flour or bread flour	550 mL
$3/4$ cup	cracked wheat	175 mL
1 cup	shredded carrots	250 mL
3 tbsp	fresh tarragon	45 mL
3 tbsp	vegetable soup mix	45 mL
2 tsp	orange zest	10 mL
$1 1/2$ tsp	bread machine yeast	7 mL

1. Measure ingredients into baking pan in the order recommended by the manufacturer. Insert pan into the oven chamber.

2. Select **Whole Wheat Cycle**.

Tips on Fresh Herbs

To store full stems: Fresh-picked herbs can last for up to 1 week with their stems standing in water. Keep the leaves out of water.

To remove leaves: Remove small leaves from the stem by running fingers down the stem in the opposite direction of growth. Larger leaves should be snipped off using scissors.

To clean and store fresh leaves: Rinse under cold running water and spin-dry in a lettuce spinner. If necessary, dry between layers of paper towels. Place a dry paper towel along with the clean herbs in a plastic bag in the refrigerator. Use within 2 to 3 days. Freeze or dry for longer storage (see below).

To measure: Pack leaves tightly into correct measure.

To snip: After measuring, transfer to a small glass and cut using the tips of sharp kitchen shears/scissors to prevent bruising the tender leaves.

To dry: Tie fresh-picked herbs together in small bunches and hang upside down in a well-ventilated location with low humidity and out of sunlight until the leaves are brittle and fully dry. If they turn brown (rather than stay green), the air is too hot. Once fully dried, strip leaves off the stems for storage. Store whole herbs in an airtight container in a cool, dark place for up to 1 year and crushed herbs for up to 6 months. (Dried herbs are stored in the dark to prevent the color from fading.) Before using, check herbs and discard any that have faded, lost flavor or smell old and musty.

To dry using the microwave: Place $1/2$ to 1 cup (125 to 250 mL) herbs between layers of paper towels. Microwave on High for 3 minutes, checking often to be sure they are not scorched. Then microwave for 10-second periods until leaves are brittle and can be pulled from stems easily.

To freeze: Lay whole herbs in a single layer on a flat surface in the freezer for 2 to 4 hours. Leave whole and pack in plastic bags. Herbs will keep in the freezer for 2 to 3 months.

Carrot Lovers' Poppy Seed Bread

Here's an exceptionally attractive loaf — confetti dots of bright orange carrot contrasting with the dark poppy seeds.

Tips

Any extra grated carrot can be frozen for later use.

To prevent the carrot from turning brown, make sure it doesn't touch the liquid.

Yes, you're reading it right: The 1.5 lb (750 g) recipe contains the *same* amount of yeast as the 2 lb (1 kg).

Variation

Substitute unpeeled, grated small zucchini for part or all of the carrots.

1.5 LB (750 G)		
3/4 cup	water	175 mL
1/4 cup	skim milk powder	50 mL
1 1/4 tsp	salt	6 mL
3 tbsp	liquid honey	45 mL
1 tbsp	vegetable oil	15 mL
2 cups	whole wheat flour	500 mL
1 cup	all-purpose flour or bread flour	250 mL
1 cup	grated carrots	250 mL
1/4 cup	poppy seeds	50 mL
2 tsp	orange zest	10 mL
1 tsp	dried thyme	5 mL
1 3/4 tsp	bread machine yeast	8 mL

2 LB (1 KG)		
1 cup	water	250 mL
1/4 cup	skim milk powder	50 mL
1 1/2 tsp	salt	7 mL
1/4 cup	liquid honey	50 mL
2 tbsp	vegetable oil	25 mL
2 1/2 cups	whole wheat flour	650 mL
1 1/2 cups	all-purpose flour or bread flour	375 mL
1 1/4 cups	grated carrots	300 mL
1/3 cup	poppy seeds	75 mL
1 tbsp	orange zest	15 mL
1 1/4 tsp	dried thyme	6 mL
1 3/4 tsp	bread machine yeast	8 mL

1. Measure ingredients into baking pan in the order recommended by the manufacturer. Insert pan into the oven chamber.
2. Select **Basic** or **Whole Wheat Cycle**.

Healthy and Hearty Grains, Seeds and Nuts

High-fiber multigrain breads have become the choice of today's health-conscious baker. Breads made from grains, seeds and nuts are excellent choices.

continued next page...

Old-Fashioned Wheat Bread

If you find that most 100% whole wheat breads are too heavy, try this one. It's lighter in texture than the traditional loaf.

Tip

If your machine has a **Rapid Whole Wheat Cycle,** you can bake either size recipe; just double the yeast.

Yes, you're reading it right: The 1.5 lb (750 g) recipe contains *more* yeast than the 2 lb (1 kg).

Variation

For a sweeter, milder-flavored bread, substitute packed brown sugar for the honey and the molasses.

1.5 LB (750 G)		
1 1/2 cups	water	375 mL
1/4 cup	skim milk powder	50 mL
1 1/2 tsp	salt	7 mL
2 tbsp	liquid honey	25 mL
1 tbsp	molasses	15 mL
2 tbsp	vegetable oil	25 mL
2 1/2 cups	whole wheat flour	625 mL
1 cup	all-purpose flour or bread flour	250 mL
1 tsp	bread machine yeast	5 mL

2 LB (1 KG)		
1 3/4 cups	water	425 mL
1/3 cup	skim milk powder	75 mL
1 1/2 tsp	salt	7 mL
2 tbsp	liquid honey	25 mL
2 tbsp	molasses	25 mL
2 tbsp	vegetable oil	25 mL
3 1/4 cups	whole wheat flour	800 mL
1 cup	all-purpose flour or bread flour	250 mL
3/4 tsp	bread machine yeast	4 mL

1. Measure ingredients into baking pan in the order recommended by the manufacturer. Insert pan into the oven chamber.
2. Select **Whole Wheat Cycle.**

Baking with Grains

- Purchase grains in small quantities and refrigerate to prevent the fat (contained in the germ of the grain kernel) from turning rancid. If stored longer than 1 month, taste before using.

- Do not use instant oats in recipes that call for rolled oats; the bread texture will be too wet and compact. Medium- or large-flake, regular or quick-cooking oats produce the best loaf.

- Cracked wheat, bulgur and other grains absorb the water and the resulting loaf can be short, heavy and compact in texture. This is especially important when using the timer. To prevent grains from touching the water, level the flour into the corners of the baking pan, then measure grains on top.

- An equal amount of bulgur can be substituted for cracked wheat.

- Bran has the effect of cutting the gluten strands, thus weakening their ability to trap air. Don't increase the amount of bran stated in the recipe or the loaf could collapse.

- The recipes in this book have been developed for unsweetened (not sweetened) cereals. If only sweetened muesli or granola are available, decrease the sugar in the recipe.

- For a contrast in texture and appearance, sprinkle extra oatmeal or barley flakes on top of the risen dough just before baking in a conventional oven or before the baking cycle of the bread machine begins. Open and close the lid quickly so no heat escapes.

Triple-Wheat Bread

This loaf is shorter than some, but with its great flavor and high fiber content, you're sure not to mind.

Tip

See the Techniques Glossary (page 370) for instructions on cooking wheat berries.

For more information on flaxseed, see page 109.

Yes, you're reading it right: The 1.5 lb (750 g) recipe contains the *same* amount of yeast as the 2 lb (1 kg).

Variation

Substitute any wheat-blend flour for the total amount of whole wheat flour and flaxseeds.

1.5 LB (750 G)		
1⅓ cups	water	325 mL
¼ cup	skim milk powder	50 mL
1½ tsp	salt	7 mL
3 tbsp	liquid honey	45 mL
2 tbsp	vegetable oil	25 mL
3 cups	whole wheat flour	750 mL
⅓ cup	cooked wheat berries	75 mL
⅓ cup	cracked wheat	75 mL
⅓ cup	flaxseed, cracked	75 mL
1½ tsp	bread machine yeast	7 mL

2 LB (1 KG)		
1½ cups	water	375 mL
⅓ cup	skim milk powder	75 mL
1¾ tsp	salt	8 mL
¼ cup	liquid honey	50 mL
3 tbsp	vegetable oil	45 mL
3¼ cups	whole wheat flour	800 mL
½ cup	cooked wheat berries	125 mL
½ cup	cracked wheat	125 mL
½ cup	flaxseed, cracked	125 mL
1½ tsp	bread machine yeast	7 mL

1. Measure ingredients into baking pan in the order recommended by the manufacturer. Insert pan into the oven chamber.
2. Select **Whole Wheat Cycle**.

Yogurt Wheat Germ Bread

Looking for a super-healthy bread with lots of fiber? Try this open-textured, nutritious loaf!

Tip

Wheat germ is one of the best sources of vitamin E. Purchase small quantities and store in the refrigerator.

Yes, you're reading it right: The 1.5 lb (750 g) recipe contains *more* yeast than the 2 lb (1 kg).

Variation

Reduce the amount of fat in this recipe by using no-fat or lower-fat yogurt.

1.5 LB (750 G)

2/3 cup	water	150 mL
2/3 cup	plain yogurt	150 mL
1 1/2 tsp	salt	7 mL
2 tbsp	liquid honey	25 mL
1 tbsp	vegetable oil	15 mL
3/4 cup	whole wheat flour	175 mL
2 cups	all-purpose flour or bread flour	500 mL
2 tbsp	wheat bran	25 mL
2 tbsp	wheat germ	25 mL
2 tsp	bread machine yeast	10 mL

2 LB (1 KG)

1 cup	water	250 mL
3/4 cup	plain yogurt	175 mL
1 3/4 tsp	salt	8 mL
3 tbsp	liquid honey	45 mL
2 tbsp	vegetable oil	25 mL
1 1/4 cups	whole wheat flour	300 mL
2 3/4 cups	all-purpose flour or bread flour	675 mL
3 tbsp	wheat bran	45 mL
3 tbsp	wheat germ	45 mL
1 1/4 tsp	bread machine yeast	6 mL

1. Measure ingredients into baking pan in the order recommended by the manufacturer. Insert pan into the oven chamber.
2. Select **Basic Cycle**.

Orange Honey Cracked Wheat Bread

Let the delicious aroma of this freshly baked bread greet you on a lazy Sunday morning. Set the timer instead of the alarm. What a way to wake up!

Tip

Zest the whole orange and freeze any leftovers for the next time you make this loaf. Be careful not to include any of the bitter white part of the orange.

Yes, you're reading it right: The 1.5 lb (750 g) recipe contains the *same* amount of yeast as the 2 lb (1 kg).

Variation

Add $1/2$ cup (125 mL) chopped walnuts, pecans or pine nuts. These can be added to the bread pan after the flour. You do not need to wait for the "add ingredient" signal.

1.5 LB (750 G)		
$1^1/_3$ cups	unsweetened orange juice	325 mL
$1/_4$ cup	skim milk powder	50 mL
$1^1/_2$ tsp	salt	7 mL
$1/_4$ cup	liquid honey	50 mL
2 tbsp	shortening or vegetable oil	25 mL
$3^1/_4$ cups	all-purpose flour or bread flour	800 mL
$2/_3$ cup	cracked wheat	150 mL
2 tsp	orange zest	10 mL
$1^1/_2$ tsp	bread machine yeast	7 mL

2 LB (1 KG)		
$1^1/_2$ cups	unsweetened orange juice	375 mL
$1/_4$ cup	skim milk powder	50 mL
$1^1/_2$ tsp	salt	7 mL
$1/_3$ cup	liquid honey	75 mL
3 tbsp	shortening or vegetable oil	45 mL
$3^3/_4$ cups	all-purpose flour or bread flour	925 mL
1 cup	cracked wheat	250 mL
1 tbsp	orange zest	15 mL
$1^1/_2$ tsp	bread machine yeast	7 mL

1. Measure ingredients into baking pan in the order recommended by the manufacturer. Insert pan into the oven chamber.
2. Select **Basic Cycle**.

The Fat/Fiber Connection

Canada's Food Guide to Healthy Eating states that we should eat 5 to 12 servings from the grain products food group each day. Included in this group are cold and hot cereals, pasta, rice and all types of breads, from bagels to hamburger buns to pitas and loaves of whole grain bread.

The guide also recommends we choose whole grain and enriched products more often. Research suggests that fiber aids in lowering blood cholesterol levels and modifies the absorption of sugar by the body. Dietary fiber is found in wheat bran, whole grains, beans, oats, fruits and vegetables. Grain products are also an excellent source of the major B vitamins and iron.

Breads containing seeds and nuts have multiple health benefits. They contain heart-healthy fats such as omega-3, as well as different types of fiber and other nutritious compounds. To lower the fat and increase the fiber in breads, make substitutions based on the values given below.

	FAT (g)	FIBER (g)
Seeds (1 cup/250 mL)		
Caraway	1	3
Flaxseed	52	43
Poppy	4	1
Pumpkin	63	5
Sesame	71	17
Sunflower	63	14
Nuts (1 cup/250 mL)		
Almonds	70	15
Hazelnuts (Filberts)	70	11
Pecans	86	11
Pistachios	55	12
Walnuts	76	4

Monique's Honey Wheat Bread

This high-fiber bread has a delicate taste of honey you will enjoy.

Tip

Be sure you don't increase the bran content (in Variation, below), since it cuts the gluten strands in the flour and the loaf will collapse.

Yes, you're reading it right: The 1.5 lb (750 g) recipe contains the *same* amount of yeast as the 2 lb (1 kg).

Variation

Substitute 1 cup (250 mL) of all-purpose or bread flour, $1/2$ cup (125 mL) natural wheat bran and the remaining amount of whole wheat flour for the total amount of wheat blend flour in the recipe.

1.5 LB (750 G)		
1 cup	water	250 mL
1	egg	1
$1/4$ cup	skim milk powder	50 mL
$1 1/4$ tsp	salt	6 mL
$1/4$ cup	liquid honey	50 mL
2 tbsp	shortening or vegetable oil	25 mL
$3 1/2$ cups	wheat blend flour	875 mL
$1 1/2$ tsp	bread machine yeast	6 mL

2 LB (1 KG) • extra large		
$1 1/3$ cups	water	325 mL
1	egg	1
$1/4$ cup	skim milk powder	50 mL
$1 1/2$ tsp	salt	7 mL
$1/4$ cup	liquid honey	50 mL
2 tbsp	shortening or vegetable oil	25 mL
$4 1/2$ cups	wheat blend flour	1125 mL
$1 1/2$ tsp	bread machine yeast	6 mL

1. Measure ingredients into baking pan in the order recommended by the manufacturer. Insert pan into the oven chamber.

2. Select **Whole Wheat Cycle**.

Irish Barm Bran Bread

This hearty barm (Gaelic for "yeast") bread was the perfect choice for a St. Patrick's Day dinner we hosted. With 176 guests, we needed (or kneaded!) 48 hearth breads — requiring the services of just about every bread machine in our test kitchen to prepare the dough.

Tips

To get the quantity exactly right, add the amount of water called for to a 2-cup (500 mL) glass measure. Then add the yogurt until the level reaches the correct total volume of both ingredients.

For instructions on cooking wheat berries, see Techniques Glossary (page 370).

Variation

Try making rolls with this recipe: Just divide the dough into 12 to 16 equal portions, then finish as directed. See page 196 for tips on forming, finishing and baking rolls.

• Baking sheet, lightly greased

1 cup	water	250 mL
1/2 cup	plain yogurt	125 mL
1 1/2 tsp	salt	7 mL
3 tbsp	liquid honey	45 mL
2 tbsp	shortening or vegetable oil	25 mL
3 cups	whole wheat flour	750 mL
1/2 cup	cooked wheat berries	125 mL
1/2 cup	quick-cooking oats	125 mL
1/2 cup	wheat bran	125 mL
1 1/2 tsp	bread machine yeast	7 mL

OATMEAL FINISH

1	egg yolk	1
1 tbsp	water	15 mL
1/4 cup	large-flake oats	50 mL

1. Measure bread ingredients into machine's baking pan in the order recommended by the manufacturer. Insert pan into the oven chamber. Select **Dough Cycle**.

2. Remove dough to a lightly floured surface. Cover with a large bowl and let rest for 10 to 15 minutes. Divide dough in half. Form each into a 6-inch (15 cm) round with a slightly flattened top. Place on prepared baking sheet. Cover and let rise in a warm, draft-free place for 30 to 45 minutes or until doubled in volume. Meanwhile, preheat oven to 350°F (180°C).

3. When dough has risen, using a pizza wheel or a sharp knife, score tops with 8 equally spaced cuts 1/2 inch (1 cm) deep.

4. *Oatmeal finish:* In a small bowl, whisk together egg yolk and water until smooth; brush over dough and sprinkle with oats.

5. Bake in preheated oven for 35 to 40 minutes or until hearth breads sound hollow when tapped on the bottom.

Seven-Grain Bran Bread

1.5 LB (750 G)		
1 1/4 cups	water	300 mL
1/4 cup	skim milk powder	50 mL
1 1/4 tsp	salt	6 mL
1 tbsp	liquid honey	15 mL
1 tbsp	molasses	15 mL
2 tbsp	shortening or vegetable oil	25 mL
3/4 cup	whole wheat flour	175 mL
2 cups	all-purpose flour or bread flour	500 mL
1/3 cup	bran cereal	75 mL
1/3 cup	7-grain cereal	75 mL
1 tsp	bread machine yeast	5 mL

2 LB (1 KG)		
1 1/2 cups	water	375 mL
1/4 cup	skim milk powder	50 mL
1 1/2 tsp	salt	7 mL
2 tbsp	liquid honey	25 mL
2 tbsp	molasses	25 mL
3 tbsp	shortening or vegetable oil	45 mL
1 cup	whole wheat flour	250 mL
2 1/4 cups	all-purpose flour or bread flour	550 mL
1/2 cup	bran cereal	125 mL
1/2 cup	7-grain cereal	125 mL
1 1/4 tsp	bread machine yeast	6 mL

1. Measure ingredients into baking pan in the order recommended by the manufacturer. Insert pan into the oven chamber.
2. Select **Whole Wheat Cycle**.

Raisin Bran Loaf

Enjoy bran muffins for breakfast? Toast a thick slice of this loaf for a rich molasses treat.

Tip

The higher the bran content of the cereal, the closer this is to a real bran muffin.

Variation

Substitute oat bran for the wheat bran, and dates or other dried fruit for the raisins.

1.5 LB (750 G)		
1 1/4 cups	water	300 mL
1/4 cup	skim milk powder	50 mL
1 1/2 tsp	salt	7 mL
2 tbsp	packed brown sugar	25 mL
1 tbsp	molasses	15 mL
2 tbsp	vegetable oil	25 mL
1 1/4 cups	whole wheat flour	300 mL
1 1/4 cups	all-purpose flour or bread flour	300 mL
1/2 cup	bran cereal	125 mL
1/4 cup	wheat bran	50 mL
3/4 cup	raisins	175 mL
1 1/4 tsp	bread machine yeast	6 mL

2 LB (1 KG)		
1 1/2 cups	water	375 mL
1/3 cup	skim milk powder	75 mL
1 3/4 tsp	salt	8 mL
3 tbsp	packed brown sugar	45 mL
2 tbsp	molasses	25 mL
2 tbsp	vegetable oil	25 mL
1 1/2 cups	whole wheat flour	375 mL
1 1/2 cups	all-purpose flour or bread flour	375 mL
3/4 cup	bran cereal	175 mL
1/2 cup	wheat bran	125 mL
1 cup	raisins	250 mL
1 1/2 tsp	bread machine yeast	7 mL

1. Measure ingredients into baking pan in the order recommended by the manufacturer. Insert pan into the oven chamber.
2. Select **Whole Wheat Cycle.**

High-Fiber Carrot Bran Bread

Plenty of fiber and just the right amount of sweetness makes a great combination in this bread.

Tips

Look for a bran cereal that contains at least 10 g fiber per $1/2$-cup (125 mL) serving.

Yes, you're reading it right: The 1.5 lb (750 g) recipe contains the *same* amount of yeast as the 2 lb (1 kg).

Other high-fiber breads include *Maple Banana Flaxseed* (see recipe, page 108), *Almond Apricot Yogurt* (see recipe, page 120) and *Amish Seed Bread* (see recipe, page 101).

1.5 LB (750 G)		
$3/4$ cup	water	175 mL
1 cup	shredded carrots	250 mL
$1^1/4$ tsp	salt	6 mL
1 tbsp	packed brown sugar	15 mL
2 tbsp	vegetable oil	25 mL
$1^1/2$ cups	whole wheat flour	375 mL
$3/4$ cup	all-purpose flour or bread flour	175 mL
$1/2$ cup	high-fiber bran cereal	125 mL
$1/3$ cup	buttermilk powder	75 mL
$1/2$ cup	pitted dates	125 mL
$1^3/4$ tsp	bread machine yeast	8 mL

2 LB (1 KG)		
1 cup	water	250 mL
1 cup	shredded carrots	250 mL
$1^1/2$ tsp	salt	7 mL
2 tbsp	packed brown sugar	25 mL
2 tbsp	vegetable oil	25 mL
2 cups	whole wheat flour	500 mL
1 cup	all-purpose flour or bread flour	250 mL
$1/2$ cup	high-fiber bran cereal	125 mL
$1/2$ cup	buttermilk powder	125 mL
$3/4$ cup	pitted dates	175 mL
$1^3/4$ tsp	bread machine yeast	8 mL

1. Measure ingredients into baking pan in the order recommended by the manufacturer. Insert pan into the oven chamber.

2. Select **Whole Wheat Cycle.**

Scandinavian Rye Bread

1.5 LB (750 G)

1 1/4 cups	beer	300 mL
1	egg	1
3/4 tsp	salt	4 mL
1 tbsp	molasses	15 mL
2 tbsp	packed brown sugar	25 mL
1 tbsp	shortening or vegetable oil	15 mL
1 3/4 cups	all-purpose flour or bread flour	450 mL
1 cup	rye flour	250 mL
1 tsp	orange zest	5 mL
1/2 tsp	anise seeds	2 mL
1/2 tsp	caraway seeds	2 mL
1/2 tsp	fennel seeds	2 mL
1 1/2 tsp	bread machine yeast	7 mL

2 LB (1 KG)

1 1/3 cups	beer	325 mL
2	eggs	2
1 1/2 tsp	salt	7 mL
2 tbsp	molasses	25 mL
2 tbsp	packed brown sugar	25 mL
2 tbsp	shortening or vegetable oil	25 mL
2 1/4 cups	all-purpose flour or bread flour	550 mL
1 1/2 cups	rye flour	375 mL
2 tsp	orange zest	10 mL
1 tsp	anise seeds	5 mL
1 tsp	caraway seeds	5 mL
1 tsp	fennel seeds	5 mL
1 3/4 tsp	bread machine yeast	8 mL

1. Measure ingredients into baking pan in the order recommended by the manufacturer. Insert pan into the oven chamber.

2. Select **Basic Cycle**.

All Bran Cereals Are Not Created Equal

We are frequently asked what we mean when we refer to "bran cereal" in a recipe. The table below lists several name-brand cereals and indicates the amount of fiber per serving in each. You'll notice that not only does the amount of fiber vary, but the serving size does too. Nutritionists recommend we eat 25 to 35 grams of fiber every day.

You can substitute either a natural wheat bran or a multigrain cereal for a bran cereal.

Cereal Name	Serving Size	Grams of Fiber/Serving
Bran Flakes	1 cup (250 mL)	4.3 to 4.6 g
All-Bran Buds	$1/3$ cup (75 mL)	13 g
All-Bran Original	$1/2$ cup (125 mL)	10 g
Raisin Bran	$3/4$ cup (175 mL)	4.6 g
100% Bran	$1/2$ cup (125 mL)	10 g
Oat Cereal with Wheat & Corn Bran	$3/4$ cup (175 mL)	4.5 g
Special K Plus	$3/4$ cup (175 mL)	2.6 g
Fiber One	$1/2$ cup (125 mL)	14 g
Shredded Wheat	$2/3$ cup (150 mL)	3.7 to 4.1 g

Swiss Rye Loaf

Tips

Because it contains neither fat nor sugar to provide food for the yeast, this loaf is heavier than most, but still fine-textured and delicious.

For instructions on cooking rye groats, see Techniques Glossary, page 370.

Yes, you're reading it right: The 1.5 lb (750 g) recipe contains the *same* amount of yeast as the 2 lb (1 kg).

Variation

For a richer loaf, use a dark rye flour and substitute cold coffee for some or all of the water.

1.5 LB (750 G)		
1 1/4 cups	water	300 mL
1 1/4 tsp	salt	6 mL
1 1/4 cups	whole wheat flour	300 mL
1 1/4 cups	all-purpose flour or bread flour	300 mL
1 1/4 cups	rye flour	300 mL
3/4 cup	cooked rye groats	175 mL
2 tsp	bread machine yeast	10 mL

2 LB (1 KG)		
1 1/2 cups	water	375 mL
1 3/4 tsp	salt	8 mL
1 1/2 cups	whole wheat flour	375 mL
1 1/2 cups	all-purpose flour or bread flour	375 mL
1 1/2 cups	rye flour	375 mL
1 cup	cooked rye groats	250 mL
2 tsp	bread machine yeast	10 mL

1. Measure ingredients into baking pan in the order recommended by the manufacturer. Insert pan into the oven chamber.

2. Select **Whole Wheat Cycle**.

Cumin Rye Bread

If you enjoy a lighter-textured rye, then this is the bread for you!

Tip

For more fiber and nutrients, replace 1 cup (250 mL) of the all-purpose or bread flour with whole wheat flour.

Yes, you're reading it right: The 1.5 lb (750 g) recipe contains the *same* amount of yeast as the 2 lb (1 kg).

Variations

Substitute malt syrup for the corn syrup.

Try caraway and fennel seeds instead of the cumin and anise seeds.

1.5 LB (750 G)

1¼ cups	water	300 mL
¼ cup	skim milk powder	50 mL
1¼ tsp	salt	6 mL
2 tbsp	corn syrup	25 mL
2 tbsp	shortening or vegetable oil	25 mL
2½ cups	all-purpose flour or bread flour	625 mL
¾ cup	rye flour	175 mL
2 tsp	cumin seeds	10 mL
2 tsp	anise seeds	10 mL
1¼ tsp	bread machine yeast	6 mL

2 LB (1 KG)

1½ cups	water	375 mL
⅓ cup	skim milk powder	75 mL
1½ tsp	salt	7 mL
3 tbsp	corn syrup	45 mL
2 tbsp	shortening or vegetable oil	25 mL
3¼ cups	all-purpose flour or bread flour	800 mL
1 cup	rye flour	250 mL
1 tbsp	cumin seeds	15 mL
2 tsp	anise seeds	10 mL
1¼ tsp	bread machine yeast	6 mL

1. Measure all ingredients into baking pan in the order recommended by the manufacturer. Insert pan into the oven chamber.
2. Select **Basic Cycle**.

Onion Rye Loaf

The mellow onion flavor of this robust rye makes for outstanding cold roast beef sandwiches. Just add a little Dijon mustard.

Tips

Do not substitute fresh onion for the dried flakes — moisture content is too high, and you'll end up with a short, weak-flavored loaf.

The 1.5 lb (750 g) loaf is perfect for a small slice.

Variation

Replace 1 cup (250 mL) of the all-purpose or bread flour with 1 cup (250 mL) whole wheat flour.

1.5 LB (750 G)

1 1/4 cups	water	300 mL
1/4 cup	skim milk powder	50 mL
1 tsp	salt	5 mL
2 tbsp	packed brown sugar	25 mL
2 tbsp	shortening or vegetable oil	25 mL
2 1/2 cups	all-purpose flour or bread flour	650 mL
1/2 cup	rye flour	125 mL
1/4 cup	dried onion flakes	50 mL
1 1/4 tsp	bread machine yeast	6 mL

2 LB (1 KG)

1 1/2 cups	water	375 mL
1/3 cup	skim milk powder	75 mL
1 1/2 tsp	salt	7 mL
3 tbsp	packed brown sugar	45 mL
3 tbsp	shortening or vegetable oil	45 mL
3 1/3 cups	all-purpose flour or bread flour	825 mL
2/3 cup	rye flour	150 mL
1/3 cup	dried onion flakes	75 mL
1 1/2 tsp	bread machine yeast	7 mL

1. Measure ingredients into baking pan in the order recommended by the manufacturer. Insert pan into the oven chamber.
2. Select **Basic Cycle**.

Southern Cornmeal Bread

Golden in color, soft in texture, with a hint of corn, this is the perfect bread to accompany a huge pot of spicy chili.

Tip

For a lighter loaf, place the cornmeal on top of the flour; be sure it doesn't touch the water.

Yes, you're reading it right: The 1.5 lb (750 g) recipe contains the *same* amount of yeast as the 2 lb (1 kg).

Variation

Choose a coarser grind of cornmeal with a deep yellow color for an attractive contrast to dark rye bread in a bread basket.

1.5 LB (750 G)		
1 cup	water	250 mL
1	egg	1
¼ cup	skim milk powder	50 mL
1½ tsp	salt	7 mL
2 tbsp	liquid honey	25 mL
2 tbsp	shortening or vegetable oil	25 mL
2½ cups	all-purpose flour or bread flour	625 mL
½ cup	cornmeal	125 mL
1 tsp	bread machine yeast	5 mL

2 LB (1 KG) • extra large		
1¼ cups	water	300 mL
2	eggs	2
¼ cup	skim milk powder	50 mL
1½ tsp	salt	7 mL
3 tbsp	liquid honey	45 mL
2 tbsp	shortening or vegetable oil	25 mL
3 cups	all-purpose flour or bread flour	750 mL
¾ cup	cornmeal	175 mL
1 tsp	bread machine yeast	5 mL

1. Measure ingredients into baking pan in the order recommended by the manufacturer. Insert pan into the oven chamber.
2. Select **Sweet Cycle**.

Wild Rice and Cranberry Loaf

This attractive
loaf is sure to bring
compliments. Its nutty
taste is a real plus.

Tips

Prepare extra wild
rice when cooking
your favorite duck or
goose dinner. Store
in the refrigerator or
freezer until needed.

See Techniques
Glossary (page 370)
for instructions on
cooking wild rice.

*Yes, you're reading it
right:* The 1.5 lb
(750 g) recipe contains
more yeast than the
2 lb (1 kg).

Variation

Substitute raw,
unsalted sunflower
seeds or unsalted
peanuts for the pine
nuts, and dried
blueberries or dried
sour cherries for the
dried cranberries.

1.5 LB (750 G)		
1 1/4 cups	water	300 mL
1/4 cup	skim milk powder	50 mL
1 1/4 tsp	salt	6 mL
2 tbsp	liquid honey	25 mL
1 tbsp	olive oil	15 mL
3 cups	all-purpose flour or bread flour	750 mL
3/4 cup	cooked wild rice	175 mL
1/4 cup	pine nuts	50 mL
3/4 tsp	celery seeds	4 mL
1/8 tsp	freshly ground black pepper	0.5 mL
1 tsp	bread machine yeast	5 mL
2/3 cup	dried cranberries	150 mL

2 LB (1 KG)		
1 1/2 cups	water	375 mL
1/3 cup	skim milk powder	75 mL
1 1/2 tsp	salt	7 mL
2 tbsp	liquid honey	25 mL
1 tbsp	olive oil	15 mL
3 3/4 cups	all-purpose flour or bread flour	925 mL
1 cup	cooked wild rice	250 mL
1/3 cup	pine nuts	75 mL
1 tsp	celery seeds	5 mL
1/8 tsp	freshly ground black pepper	0.5 mL
3/4 tsp	bread machine yeast	4 mL
3/4 cup	dried cranberries	175 mL

1. Measure all ingredients *except dried cranberries* into baking pan in the order recommended by the manufacturer. Insert pan into the oven chamber. Select **Basic Cycle**. Add dried cranberries at the "add ingredient" signal.

Granary Bread

MAKES 1 LOAF

You won't find many breads with such a collection of grains — wheat, buckwheat, oats, barley and rye. The name says it all!

Tips

Remember that only wheat and rye contain gluten. Increasing the amount of other grains will result in an even heavier loaf.

See the Techniques Glossary (page 370) for instructions on cooking rye groats.

Yes, you're reading it right: The 1.5 lb (750 g) recipe contains the *same* amount of yeast as the 2 lb (1 kg).

Variation

Substitute quinoa, spelt, amaranth or kamut for one or more of the grains, but not the bread flour.

1.5 LB (750 G)		
1 1/4 cups	water	300 mL
1/4 cup	skim milk powder	50 mL
1 1/2 tsp	salt	7 mL
2 tbsp	packed brown sugar	25 mL
1 tbsp	molasses	15 mL
2 tbsp	shortening or vegetable oil	25 mL
2 3/4 cups	all-purpose flour or bread flour	675 mL
1/4 cup	buckwheat flour	50 mL
1/4 cup	quick-cooking oats	50 mL
1/4 cup	barley flakes	50 mL
1/4 cup	cooked rye groats	50 mL
1 1/4 tsp	bread machine yeast	6 mL

2 LB (1 KG)		
1 1/2 cups	water	375 mL
1/3 cup	skim milk powder	75 mL
1 3/4 tsp	salt	8 mL
2 tbsp	packed brown sugar	25 mL
2 tbsp	molasses	25 mL
2 tbsp	shortening or vegetable oil	25 mL
3 cups	all-purpose flour or bread flour	750 mL
1/3 cup	buckwheat flour	75 mL
1/3 cup	quick-cooking oats	75 mL
1/3 cup	barley flakes	75 mL
1/3 cup	cooked rye groats	75 mL
1 1/4 tsp	bread machine yeast	6 mL

1. Measure ingredients into baking pan in the order recommended by the manufacturer. Insert pan into the oven chamber.
2. Select **Whole Wheat Cycle.**

Mock Spoon Bread

If you love cornbread, the sharp Cheddar and smoky bacon flavors in this bread will make you think you've gone to heaven.

Tip

For cheese weight/volume equivalents, see Ingredient Glossary (page 360).

Yes, you're reading it right: The 1.5 lb (750 g) recipe contains the *same* amount of yeast as the 2 lb (1 kg).

Variation

Substitute 3 to 4 oz (90 to 120 g) of cooked smoked ham for the bacon.

1.5 LB (750 G)		
1/4 cup	milk	50 mL
1	can (10 oz/284 mL) cream-style corn	1
1 tsp	salt	5 mL
1 tbsp	liquid honey	15 mL
2 3/4 cups	all-purpose flour or bread flour	675 mL
3	slices crisp bacon, crumbled	3
1/3 cup	cornmeal	75 mL
1/2 cup	shredded old Cheddar cheese	125 mL
1 tsp	bread machine yeast	5 mL

2 LB (1 KG)		
1/2 cup	milk	125 mL
1	can (10 oz/284 mL) cream-style corn	1
1 tsp	salt	5 mL
1 tbsp	liquid honey	15 mL
3 cups	all-purpose flour or bread flour	750 mL
4	slices crisp bacon, crumbled	4
1/2 cup	cornmeal	125 mL
3/4 cup	shredded old Cheddar cheese	175 mL
1 tsp	bread machine yeast	5 mL

1. Measure ingredients into baking pan in the order recommended by the manufacturer. Insert pan into the oven chamber.
2. Select **Basic Cycle**.

Maple Banana Flaxseed Bread (page 108)

Overleaf: Sun-Dried Tomato Lavosh (page 131) and Sourdough Baguettes (page 183)

MAKES 1 LOAF

Oatmeal Molasses Bread

Oatmeal breads always have a moist, heavy texture. You will enjoy this strong-flavored, slightly tart recipe.

Tips

This loaf frequently has a rough top, since neither the oatmeal nor the grain cereal contain enough cell-building gluten to form a rounded crown.

Use a medium-flaked oatmeal, not an instant, for the best texture in this loaf.

Yes, you're reading it right: The 1.5 lb (750 g) recipe contains the *same* amount of yeast as the 2 lb (1 kg).

Variation

Substitute a 12-grain cereal or muesli for the 7-grain.

1.5 LB (750 G)		
1 1/4 cups	water	300 mL
1/4 cup	skim milk powder	50 mL
1 1/2 tsp	salt	6 mL
3 tbsp	molasses	40 mL
2 tbsp	shortening or vegetable oil	25 mL
1 1/2 cups	whole wheat flour	400 mL
3/4 cup	all-purpose flour or bread flour	200 mL
2/3 cup	quick-cooking oats	150 mL
1/3 cup	7-grain cereal	75 mL
1 1/2 tsp	bread machine yeast	6 mL

2 LB (1 KG)		
1 1/2 cups	water	375 mL
1/4 cup	skim milk powder	50 mL
1 1/2 tsp	salt	7 mL
1/4 cup	molasses	50 mL
2 tbsp	shortening or vegetable oil	25 mL
2 cups	whole wheat flour	500 mL
1 1/4 cups	all-purpose flour or bread flour	300 mL
3/4 cup	quick-cooking oats	175 mL
1/2 cup	7-grain cereal	125 mL
1 1/2 tsp	bread machine yeast	6 mL

1. Measure ingredients into baking pan in the order recommended by the manufacturer. Insert pan into the oven chamber.
2. Select **Whole Wheat Cycle**.

Autumn Pumpkin Seed Bread (page 114)

Tip

Store wheat germ in
the refrigerator since it
becomes rancid quickly.
Taste before adding.

*Yes, you're reading it
right:* The 1.5 lb
(750 g) recipe contains
the *same* amount of
yeast as the 2 lb (1 kg).

Variation

Substitute an equal
amount of oat bran
for the wheat bran. It
will result in a slightly
sweeter loaf.

Pilgrims' Multigrain Bread

1.5 LB (750 G)		
1 1/4 cups	water	300 mL
1	egg	1
1 1/2 tsp	salt	7 mL
2 tbsp	liquid honey	25 mL
2 tbsp	vegetable oil	25 mL
3 cups	all-purpose flour or bread flour	750 mL
1/3 cup	buttermilk powder	75 mL
1/4 cup	quick-cooking oats	50 mL
1/4 cup	wheat bran	50 mL
2 tbsp	wheat germ	25 mL
1 tbsp	sesame seeds	15 mL
1 1/2 tsp	bread machine yeast	7 mL

2 LB (1 KG) • extra large		
1 1/3 cups	water	325 mL
2	eggs	2
1 1/2 tsp	salt	7 mL
3 tbsp	liquid honey	45 mL
2 tbsp	vegetable oil	25 mL
3 1/2 cups	all-purpose flour or bread flour	875 mL
1/2 cup	buttermilk powder	125 mL
1/3 cup	quick-cooking oats	75 mL
1/3 cup	wheat bran	75 mL
3 tbsp	wheat germ	45 mL
2 tbsp	sesame seeds	25 mL
1 1/2 tsp	bread machine yeast	7 mL

1. Measure ingredients into baking pan in the order recommended by the manufacturer. Insert pan into the oven chamber.

2. Select **Basic Cycle**.

Ancient Grains Bread

*Here's a quartet of
unusual ingredients —
spelt, amaranth, kamut,
quinoa (pronounced
"keen–wa") — combined
in a light-textured,
nutritious loaf.*

Tip

Purchase grains in
small amounts at bulk
or health food stores.
Store in airtight
containers in the
refrigerator.

Variation

Semolina or cornmeal
can be substituted for
one of the ancient
grains.

1.5 LB (750 G)		
1¼ cups	water	300 mL
¼ cup	skim milk powder	50 mL
1 tsp	salt	5 mL
2 tbsp	packed brown sugar	25 mL
2 tbsp	vegetable oil	25 mL
2½ cups	all-purpose flour or bread flour	625 mL
½ cup	spelt flour	125 mL
¼ cup	amaranth flour	50 mL
¼ cup	kamut flour	50 mL
¼ cup	quinoa flour	50 mL
1¼ tsp	bread machine yeast	6 mL

2 LB (1 KG)		
1½ cups	water	375 mL
⅓ cup	skim milk powder	75 mL
1½ tsp	salt	7 mL
3 tbsp	packed brown sugar	45 mL
3 tbsp	vegetable oil	45 mL
3 cups	all-purpose flour or bread flour	750 mL
⅔ cup	spelt flour	150 mL
⅓ cup	amaranth flour	75 mL
⅓ cup	kamut flour	75 mL
⅓ cup	quinoa flour	75 mL
1¾ tsp	bread machine yeast	8 mL

1. Measure ingredients into baking pan in the order
   recommended by the manufacturer. Insert pan into
   the oven chamber.
2. Select **Basic Cycle**.

Country Harvest Bread

One of our personal favorites, this is a perfect sandwich bread. Smoked turkey, sliced tomatoes and a thin spread of honey Dijon dressing is all you need.

Tip

To prevent the seeds from becoming rancid, store in an airtight container in the refrigerator.

For more information on flaxseed, see page 109.

Yes, you're reading it right: The 1.5 lb (750 g) recipe contains the *same* amount of yeast as the 2 lb (1 kg).

Variation

Try different types of seeds in the recipe, but keep the total amount the same. Choices include pumpkin or poppy seeds.

1.5 LB (750 G)		
1¼ cups	water	300 mL
¼ cup	skim milk powder	50 mL
1½ tsp	salt	7 mL
2 tbsp	liquid honey	25 mL
2 tbsp	shortening or vegetable oil	25 mL
1 cup	whole wheat flour	250 mL
2 cups	all-purpose flour or bread flour	500 mL
¼ cup	flaxseed, cracked	50 mL
2 tbsp	sunflower seeds, raw, unsalted	25 mL
1 tbsp	sesame seeds	15 mL
1¾ tsp	bread machine yeast	8 mL

2 LB (1 KG)		
1⅓ cups	water	325 mL
¼ cup	skim milk powder	50 mL
1½ tsp	salt	7 mL
3 tbsp	liquid honey	45 mL
3 tbsp	shortening or vegetable oil	45 mL
1¼ cups	whole wheat flour	300 mL
2⅓ cups	all purpose flour or bread flour	575 mL
⅓ cup	flaxseed, cracked	75 mL
¼ cup	sunflower seeds, raw, unsalted	50 mL
2 tbsp	sesame seeds	25 mL
1¾ tsp	bread machine yeast	8 mL

1. Measure ingredients into baking pan in the order recommended by the manufacturer. Insert pan into the oven chamber.
2. Select **Whole Wheat Cycle**.

Amish Seed Bread

With its rough top studded by sesame seeds, this loaf has a heavier texture than most. Its sharp, sourdough-like taste is deliciously distinctive — but may not appeal to everyone.

Tip

For a lighter texture, substitute 1 cup (250 mL) all-purpose or bread flour for 1 cup (250 mL) of the whole wheat flour.

Variation

Use any flavor of liquid honey. Orange-blossom or clover honey will produce a milder-flavored loaf than buckwheat.

1.5 LB (750 G)		
¼ cup	water	50 mL
¾ cup	plain yogurt	175 mL
1	egg	1
1¼ tsp	salt	6 mL
3 tbsp	buckwheat honey	45 mL
1 tbsp	shortening or vegetable oil	15 mL
2¾ cups	whole wheat flour	675 mL
⅓ cup	quick-cooking oats	75 mL
3 tbsp	wheat bran	45 mL
3 tbsp	sesame seeds	45 mL
1½ tsp	bread machine yeast	7 mL

2 LB (1 KG)		
½ cup	water	125 mL
1 cup	plain yogurt	250 mL
1	egg	1
1¼ tsp	salt	6 mL
¼ cup	buckwheat honey	50 mL
1 tbsp	shortening or vegetable oil	15 mL
3 cups	whole wheat flour	750 mL
½ cup	quick-cooking oats	125 mL
¼ cup	wheat bran	50 mL
¼ cup	sesame seeds	50 mL
2 tsp	bread machine yeast	10 mL

1. Measure ingredients into baking pan in the order recommended by the manufacturer. Insert pan into the oven chamber.

2. Select **Whole Wheat Cycle.**

Brown Seed Bread

Here you'll find poppy seeds and sesame seeds — and plenty of extra goodness.

Tip

To get the quantity exactly right, add the amount of water called for to a 2-cup (500 mL) glass measure. Then add the cottage cheese until the level reaches the correct total volume of both ingredients.

Yes, you're reading it right: The 1.5 lb (750 g) recipe contains the *same* amount of yeast as the 2 lb (1 kg).

Variation

Substituting ricotta cheese for the cottage cheese gives a slightly creamier texture.

1.5 LB (750 G)		
1 cup	water	250 mL
1/2 cup	cottage cheese	125 mL
1 1/2 tsp	salt	7 mL
1/4 cup	liquid honey	50 mL
2 tbsp	shortening or vegetable oil	25 mL
2 cups	whole wheat flour	500 mL
1 cup	all-purpose flour or bread flour	250 mL
1/2 cup	barley flakes	125 mL
1/2 cup	bran cereal	125 mL
1/4 cup	poppy seeds	50 mL
1/4 cup	sesame seeds	50 mL
2 tsp	bread machine yeast	10 mL

2 LB (1 KG)		
1 1/4 cups	water	300 mL
3/4 cup	cottage cheese	175 mL
1 3/4 tsp	salt	8 mL
1/3 cup	liquid honey	75 mL
3 tbsp	shortening or vegetable oil	45 mL
2 1/2 cups	whole wheat flour	625 mL
1 1/4 cups	all-purpose flour or bread flour	300 mL
1/2 cup	barley flakes	125 mL
1/2 cup	bran cereal	125 mL
1/3 cup	poppy seeds	75 mL
1/3 cup	sesame seeds	75 mL
2 tsp	bread machine yeast	10 mL

1. Measure ingredients into baking pan in the order recommended by the manufacturer. Insert pan into the oven chamber.
2. Select **Whole Wheat Cycle**.

Five-Seed Rye Bread

1.5 LB (750 G)		
1 1/4 cups	water	300 mL
1/4 cup	skim milk powder	50 mL
1 1/4 tsp	salt	6 mL
2 tbsp	packed brown sugar	25 mL
2 tbsp	shortening or vegetable oil	25 mL
3 1/4 cups	all-purpose flour or bread flour	625 mL
1/2 cup	rye flour	125 mL
2 tbsp	flaxseed, cracked	25 mL
2 tbsp	poppy seeds	25 mL
2 tbsp	sesame seeds	25 mL
1/2 tsp	caraway seeds	2 mL
1/2 tsp	fennel seeds	2 mL
1 tsp	bread machine yeast	5 mL

2 LB (1 KG)		
1 1/2 cups	water	375 mL
1/4 cup	skim milk powder	50 mL
1 1/2 tsp	salt	7 mL
2 tbsp	packed brown sugar	25 mL
2 tbsp	shortening or vegetable oil	25 mL
3 cups	all-purpose flour or bread flour	750 mL
3/4 cup	rye flour	175 mL
1/4 cup	flaxseed, cracked	50 mL
1/4 cup	poppy seeds	50 mL
1/4 cup	sesame seeds	50 mL
1 tsp	caraway seeds	5 mL
1 tsp	fennel seeds	5 mL
1 1/2 tsp	bread machine yeast	7 mL

1. Measure ingredients into baking pan in the order recommended by the manufacturer. Insert pan into the oven chamber.
2. Select **Basic Cycle**.

Seed-and-Soy Loaf

MAKES 1 LOAF

With its dark gold, shiny crust studded with seeds, this loaf is so attractive, you'll forget it's healthy too.

Tip

Because soy flour contains no gluten at all, you can't use too much in yeast breads.

Yes, you're reading it right: The 1.5 lb (750 g) recipe contains the *same* amount of yeast as the 2 lb (1 kg).

Variation

Substitute any gluten-free flour for the soy flour.

1.5 LB (750 G)

1 1/4 cups	water	300 mL
1/4 cup	skim milk powder	50 mL
1 1/2 tsp	salt	7 mL
2 tbsp	liquid honey	25 mL
1 tbsp	molasses	15 mL
2 tbsp	vegetable oil	25 mL
1 1/4 cups	whole wheat flour	300 mL
1 1/4 cups	all-purpose flour or bread flour	300 mL
1/2 cup	soy flour	125 mL
1/4 cup	sesame seeds	50 mL
1/4 cup	sunflower seeds, raw, unsalted	50 mL
1 tbsp	caraway seeds	15 mL
1 1/2 tsp	bread machine yeast	7 mL

2 LB (1 KG)

1 1/2 cups	water	375 mL
1/3 cup	skim milk powder	75 mL
1 3/4 tsp	salt	8 mL
3 tbsp	liquid honey	45 mL
2 tbsp	molasses	25 mL
2 tbsp	vegetable oil	25 mL
1 1/2 cups	whole wheat flour	375 mL
1 1/2 cups	all-purpose flour or bread flour	375 mL
3/4 cup	soy flour	175 mL
1/3 cup	sesame seeds	75 mL
1/3 cup	sunflower seeds, raw, unsalted	75 mL
1 tbsp	caraway seeds	15 mL
1 1/2 tsp	bread machine yeast	7 mL

1. Measure ingredients into baking pan in the order recommended by the manufacturer. Insert pan into the oven chamber.
2. Select **Whole Wheat Cycle.**

Honey Berry Seed Bread

We held a contest among our newsletter readers to name this bread. The winning entry came from Sue Phillips of Sorrento, British Columbia, who was inspired by the "very delightful taste of honey, wheat berries and a combination of sesame, sunflower and poppy seeds — a real comfort food!"

Tips

For instructions on cooking wheat berries, see Techniques Glossary, page 370.

Cook enough wheat berries for several loaves. Store in the refrigerator in an airtight container for 3 to 4 weeks or in the freezer for longer storage.

Variation

Substitute cracked wheat or bulgur for the wheat berries.

1.5 LB (750 G)		
1¼ cups	water	300 mL
1½ tsp	salt	7 mL
2 tbsp	liquid honey	25 mL
2 tbsp	shortening or vegetable oil	25 mL
1¼ cups	whole wheat flour	300 mL
1¼ cups	all-purpose flour or bread flour	300 mL
⅓ cup	buttermilk powder	75 mL
⅓ cup	cooked wheat berries	75 mL
¼ cup	sesame seeds	50 mL
¼ cup	sunflower seeds, raw, unsalted	50 mL
¼ cup	poppy seeds	50 mL
1¼ tsp	bread machine yeast	6 mL

2 LB (1 KG)		
1⅓ cups	water	325 mL
1½ tsp	salt	7 mL
3 tbsp	liquid honey	45 mL
2 tbsp	shortening or vegetable oil	25 mL
1½ cups	whole wheat flour	375 mL
1¼ cups	all-purpose flour or bread flour	300 mL
½ cup	buttermilk powder	125 mL
½ cup	cooked wheat berries	125 mL
⅓ cup	sesame seeds	75 mL
⅓ cup	sunflower seeds, raw, unsalted	75 mL
¼ cup	poppy seeds	50 mL
1½ tsp	bread machine yeast	7 mL

1. Measure ingredients into baking pan in the order recommended by the manufacturer. Insert pan into the oven chamber.
2. Select **Whole Wheat Cycle**.

European Black Bread with Anise Seeds

Tips

Use cold leftover coffee to replace the water and instant coffee granules.

Be sure you don't use onion salt for onion powder in bread machine recipes.

Variation

Add 2 to 3 tsp (10 to 15 mL) dill, fennel or caraway seeds after the flour.

1.5 LB (750 G)

1 1/4 cups	water	300 mL
2 tbsp	white vinegar	25 mL
1 tsp	salt	5 mL
1/4 cup	molasses	50 mL
2 tbsp	shortening or vegetable oil	25 mL
2 1/3 cups	all-purpose flour or bread flour	575 mL
3/4 cup	rye flour	175 mL
1/3 cup	buttermilk powder	75 mL
1 tbsp	unsweetened cocoa powder	15 mL
2 tsp	anise seeds	10 mL
1 tsp	instant coffee granules	5 mL
1 tsp	onion powder	5 mL
1 1/4 tsp	bread machine yeast	6 mL

2 LB (1 KG)

1 1/2 cups	water	375 mL
3 tbsp	white vinegar	45 mL
1 1/4 tsp	salt	6 mL
1/4 cup	molasses	50 mL
2 tbsp	shortening or vegetable oil	25 mL
3 1/2 cups	all-purpose flour or bread flour	875 mL
1 cup	rye flour	250 mL
1/2 cup	buttermilk powder	125 mL
1 tbsp	unsweetened cocoa powder	15 mL
1 tbsp	anise seeds	15 mL
2 tsp	instant coffee granules	10 mL
1 1/2 tsp	onion powder	7 mL
1 1/2 tsp	bread machine yeast	7 mL

1. Measure ingredients into baking pan in the order recommended by the manufacturer. Insert pan into the oven chamber.

2. Select **Basic Cycle**.

Homemade Mixes: Economical, Convenient and Great Tasting!

Sometimes you are just too busy to take the time to bake a loaf of bread. Just the thought of taking out and measuring the flour, sugar, seeds and grains seems like too much work. Wouldn't a mix be handy at these times?

You can make your own mixes from any of the recipes contained in this cookbook. Here are some hints:

- Next time you bake a loaf, measure 3 or 4 extra sets of ingredients into plastic bags. Mixes should contain all the dry ingredients except the yeast; the extra exposure to air stales the yeast too quickly.

- Substitute granulated sugar for honey and brown sugar for molasses.

- The nuts and seeds can be part of the mix, but don't include anything you would normally add at the "add ingredient" signal. These can be measured into smaller sandwich bags to have ready.

- Label your plastic bags with the recipe name, cycle to use and size of loaf, as well as the date. List on the label the amounts of ingredients that must be added to the mix to finish the loaf.

- The mix can be stored at room temperature for 2 to 3 weeks or frozen for up to 6 weeks. Bring to room temperature before using.

- Be sure to mix well to distribute the ingredients evenly before adding to baking pan.

- A bread machine mix with instructions for finishing, presented in a fancy wicker basket along with some jam or jelly, makes an excellent hostess gift.

Maple Banana Flaxseed Bread

As it bakes, the aroma of this bread brings back memories of a farm kitchen from long ago.

Tip

Mash and freeze ripe bananas so they're ready when you need them. Thaw and warm to room temperature before using.

Yes, you're reading it right: The 1.5 lb (750 g) recipe contains the *same* amount of yeast as the 2 lb (1 kg).

Variation

Light or regular pancake syrup, or honey, can be substituted for the maple syrup.

1.5 LB (750 G)		
1/3 cup	water	75 mL
1 cup	mashed bananas	250 mL
1/4 cup	skim milk powder	50 mL
1 1/2 tsp	salt	7 mL
2 tbsp	maple syrup	25 mL
2 tbsp	shortening or vegetable oil	25 mL
3/4 cup	whole wheat flour	175 mL
1 1/2 cups	all-purpose flour or bread flour	375 mL
1/4 cup	flaxseed, cracked	50 mL
1/4 cup	chopped walnuts	50 mL
1/2 tsp	ground cinnamon	2 mL
1/4 tsp	ground ginger	1 mL
2 tsp	bread machine yeast	10 mL

2 LB (1 KG)		
1/2 cup	water	125 mL
1 cup	mashed bananas	250 mL
1/3 cup	skim milk powder	75 mL
1 1/2 tsp	salt	7 mL
3 tbsp	maple syrup	45 mL
2 tbsp	shortening or vegetable oil	25 mL
1 cup	whole wheat flour	250 mL
2 cups	all-purpose flour or bread flour	500 mL
1/3 cup	flaxseed, cracked	75 mL
1/3 cup	chopped walnuts	75 mL
1/2 tsp	ground cinnamon	2 mL
1/4 tsp	ground ginger	1 mL
2 tsp	bread machine yeast	10 mL

1. Measure ingredients into baking pan in the order recommended by the manufacturer. Insert pan into the oven chamber.
2. Select **Whole Wheat Cycle**.

Tips on Using Flaxseed

Thin and oval in shape, dark brown or golden in color, flaxseed adds a crunchy texture to baked products. Ground flaxseed (also known as linseed) is often used as part of the fat component of recipes.

Baked goods containing ground flaxseed tend to brown more rapidly, so use the light crust setting.

To crack: Pulse in a coffee grinder, blender or food processor just long enough to break the seed coat but not grind completely. This allows the body to digest and absorb the nutrients.

To grind: Place whole seeds in a coffee grinder or blender. Grind only the amount required.

To store: Whole flaxseed can be stored at room temperature for up to a year. Ground flaxseed should be refrigerated in an airtight opaque container, as it can become rancid at room temperature. Use it within 1 month.

Whole Wheat Flaxseed Bread

Here's a crunchy, nutty, whole wheat loaf that's loaded with flaxseed.

Tips

Flaxseed can aid in lowering cholesterol levels.

For more information on flaxseed, see page 109.

Variation

For a lighter-textured loaf, substitute 1 cup (250 mL) all-purpose or bread flour for 1 cup (250 mL) of the whole wheat flour.

1.5 LB (750 G)

1¼ cups	water	300 mL
¼ cup	skim milk powder	50 mL
1¼ tsp	salt	6 mL
1 tbsp	packed brown sugar	15 mL
2 tbsp	shortening or vegetable oil	25 mL
3 cups	whole wheat flour	750 mL
½ cup	flaxseed, cracked	125 mL
1 tsp	bread machine yeast	5 mL

2 LB (1 KG)

1½ cups	water	375 mL
¼ cup	skim milk powder	50 mL
1½ tsp	salt	7 mL
2 tbsp	packed brown sugar	25 mL
2 tbsp	shortening or vegetable oil	25 mL
3½ cups	whole wheat flour	875 mL
¾ cup	flaxseed, cracked	175 mL
1½ tsp	bread machine yeast	7 mL

1. Measure ingredients into baking pan in the order recommended by the manufacturer. Insert pan into the oven chamber.
2. Select **Whole Wheat Cycle**.

Whole Wheat Harvest Seed Bread

This variation of our
Country Harvest
Bread *is for the true*
whole wheat lover.

Tips

Store flaxseed, sesame
and sunflower seeds
in the refrigerator to
keep them fresh.

For more information
on flaxseed, see
page 109.

Variation

For an interesting
flavor, substitute
$1/4$ cup (50 mL) of
rye flour for $1/4$ cup
(50 mL) of the whole
wheat flour.

1.5 LB (750 G)		
1$1/4$ cups	water	300 mL
1$1/2$ tsp	salt	7 mL
2 tbsp	packed brown sugar	25 mL
2 tbsp	vegetable oil	25 mL
2$3/4$ cups	whole wheat flour	675 mL
$1/3$ cup	buttermilk powder	75 mL
$1/4$ cup	flaxseed, cracked	50 mL
$1/4$ cup	sesame seeds	50 mL
$1/4$ cup	sunflower seeds raw, unsalted	50 mL
1$1/4$ tsp	bread machine yeast	6 mL

2 LB (1 KG)		
1$1/3$ cups	water	325 mL
1$1/2$ tsp	salt	7 mL
3 tbsp	packed brown sugar	45 mL
3 tbsp	vegetable oil	45 mL
3$1/2$ cups	whole wheat flour	875 mL
$1/2$ cup	buttermilk powder	125 mL
$1/3$ cup	flaxseed, cracked	75 mL
$1/3$ cup	sesame seeds	75 mL
$1/3$ cup	sunflower seeds, raw, unsalted	75 mL
1$1/2$ tsp	bread machine yeast	7 mL

1. Measure ingredients into baking pan in the order
   recommended by the manufacturer. Insert pan into
   the oven chamber.
2. Select **Whole Wheat Cycle**.

Double-Crunch Wheat Bread

French toast made from this bread is scrumptious — the perfect treat for a holiday brunch.

Tip

Don't use roasted, salted sunflower seeds for this recipe. The fat and salt will make the loaf short and heavy.

Yes, you're reading it right: The 1.5 lb (750 g) recipe contains *more* yeast than the 2 lb (1 kg).

Variation

For an even crunchier loaf, substitute bulgur for the cracked wheat.

1.5 LB (750 G)		
1⅓ cups	water	325 mL
¼ cup	skim milk powder	50 mL
1 tsp	salt	5 mL
2 tbsp	liquid honey	25 mL
2 tbsp	vegetable oil	25 mL
3 cups	all-purpose flour or bread flour	750 mL
⅔ cup	cracked wheat	150 mL
⅔ cup	sunflower seeds, raw, unsalted	150 mL
1½ tsp	bread machine yeast	7 mL

2 LB (1 KG)		
1½ cups	water	375 mL
⅓ cup	skim milk powder	75 mL
1¼ tsp	salt	6 mL
3 tbsp	liquid honey	45 mL
2 tbsp	vegetable oil	25 mL
3¼ cups	all-purpose flour or bread flour	800 mL
¾ cup	cracked wheat	175 mL
¾ cup	sunflower seeds, raw, unsalted	175 mL
1¼ tsp	bread machine yeast	6 mL

1. Measure ingredients into baking pan in the order recommended by the manufacturer. Insert pan into the oven chamber.
2. Select **Basic Cycle**.

Poppy Thyme Bread

1.5 LB (750 G)		
3/4 cup	water	175 mL
2	eggs	2
1 1/4 tsp	salt	6 mL
2 tbsp	liquid honey	25 mL
2 tbsp	butter	25 mL
2 2/3 cups	all-purpose flour or bread flour	650 mL
1/4 cup	poppy seeds	50 mL
1 tsp	dried thyme (or 1 tbsp/15 mL snipped fresh thyme)	5 mL
3/4 tsp	bread machine yeast	3 mL

2 LB (1 KG)		
1 cup	water	250 mL
2	eggs	2
1 1/2 tsp	salt	7 mL
2 tbsp	liquid honey	25 mL
3 tbsp	butter	45 mL
3 cups	all-purpose flour or bread flour	750 mL
1/3 cup	poppy seeds	75 mL
1 1/2 tsp	dried thyme (or 2 tbsp/25 mL snipped fresh thyme)	7 mL
3/4 tsp	bread machine yeast	3 mL

1. Measure ingredients into baking pan in the order recommended by the manufacturer. Insert pan into the oven chamber.
2. Select **Basic Cycle**.

Autumn Pumpkin Seed Bread

A fall celebration of color, texture and flavor, this bread has toasted pumpkin seeds for crunch.

Tips

Canned pumpkin purée must be at room temperature or the loaf will be short and heavy.

When using fresh pumpkin, ensure that it has the same consistency as canned.

See Techniques Glossary, page 369, for instructions on toasting nuts and seeds.

Yes, you're reading it right: The 1.5 lb (750 g) recipe contains *more* yeast than the 2 lb (1 kg).

Variation

Substitute fresh pumpkin, cooked and puréed, for the canned — but not pumpkin pie filling — also at room temperature.

1.5 LB (750 G)		
1/3 cup	water	75 mL
2/3 cup	canned pumpkin purée	150 mL
1	egg	1
1/4 cup	skim milk powder	50 mL
1 tsp	salt	5 mL
1/4 cup	packed brown sugar	50 mL
2 tbsp	shortening or vegetable oil	25 mL
3/4 cup	whole wheat flour	175 mL
1 3/4 cups	all-purpose flour or bread flour	400 mL
1/3 cup	pumpkin seeds, toasted	75 mL
1/2 tsp	ground allspice	2 mL
1/4 tsp	ground ginger	1 mL
1/4 tsp	ground nutmeg	1 mL
1 3/4 tsp	bread machine yeast	8 mL

2 LB (1 KG)		
1/2 cup	water	125 mL
1 cup	canned pumpkin purée	250 mL
1	egg	1
1/4 cup	skim milk powder	50 mL
1 1/2 tsp	salt	7 mL
1/3 cup	packed brown sugar	75 mL
2 tbsp	shortening or vegetable oil	25 mL
1 cup	whole wheat flour	250 mL
2 1/4 cups	all-purpose flour or bread flour	550 mL
1/2 cup	pumpkin seeds, toasted	125 mL
3/4 tsp	ground allspice	3 mL
1/2 tsp	ground ginger	2 mL
1/4 tsp	ground nutmeg	1 mL
1 1/2 tsp	bread machine yeast	7 mL

1. Measure ingredients into baking pan in the order recommended by the manufacturer. Insert pan into the oven chamber.
2. Select **Whole Wheat Cycle**.

For Those Who Love Oven-Baked Bread

You can bake any of the recipes in this book in your oven instead of in the bread machine. Here's how:

Choose any 1.5 lb (750 g) loaf recipe, but select the **Dough Cycle**. Then remove the dough to a lightly floured surface. Cup the fingers of one hand together while holding the bread machine baking pan with the other. This allows you to get under the dough and tip it out.

Doughs may be sticky until they cool to room temperature. Resist the urge to add more flour, as added flour toughens the texture of the finished loaf. Don't rush this resting period, as it allows the gluten developed during kneading to relax. The dough will be more elastic and easier to work with.

Once the dough has cooled, roll it out or pull it into an 8- by 10-inch (20 by 25 cm) rectangle. Working from the short side, roll jellyroll-style. Press the dough surfaces together with the heel of your hand at each turn. Start at one end and work the heel down to the other with short pats.

Seal the seam by pinching the dough between the thumb and forefinger. Holding the loaf in both hands, with the seam down, tuck the ends under. Place the dough seam side down in the pan.

Lightly spray the top of the loaf so it does not dry out during rising. Cover with a sheet of waxed paper, then a lint-free towel. Set in a warm, draft-free place until it doubles in volume. This will take between 30 minutes and 2 hours. The sweeter and denser breads take longer to rise.

To test for doneness, press your baby finger into the dough, near the side of the pan; if the indent stays, the loaf has risen enough. If the indent slowly fills in, wait another 10 to 15 minutes and try again. Do not let the dough over-rise, as it rises a bit more in the oven (called "oven bloom"). It could collapse during baking if over-risen.

Bake bread at 350°F (180°C) for 40 to 50 minutes. Sometimes the loaf browns on the top before it is actually finished baking. To test for doneness, invert the loaf and tap it on the bottom with your knuckles. It will sound hollow when it is baked. If the top of a sweet loaf is browning too quickly, tent it with foil for the last 10 minutes. Remove the baked loaf from the pan immediately and set on a rack to cool.

Sesame Semolina Bread

Tip

Look for semolina flour in bulk food stores or in the pasta or specialty food section of your supermarket.

Variation

Pasta flour or a very fine grind of cornmeal can be substituted for the semolina.

1.5 LB (750 G)		
1¼ cups	water	300 mL
¼ cup	skim milk powder	50 mL
1¼ tsp	salt	6 mL
2 tbsp	granulated sugar	25 mL
2 tbsp	olive oil	25 mL
2 cups	all-purpose flour or bread flour	500 mL
1 cup	semolina flour	250 mL
⅓ cup	sesame seeds	75 mL
1 tsp	bread machine yeast	5 mL

2 LB (1 KG)		
1½ cups	water	375 mL
⅓ cup	skim milk powder	75 mL
1½ tsp	salt	7 mL
2 tbsp	granulated sugar	25 mL
3 tbsp	olive oil	45 mL
2½ cups	all-purpose flour or bread flour	625 mL
1 cup	semolina flour	250 mL
½ cup	sesame seeds	125 mL
1¼ tsp	bread machine yeast	6 mL

1. Measure ingredients into baking pan in the order recommended by the manufacturer. Insert pan into the oven chamber.
2. Select **Basic Cycle**.

Apple Date Granola Bread

1.5 LB (750 G)		
3/4 cup	unsweetened apple juice	175 mL
2/3 cup	unsweetened applesauce	150 mL
1 tsp	salt	5 mL
2 tbsp	liquid honey	25 mL
2 tbsp	shortening or vegetable oil	25 mL
1 cup	whole wheat flour	250 mL
2 cups	all-purpose flour or bread flour	500 mL
2/3 cup	whole pitted dates	150 mL
1/3 cup	granola	75 mL
1 tsp	ground cinnamon	5 mL
1 1/2 tsp	bread machine yeast	7 mL

2 LB (1 KG)		
1 cup	unsweetened apple juice	250 mL
2/3 cup	unsweetened applesauce	150 mL
1 1/4 tsp	salt	6 mL
2 tbsp	liquid honey	25 mL
2 tbsp	shortening or vegetable oil	25 mL
1 1/2 cups	whole wheat flour	375 mL
2 cups	all-purpose flour or bread flour	500 mL
3/4 cup	whole pitted dates	175 mL
1/2 cup	granola	125 mL
1 1/4 tsp	ground cinnamon	6 mL
1 1/2 tsp	bread machine yeast	7 mL

1. Measure ingredients into baking pan in the order recommended by the manufacturer. Insert pan into the oven chamber.
2. Select **Whole Wheat Cycle**.

Granola Currant Loaf

Tip

Unsweetened granola can be purchased at bulk food stores. If all you can find is the sweetened variety, decrease the sugar by half.

Yes, you're reading it right: The 1.5 lb (750 g) recipe contains the *same* amount of yeast as the 2 lb (1 kg).

Variation

For a nuttier, slightly sweeter taste, substitute an equal amount of muesli for the granola, and raisins for the dried currants.

1.5 LB (750 G)

1 1/4 cups	water	300 mL
1/4 cup	skim milk powder	50 mL
1 1/2 tsp	salt	7 mL
2 tbsp	packed brown sugar	25 mL
1 tbsp	vegetable oil	15 mL
2 3/4 cups	all-purpose flour or bread flour	675 mL
1 cup	unsweetened granola	250 mL
1 1/2 tsp	bread machine yeast	7 mL
1/2 cup	dried currants	125 mL

2 LB (1 KG)

1 1/2 cups	water	375 mL
1/3 cup	skim milk powder	75 mL
1 3/4 tsp	salt	8 mL
2 tbsp	packed brown sugar	25 mL
2 tbsp	vegetable oil	25 mL
3 cups	all-purpose flour or bread flour	750 mL
1 1/4 cups	unsweetened granola	300 mL
1 1/2 tsp	bread machine yeast	7 mL
3/4 cup	dried currants	175 mL

1. Measure all ingredients *except dried currants* into baking pan in the order recommended by the manufacturer. Insert pan into the oven chamber.
2. Select **Basic Cycle**.
3. Add currants at the "add ingredient" signal.

Trail Bread

The tang of yogurt enhances the mix of fruits in this bread, while the nuts provide a delightful crunch.

Tip

Different types of trail mix will affect the taste and appearance of this bread. Try making it with Sierra, Harvest or Manhattan Mix.

Yes, you're reading it right: The 1.5 lb (750 g) recipe contains the *same* amount of yeast as the 2 lb (1 kg).

1.5 LB (750 G)		
1/2 cup	water	125 mL
3/4 cup	fruit-flavored yogurt	175 mL
1 tsp	salt	5 mL
3 tbsp	granulated sugar	45 mL
1 tbsp	shortening or vegetable oil	15 mL
2 3/4 cups	all-purpose flour or bread flour	675 mL
3/4 cup	trail mix (see Tip, at left)	175 mL
1 1/2 tsp	bread machine yeast	7 mL

2 LB (1 KG)		
1 cup	water	250 mL
3/4 cup	fruit-flavored yogurt	175 mL
1 1/2 tsp	salt	7 mL
3 tbsp	granulated sugar	45 mL
2 tbsp	shortening or vegetable oil	25 mL
3 3/4 cups	all-purpose flour or bread flour	925 mL
1 1/2 cups	trail mix (see Tip, at left)	375 mL
1 1/2 tsp	bread machine yeast	7 mL

1. Measure ingredients into baking pan in the the order recommended by the manufacturer. Insert pan into the oven chamber.
2. Select **Sweet Cycle**.

Almond Apricot Yogurt Bread

With its flecks of golden apricots, this sweet bread is a treat for the eye — and tastebuds! Serve it with fresh fruit for a late Sunday brunch.

Tips

Use scissors to snip dried apricots into 6 pieces.

For instructions on toasting almonds and other nuts, see Techniques Glossary, page 368.

This recipe was developed using both apricot- and peach-flavored yogurt — in regular, lower-fat and fat-free varieties. Each type resulted in a slightly different bread, but they all tasted great.

1.5 LB (750 G)		
1/2 cup	water	125 mL
1/2 cup	fruit-flavored yogurt (see note, at left)	125 mL
1	egg	1
1 1/4 tsp	salt	6 mL
2 tbsp	granulated sugar	25 mL
2 tbsp	butter	25 mL
2 1/2 cups	all-purpose flour or bread flour	625 mL
1 tsp	ground nutmeg	5 mL
1 1/2 tsp	bread machine yeast	7 mL
2/3 cup	slivered almonds, toasted	150 mL
2/3 cup	snipped dried apricots	150 mL

2 LB (1 KG) • extra large		
2/3 cup	water	150 mL
2/3 cup	fruit-flavored yogurt (see note, at left)	150 mL
1	egg	1
1 1/2 tsp	salt	7 mL
2 tbsp	granulated sugar	25 mL
2 tbsp	butter	25 mL
3 cups	all-purpose flour or bread flour	750 mL
1 1/2 tsp	ground nutmeg	7 mL
2 tsp	bread machine yeast	10 mL
3/4 cup	slivered almonds, toasted	175 mL
3/4 cup	snipped dried apricots	175 mL

1. Measure all ingredients *except almonds and dried apricots* into baking pan in the order recommended by the manufacturer. Insert pan into the oven chamber. Select **Sweet Cycle**. Add almonds and dried apricots at "add ingredient" signal.

Peanut Rye Loaf

Tips

Rye flour is much lower in gluten than wheat flour, so this loaf is quite compact.

Use either smooth or crunchy peanut butter.

The peanuts can be added directly with the flour; no need to wait for the "add ingredient" signal.

Yes, you're reading it right: The 1.5 lb (750 g) recipe contains the *same* amount of yeast as the 2 lb (1 kg).

1.5 LB (750 G)		
1½ cups	water	375 mL
¼ cup	skim milk powder	50 mL
1½ tsp	salt	7 mL
2 tbsp	packed brown sugar	25 mL
2 tbsp	peanut butter	25 mL
2¾ cups	all-purpose flour or bread flour	675 mL
¾ cup	rye flour	175 mL
⅔ cup	unsalted peanuts	150 mL
1½ tsp	bread machine yeast	7 mL

2 LB (1 KG) • extra large		
1⅔ cups	water	400 mL
⅓ cup	skim milk powder	75 mL
1½ tsp	salt	7 mL
3 tbsp	packed brown sugar	45 mL
3 tbsp	peanut butter	45 mL
4 cups	all-purpose flour or bread flour	1000 mL
¾ cup	rye flour	175 mL
¾ cup	unsalted peanuts	175 mL
1½ tsp	bread machine yeast	7 mL

1. Measure ingredients into baking pan in the order recommended by the manufacturer. Insert pan into the oven chamber.
2. Select **Basic Cycle**.

Sweet Potato Pecan Bread

1.5 LB (750 G)		
2/3 cup	water	150 mL
1/2 cup	mashed sweet potato	125 mL
1/2 cup	chopped apple, with peel	125 mL
1/4 cup	skim milk powder	50 mL
1 tsp	salt	5 mL
2 tbsp	granulated sugar	25 mL
2 tbsp	shortening or vegetable oil	25 mL
3 cups	all-purpose flour or bread flour	750 mL
1/2 tsp	ground cinnamon	2 mL
1/4 tsp	ground nutmeg	1 mL
1 tsp	bread machine yeast	5 mL
1/3 cup	chopped pecans	75 mL
1/4 cup	raisins	50 mL

2 LB (1 KG)		
3/4 cup	water	175 mL
2/3 cup	mashed sweet potato	150 mL
2/3 cup	chopped apple, with peel	150 mL
1/4 cup	skim milk powder	50 mL
1 1/2 tsp	salt	8 mL
3 tbsp	granulated sugar	45 mL
3 tbsp	shortening or vegetable oil	45 mL
3 1/2 cups	all-purpose flour or bread flour	875 mL
1 tsp	ground cinnamon	5 mL
1/2 tsp	ground nutmeg	2 mL
1 1/4 tsp	bread machine yeast	6 mL
1/2 cup	chopped pecans	125 mL
1/3 cup	raisins	75 mL

1. Measure all ingredients *except pecans and raisins* into baking pan in the order recommended by the manufacturer. Insert pan into the oven chamber.
2. Select **Sweet Cycle**.
3. Add pecans and raisins at "add ingredient" signal.

Pecans (Peek-anns or Pe-kawns)

Nutritional value

Pecans contain more than 19 vitamins and minerals, including vitamins A and E, folic acid, calcium, magnesium, phosphorous, potassium, several B vitamins and zinc. Half the fat is monounsaturated and a quarter is polyunsaturated. Pecans contain antioxidants that may have a protective effect against certain cancers and heart disease and that aid in lowering cholesterol. Pecans are a protein and also increase fiber when added to breads.

Purchasing

A fresh crop arrives in the stores in November each year. Shells should crack easily and release most of the kernel (nut meat) in one or more large pieces. The kernel should be a very light color, without stains or dark spots, and the texture should be crisp, not soft (green) or brittle (old). There should be no hint of bitterness in the flavor. Pecans can be purchased in the shell or shelled. Shelled nuts are sold in perfect halves or in pieces, granules or meal. Purchase plump nuts that are uniform in color and size. Pieces are usually less expensive.

1 lb (450 g) in-shell pecans yields 8 to 9 oz (240 to 270 g) pecan halves
1 cup (250 mL) chopped pecans weighs 5 oz (150 g)

Storing

Protect from moisture, light, heat and air to keep fresh. Store in an airtight container to prevent absorption of moisture, gases and odors. In-shell pecans can be stored in a cool, dry place for 6 to 12 months. Shelled pecans can be kept in airtight containers in the refrigerator for up to 9 months or in sealed plastic bags in the freezer for up to 2 years. Pecans can be thawed and re-frozen without loss of flavor or texture.

Java Chocolate Crunch Loaf

Tip

Chances are you'll have to shell the pistachio nuts yourself. But if you can find pre-shelled nuts, use them — you'll save a lot of time.

Yes, you're reading it right: The 1.5 lb (750 g) recipe contains *more* yeast than the 2 lb (1 kg).

Variation

Substitute espresso coffee for the regular brewed.

1.5 LB (750 G)		
³/₄ cup	water	175 mL
¹/₃ cup	lukewarm coffee	75 mL
¹/₄ cup	skim milk powder	50 mL
1¹/₄ tsp	salt	6 mL
2 tbsp	liquid honey	25 mL
2 tbsp	vegetable oil	25 mL
3 cups	all-purpose flour or bread flour	750 mL
1 tbsp	unsweetened cocoa powder	15 mL
¹/₃ cup	pistachio nuts	75 mL
1¹/₂ tsp	bread machine yeast	7 mL

2 LB (1 KG)		
1 cup	water	250 mL
¹/₂ cup	lukewarm coffee	125 mL
¹/₃ cup	skim milk powder	75 mL
1¹/₂ tsp	salt	7 mL
2 tbsp	liquid honey	25 mL
2 tbsp	vegetable oil	25 mL
3³/₄ cups	all-purpose flour or bread flour	925 mL
2 tbsp	unsweetened cocoa powder	25 mL
¹/₂ cup	pistachio nuts	125 mL
1¹/₄ tsp	bread machine yeast	6 mL

1. Measure all ingredients into baking pan in the order recommended by the manufacturer. Insert pan into the oven chamber.
2. Select **Sweet Cycle**.

Chunky Walnut Bread

Serve as an after-school snack with wedges of old Cheddar cheese.

Tips

Taste the walnuts for freshness before adding.

Use olive oil if walnut oil is not available.

Variation

Substitute an equal amount of pecans or shredded unsweetened coconut for the walnuts.

1.5 LB (750 G)		
1 1/4 cups	water	300 mL
1/4 cup	skim milk powder	50 mL
1 1/4 tsp	salt	6 mL
1 tbsp	packed brown sugar	15 mL
1 tbsp	walnut oil	15 mL
3 cups	all-purpose flour or bread flour	750 mL
3/4 cup	chopped walnuts	175 mL
1 tsp	bread machine yeast	5 mL

2 LB (1 KG)		
1 1/3 cups	water	325 mL
1/4 cup	skim milk powder	50 mL
1 1/2 tsp	salt	7 mL
3 tbsp	packed brown sugar	45 mL
2 tbsp	walnut oil	25 mL
3 1/2 cups	all-purpose flour or bread flour	875 mL
1 cup	chopped walnuts	250 mL
1 1/4 tsp	bread machine yeast	6 mL

1. Measure ingredients into baking pan in the order recommended by the manufacturer. Insert the pan into the oven chamber.
2. Select **Basic Cycle**.

Applesauce Oatmeal Walnut Bread

Try this heavier-textured bread, which has the sweet taste of apples and the crunch of walnuts.

Tip

Choose unsweetened applesauce for this recipe; the sweetened variety may affect the loaf's appearance.

Yes, you're reading it right: The 1.5 lb (750 g) recipe contains the *same* amount of yeast as the 2 lb (1 kg).

Variation

You can add up to $1/4$ cup (50 mL) extra grated apple or chunks of apple without changing the appearance of the loaf.

1.5 LB (750 G)

$1/2$ cup	grated apple	125 mL
$1/2$ cup	unsweetened applesauce	125 mL
1	egg	1
$1 1/2$ tsp	salt	7 mL
3 tbsp	granulated sugar	45 mL
2 tbsp	shortening or vegetable oil	25 mL
1 cup	whole wheat flour	250 mL
$1 1/4$ cups	all-purpose flour or bread flour	300 mL
$1/2$ cup	quick-cooking oats	125 mL
$1/2$ cup	chopped walnuts	125 mL
$1 1/2$ tsp	bread machine yeast	7 mL

2 LB (1 KG) • extra large

$2/3$ cup	grated apple	150 mL
$2/3$ cup	unsweetened applesauce	150 mL
2	eggs	2
$1 1/2$ tsp	salt	7 mL
3 tbsp	granulated sugar	45 mL
2 tbsp	shortening or vegetable oil	25 mL
$1 1/2$ cups	whole wheat flour	375 mL
2 cups	all-purpose flour or bread flour	500 mL
$3/4$ cup	quick-cooking oats	175 mL
$3/4$ cup	chopped walnuts	175 mL
$1 1/2$ tsp	bread machine yeast	7 mL

1. Measure ingredients into baking pan in the order recommended by the manufacturer. Insert pan into the oven chamber.
2. Select **Whole Wheat Cycle.**

Savory Wraps, Flatbreads and Filled Breads

Today's busy lifestyle means most of us eat on the run. With your bread machine preparing the dough for these wraps and flatbreads, your life will be less complicated. Make a meal or a snack for hungry teens with filled breads, or serve with a salad on a busy Friday night. These recipes will be a hit with your family. Let them choose and help prepare the toppings and fillings.

continued next page...

Ciabatta

• *Baking sheet, lightly floured*

1 1/2 cups	water	375 mL
1 1/2 tsp	salt	7 mL
1 tsp	granulated sugar	5 mL
1 tbsp	olive oil	15 mL
3 1/4 cups	all-purpose flour or bread flour	800 mL
1 1/2 tsp	bread machine yeast	7 mL

Tip

When dusting with flour, do not use any other finish or the crust will be sticky. Use a flour sifter for a light, even dusting.

Variation

Dust with sweet rice or rye flour for an interesting color contrast.

1. Measure ingredients into baking pan in the order recommended by the manufacturer. Insert pan into the oven chamber. Select **Dough Cycle**.

2. Remove dough to a lightly floured surface. (This is a very sticky and moist dough, but resist the urge to add more flour). Cover with a large bowl and let the dough rest for 10 to 15 minutes. Divide the dough into half. Form each into a 13- by 4-inch (33 by 10 cm) oval. Place on prepared baking sheet. With floured fingers, make deep indentations all over each loaf, making sure to press all the way down to the baking sheet. Dust the ovals lightly with flour.

3. Cover and allow to rise in a warm, draft-free place for 30 to 45 minutes, or until doubled in volume. Meanwhile, preheat oven to 425°F (220°C).

4. Make indents in the loaves a second time. Bake on the middle rack in preheated oven for 25 to 30 minutes, or until the bread sounds hollow when tapped on bottom. For a crispier crust, put 12 ice cubes into a 13- by 9-inch (3 L) metal baking pan on bottom oven rack. During baking, spritz loaves with water every 5 to 10 minutes.

The specks of tomato in this flatbread provide bursts of flavor.

Tips

To give a warm tomato color to the ciabatta, snip the sun-dried tomatoes into bite-size pieces before adding with the liquid. Use dry, not oil-packed, sun-dried tomatoes.

The dough should be slightly sticky — resist the temptation to add flour.

Dust the baking sheet and ciabatta with sweet rice flour. It doesn't brown the way wheat flour does during baking.

Tomato Rosemary Ciabatta

• Baking sheet, lightly floured

1¹/₂ cups	water	375 mL
¹/₃ cup	sun-dried tomatoes, snipped into small pieces	75 mL
1¹/₂ tsp	salt	7 mL
1 tsp	granulated sugar	5 mL
1 tbsp	olive oil	15 mL
1¹/₄ cups	whole wheat flour	300 mL
2 cups	all-purpose flour or bread flour	500 mL
1 tsp	dry rubbed rosemary	5 mL
1¹/₂ tsp	bread machine yeast	7 mL

1. Measure all ingredients into machine's baking pan in the order recommended by the manufacturer. Insert pan into the oven chamber. Select **Dough Cycle**.

2. Remove dough to a lightly floured surface. Cover with a large bowl and let rest for 10 to 15 minutes. Divide the dough in half. Form each into a 13- by 4-inch (33 by 10 cm) oval. Place on prepared baking sheet. With floured fingers, make deep indentations all over each loaf, making sure to press all the way down to the baking sheet. Dust the ovals lightly with flour.

3. Cover and let rise in a warm, draft-free place for 30 to 45 minutes, or until doubled in volume. Meanwhile, preheat oven to 425°F (220°C).

4. Make indents in the loaves a second time. Bake in preheated oven for 25 to 30 minutes, or until ciabatta sound hollow when tapped on the bottom.

Sun-Dried Tomato Lavosh

Tips

Store in an airtight container, and the lavosh will keep crisp for weeks.

To make sure the lavosh isn't tough, roll the dough as thinly as possible.

Variation

Any flavored olive oil can be used in this recipe. Try adding dried herbs (such as oregano, rosemary or thyme) to complement the oil.

• Preheated baking stone or baking sheet

1¼ cups	water	300 mL
⅓ cup	sun-dried tomatoes, snipped into small pieces	75 mL
1 tsp	salt	5 mL
1 tsp	granulated sugar	5 mL
2 tbsp	roasted garlic and basil–flavored olive oil	25 mL
3½ cups	all-purpose flour or bread flour	875 mL
2 tsp	dried basil	10 mL
1¼ tsp	bread machine yeast	6 mL
1 cup	shredded Parmesan or old Cheddar cheese	250 mL

1. Measure all ingredients *except cheese* into machine's baking pan in the order recommended by the manufacturer. Insert pan into the oven chamber. Select **Dough Cycle**.

2. Remove dough to a lightly floured surface. Cover with a large bowl and let rest for 10 to 15 minutes. Meanwhile, preheat oven to 375°F (190°C).

3. Divide the dough into 4 portions. Sprinkle ¼ cup (50 mL) of the cheese on a cutting board. Place one portion of the dough on top of the cheese and roll as thinly as possible into a 7-inch (18 cm) wide rectangle, turning over frequently to press the cheese into the dough. With a pizza cutter or sharp knife, score into triangles with a base of 2 to 2½ inches (5 to 6 cm), being careful not to cut all the way through. Repeat with remaining portions.

4. Place one rectangle at a time on prepared baking sheet or preheated baking stone. Bake in preheated oven for 13 to 18 minutes, or until golden brown. Remove from oven and allow to cool. Break into long, thin triangles.

Lavosh Crisps with Sesame Seeds

This thin, crisp Armenian flatbread is covered with sesame seeds, which toast as it bakes. Your guests will wonder how you prepared the crisps.

Tips

Store in an airtight container for up to 2 to 3 months. Crisp in the oven, if necessary, before serving.

The thinner the dough is rolled, the more authentic the bread will be.

Variation

Break this thin, crunchy bread into crisps to serve with soups, salads or dips.

• Preheated baking stone or baking sheet

1¼ cups	water	300 mL
¼ cup	skim milk powder	50 mL
1½ tsp	salt	7 mL
1 tsp	granulated sugar	5 mL
2 tbsp	shortening or vegetable oil	25 mL
3½ cups	all purpose flour or bread flour	875 mL
1¼ tsp	bread machine yeast	6 mL
1 cup	sesame seeds	250 mL

1. Measure all ingredients *except sesame seeds* into baking pan in the order recommended by the manufacturer. Insert pan into the oven chamber. Select **Dough Cycle**.

2. Remove dough to a lightly floured board; cover with a large bowl and let rest for 10 to 15 minutes. Meanwhile, preheat oven to 375°F (190°C).

3. Divide the dough into 4 equal portions. Spread ¼ cup (50 mL) sesame seeds on the board. Roll one portion of dough as thinly as possible, turning over frequently to press the seeds into the dough. Repeat with the remaining portions.

4. Bake in preheated oven for 13 to 18 minutes, until golden brown and large bubbles form. Remove from the oven; allow to cool and break into large pieces.

Moroccan Anise Bread

• *Two baking sheets, sprinkled with cornmeal*

Making dough doesn't get much easier (or faster) than this. Hands-on preparation time is less than 15 minutes.

1⅓ cups	water	325 mL
1½ tsp	salt	7 mL
1½ cups	whole wheat flour	375 mL
2 cups	all-purpose flour or bread flour	500 mL
¼ cup	cornmeal	50 mL
2 tsp	anise seeds	10 mL
1 tsp	bread machine yeast	5 mL

Tip

Baking the flatbread directly on the oven rack gives a crispier bottom crust.

Variation

Roll out the dough to one 10-inch (25 cm) circle and finish as a hearth bread.

1. Measure ingredients into machine's baking pan in the order recommended by the manufacturer. Insert pan into the oven chamber. Select **Dough Cycle**.

2. Remove dough to a lightly floured surface. Cover with a large bowl and let rest for 10 to 15 minutes. Meanwhile, preheat oven to 400°F (200°C).

3. Divide dough in half. Form or roll out each half into a 10-inch (25 cm) round. Place on prepared baking sheets. Cover and let rise in a warm, draft-free place for 20 to 25 minutes or until almost doubled in volume.

4. Pierce the dough all the way through with a fork. Bake in preheated oven for 10 minutes. Remove from baking sheet and place directly onto the oven rack; continue baking for 8 to 10 minutes, or until flatbreads sound hollow when tapped on the bottom.

Middle-Eastern Flatbread

This bread complements a grilled salmon steak and a spicy corn and black bean salsa.

Tip

Quickly immerse this flatbread in water, blot dry and roll up jellyroll-style around deli meats for a delicious luncheon treat to go.

Variation

Grill the flatbread dough quickly on your outdoor barbecue. Place dough on 2 baking sheets stacked together, then cook on the grill. This will help prevent burning.

• *Preheated baking stone or baking sheet*

1 1/4 cups	water	300 mL
1/4 cup	skim milk powder	50 mL
1 1/2 tsp	salt	7 mL
1 tsp	liquid honey	5 mL
2 tbsp	olive oil	25 mL
3 1/2 cups	all purpose flour or bread flour	875 mL
1 1/4 tsp	bread machine yeast	6 mL

TOPPING

2 tbsp	olive oil	25 mL
1 tbsp	lemon juice	15 mL
2 tsp	Zahtar spice mix	10 mL

1. Measure ingredients into baking pan in the order recommended by the manufacturer. Insert pan into the oven chamber. Select **Dough Cycle**.

2. Remove dough to a lightly floured board; cover with a large bowl and let rest for 10 to 15 minutes. Meanwhile, preheat oven to 425°F (220°C).

3. Flatten dough into a circle. Cut into 8 wedges. Stretch each into a triangle 1/4 inch (5 mm) thick. Place on a baking sheet, cover and let rest for 15 minutes.

4. *Topping:* In a small bowl, combine all topping ingredients. Brush over each triangle.

5. Bake in preheated oven for 10 minutes or until golden brown.

Indian-Style Naan

• Baking sheet, sprinkled with cornmeal

In India this golden puffed bread is served right off the sides of a tandoor oven. Naan is a must to accompany curry dishes.

³/₄ cup	water	175 mL
¹/₂ cup	plain yogurt	125 mL
1	egg yolk	1
1¹/₂ tsp	salt	7 mL
1 tbsp	butter	15 mL
3¹/₃ cups	all-purpose flour or bread flour	825 mL
1¹/₂ tsp	baking powder	7 mL
1¹/₂ tsp	bread machine yeast	7 mL

TOPPING

2 tsp	melted butter	10 mL
2 tsp	sesame seeds or minced onion	10 mL

Tips

Cool the melted butter slightly before brushing on the risen dough.

Bake these teardrop-shaped breads just until lightly browned or they will toughen.

Variation

Grill on the barbecue over medium-high heat, directly on the grill rack, with the lid closed, for 3 to 4 minutes per side.

1. Measure ingredients into baking pan in the order recommended by the manufacturer. Insert pan into the oven chamber. Select **Dough Cycle**.

2. Remove dough to a lightly floured surface; cover with a large bowl and let rest for 10 to 15 minutes. Meanwhile, preheat oven to 375°F (190°C).

3. Divide the dough into 8 pieces and roll into balls. Cover and let rest for 10 minutes. Gently stretch into a teardrop shape about ¹/₄ inch (5 mm) thick. Cover and let rest for 15 minutes.

4. *Topping:* Brush the dough with melted butter. Sprinkle with sesame seeds or minced onion.

5. Bake in preheated oven for 8 to 10 minutes, or until the naan sounds hollow when tapped on the bottom.

English Muffins

A popular breakfast or brunch treat, just split with a fork and toast.

Tip

Follow the directions when rolling out the dough. If too thick, the muffins will brown before cooking through. Turn just once, but do not press or flatten the tops.

Variation

Try substituting 1 cup (250 mL) whole wheat flour for 1 cup (250 mL) of all-purpose or bread flour.

• *Baking sheet, sprinkled with cornmeal*

1 cup	milk	250 mL
2	eggs	2
1 tsp	salt	5 mL
2 tbsp	granulated sugar	25 mL
2 tbsp	shortening or vegetable oil	25 mL
3 cups	all-purpose flour or bread flour	750 mL
1¼ tsp	bread machine yeast	6 mL
	Cornmeal for topping	

1. Measure all ingredients *except the cornmeal* into baking pan in the order recommended by the manufacturer. Insert pan into the oven chamber. Select **Dough Cycle**.

2. Remove dough to a lightly floured board; cover with a large bowl and let rest for 10 to 15 minutes.

3. Roll out dough to ¼-inch (5 mm) thickness. Cut into 3-inch (7.5 cm) circles. Place on prepared baking sheet. Brush with water and sprinkle tops with cornmeal. Cover and allow to rise in a warm, draft-free place for 30 to 45 minutes, or until doubled in volume. Meanwhile, preheat grill to 500°F (260°C).

4. Grill for 6 to 7 minutes on each side, or until golden brown.

Nothing beats the simple pleasure of a toasted English muffin. Try this whole wheat version for added fiber in your diet.

Tips

Make sure English muffins are not too thick or they will burn on the outside before cooking through to the center.

The slight indent on the sides of the English muffin makes a perfect place to split with a fork before toasting.

Whole Wheat English Muffins

• *Baking sheet, sprinkled with cornmeal*

1 cup	milk	250 mL
2	eggs	2
1 tsp	salt	5 mL
1 tbsp	liquid honey	15 mL
1 tbsp	molasses	15 mL
2 tbsp	shortening or vegetable oil	25 mL
3 1/3 cups	whole wheat flour	825 mL
1 1/4 tsp	bread machine yeast	6 mL
	Cornmeal for topping	

ORANGE HONEY BUTTER

1/3 cup	soft butter	75 mL
2 tbsp	creamed honey	25 mL
1 tsp	orange zest	5 mL

1. Measure muffin ingredients, *except the cornmeal,* into machine's baking pan in the order recommended by the manufacturer. Insert pan into the oven chamber. Select **Dough Cycle**.

2. Remove dough to a lightly floured surface. Cover with a large bowl and let rest for 10 to 15 minutes.

3. Roll out the dough to 1/4-inch (5 mm) thickness. Cut into 3-inch (7.5 cm) circles. Place on prepared baking sheet. Brush with water and sprinkle tops with cornmeal. Cover and let rise in a warm, draft-free place for 30 to 45 minutes, or until doubled in volume. Meanwhile, preheat grill to 500°F (260°C).

4. Grill muffins for 6 to 7 minutes per side, or until golden.

5. *Honey Butter:* In a small bowl, cream together butter, honey and orange zest. Spread on toasted English muffins. Store in refrigerator if not using immediately; warm to room temperature before spreading.

Beaver Tails

1 cup	milk	250 mL
1	egg	1
3/4 tsp	salt	4 mL
3 tbsp.	granulated sugar	40 mL
1 tbsp	butter	15 mL
3 1/4 cups	all-purpose flour or bread flour	800 mL
3/4 tsp	bread machine yeast	4 mL

Served warm, these rich sweet treats have become a must-have during the winter. Beaver tails, as they are called in Canada, are similar to the American bear claws or elephant ears.

Tip

Stretch dough gently over your fingertips. The edges will be slightly thicker.

1. Measure ingredients into baking pan in the order recommended by the manufacturer. Insert pan into the oven chamber. Select **Dough Cycle**.

2. Remove dough to a lightly floured surface; cover with a large bowl and let rest for 10 to 15 minutes. Meanwhile, preheat oil in deep fryer to 350°F (180°C).

3. Divide the dough into 10 pieces. Gently stretch into 8- by 6-inch (20 by 15 cm) ovals.

4. Deep-fry for 30 to 45 seconds, holding the beaver tails under the fat until lightly browned, turning once. Drain well on paper towels.

5. Top the warm beaver tails with 1 to 2 tbsp (15 to 25 mL) of your choice of topping.

Suggested Toppings

Try your own favorite topping or one of the suggestions listed below:
- Sugar and cinnamon
- Sausage
- Cream cheese and green onion
- Jam
- Apple and cinnamon
- Chocolate and hazelnut
- Killaloe sunrise (sugar, cinnamon and lemon)
- Maple butter

Bruschetta (Basic Dough)

Begin with this baguette recipe. Prepare it early in the day and cool completely.

• *Baking sheet, sprinkled with cornmeal*

1¼ cups	water	300 mL
1 tsp	salt	5 mL
2 tsp	granulated sugar	10 mL
3½ cups	all-purpose flour or bread flour	875 mL
1½ tsp	bread machine yeast	7 mL
1	egg white	1
1 tbsp	water	15 mL

1. Measure all ingredients *except egg white and 1 tbsp (15 mL) water* into baking pan in the order recommended by the manufacturer. Insert pan into the oven chamber. Select **Dough Cycle**.

2. Remove dough to a lightly floured board; cover with a large bowl and let rest for 10 to 15 minutes. Divide the dough in half; form each into a long, thin rope, 1 inch (2.5 cm) in diameter and 16 inches (40 cm) long. (Ropes should be thicker in the middle and tapered at the ends.) Place on prepared baking sheet; cover and let dough rise in a warm, draft-free place for 30 to 45 minutes, or until doubled in volume. Meanwhile, preheat oven to 375°F (190°C).

3. With a sharp knife or a lame, make 3 to 5 diagonal slits, ⅛ inch (2 mm) deep, across the top of each loaf. Brush with the egg white beaten with water. Bake in preheated oven for 30 minutes, or until loaves sound hollow when tapped on the bottom. For a crispier crust, place a pan of hot water in the oven and spritz the loaves with water every 5 to 10 minutes during baking.

4. Diagonally slice each loaf into 1-inch (2.5 cm) thick slices, toast one side, and top the untoasted side with your favorite bruschetta mixture. Three of our favorites are presented on pages 140 and 141.

Mozzarella Toast

• *Preheat broiler*

1/3 cup	softened butter	75 mL
6	anchovy fillets, minced	6
2	cloves garlic, minced	2
1/3 cup	grated mozzarella cheese	75 mL
1 to 2 tsp	dried basil	5 to 10 mL
1	baguette, diagonally sliced 1 inch (2.5 cm) thick, toasted on one side	1

1. In a medium bowl, combine butter, anchovies and garlic. Spread mixture on untoasted side of baguette slices. Sprinkle with cheese and top each with a pinch of basil. Toast under broiler just until the cheese melts.

A tasty bread to complement a vegetable stir-fry.

Tip

Preheat broiler for 8 to 10 minutes to quickly melt the cheese rather than bake it.

Variation

Try a Havarti and goat cheese combination and grill on the barbecue.

Fresh Tomato Basil Topping

• *Preheat broiler*

2 tbsp	extra virgin olive oil	25 mL
2	cloves garlic, minced	2
4	ripe tomatoes, chopped	4
1/4 cup	chopped fresh parsley	50 mL
1	baguette, diagonally sliced 1 inch (2.5 cm) thick, toasted on one side	1
1 tbsp	snipped fresh basil	15 mL
1/2 cup	grated mozzarella cheese	125 mL

1. In a bowl, combine olive oil, tomatoes, garlic, parsley and basil.
2. Spread mixture on untoasted side of baguette slices.
3. Sprinkle with cheese.
4. Toast under broiler just until cheese melts.

Enjoy the late-summer crop of fresh tomatoes with fresh basil from your garden in this delicious topping.

Tips

Choose a meaty plum tomato such as Roma or San Marzone.

To snip basil, place in a cup and cut with kitchen shears. Pack tightly to measure. If the flavor is too strong, use half basil and half parsley.

Variation

Substitute an equal amount of oregano or thyme for the basil.

Roasted Red Pepper with Shrimp and Garlic

Bright red peppers, piled high on each bruschetta slice, will whet the appetite of your guests at your next barbecue. The balsamic vinegar gives this colorful topping a rich, fruity character.

Tip

Place blistered roasted red peppers in a paper bag for 10 to 15 minutes, then peel. The skin will slip off easily.

Variation

Substitute yellow and orange bell peppers for an interesting color combination.

4	roasted red bell peppers, chopped	4
1	clove garlic, minced	1
1/2 cup	chopped fresh parsley	125 mL
2 tbsp	balsamic vinegar	25 mL
2 tsp	olive oil	10 mL
	Freshly ground pepper	
1	baguette, diagonally sliced 1 inch (2.5 cm) thick, toasted on one side	1
48	cooked salad shrimp	48

1. *To roast peppers:* Place seeded pepper halves, skin-side up, on a baking sheet. Bake at 375°F (190°C) for 30 to 45 minutes, or until the skins are well blistered. Place peppers in a paper or plastic bag; seal well and set aside for 10 to 15 minutes. Remove from bag; the skins will loosen and peel easily.

2. In a medium bowl, combine garlic, parsley, balsamic vinegar and olive oil; stir gently. Season with pepper to taste. Add the mixture to the roasted peppers. Toss gently.

3. Heap mixture onto untoasted side of baguette slices. Top each with 3 shrimp.

Focaccia

This slightly raised Italian flatbread has a pebbled, dimpled surface. Serve plain or in combination with your favorite fresh herbs, ripe olives or red onions.

Tip

See Equipment Glossary, page 357, for instructions on preheating the baking stone.

• Two baking sheets, lightly greased, or preheated baking stone

1 1/3 cups	water	325 mL
1 1/2 tsp	salt	7 mL
1 tsp	granulated sugar	5 mL
3 1/3 cups	all-purpose flour or bread flour	825 mL
2 1/4 tsp	bread machine yeast	11 mL

1. Measure ingredients into baking pan in the order recommended by the manufacturer. Insert pan into the oven chamber. Select **Dough Cycle**.

2. Remove dough to a lightly floured board; cover with a large bowl and let rest for 10 to 15 minutes.

3. Divide the dough in half. Stretch each half into a 10- by 8-inch (25 by 20 cm) rectangle. Dimple with flour-coated fingertips. Cover and let rise in a warm, draft-free place for 30 minutes. Meanwhile, preheat oven to 375°F (190°C).

4. Re-dimple dough and cover with preferred topping mixture (recipes follow).

5. Place dough on prepared baking sheet or preheated baking stone and bake on the lowest rack of the preheated oven for 20 to 30 minutes, or until golden.

Caramelized Vidalia Onion Topping

Top focaccia with generous amounts of thinly sliced sweet onions, slowly cooked in a very small amount of olive oil until lightly golden.

Tip

No need for extra oil; keep onions covered and add 1 tbsp (15 mL) white wine or water to prevent sticking.

2 tbsp	olive oil	25 mL
3 cups	sliced Vidalia onions	750 mL
1 tbsp	balsamic vinegar	15 mL
8	Kalamata olives, sliced	8
1/3 cup	crumbled feta cheese	75 mL
1 tbsp	snipped fresh thyme	15 mL

1. In a saucepan, heat oil over medium heat. Add onions and sauté until soft but not browned. Add vinegar and stir well. Spoon over prepared focaccia.

2. Sprinkle remaining ingredients over the onions.

Tip

Use the amounts of
cheese stated in the
recipe; too much will
make the focaccia
greasy.

Variation

Substitute cheeses
with your favorite
lower-fat varieties.

Triple-Cheese Topping

1 to 2 tbsp	olive oil	15 to 25 mL
2	cloves garlic, minced	2
1 tsp	dried basil	5 mL
1/2 to 1 cup	prepared salsa	125 to 250 mL
1/2 cup	shredded Asiago cheese	125 mL
1/2 cup	shredded mozzarella cheese	125 mL
1/4 cup	grated Parmesan cheese	50 mL
	Salsa for garnish	

1. Mix together olive oil and garlic. Drizzle over the dough; allow to puddle in the dimples. Top with basil and salsa.
2. Mix the 3 cheeses together. Sprinkle over salsa.
3. Serve with salsa for garnish.

*Walnuts with freshly
grated Parmesan cheese
is a combination of
flavors sure to please.*

Tip

Store walnuts in the
refrigerator and taste
for freshness before
using.

Variation

Pine nuts can be
substituted for walnuts
and Romano cheese
for the Parmesan.

Parmesan Walnut Topping

2 tbsp	olive oil	25 mL
2	cloves garlic, minced	2
1/2 cup	chopped walnuts	125 mL
2 tbsp	grated Parmesan cheese	25 mL

1. Mix together olive oil and garlic. Drizzle over the dough; allow to puddle in the dimples.
2. Top the dough with walnuts and Parmesan cheese.

Easy Baking Tips for Crisp Crusts and Focaccia

1. Use a baking stone
Baking stones, available in different sizes and shapes, are made of unglazed quarry or ceramic tile. Preheat on the bottom rack of oven set to 450°F (230°C) for at least 10 to 15 minutes before using. Cool completely, then scrape off any burnt matter. Wipe the stone with a damp cloth. Use for pitas, pizza and naan bread when a crisp crust is desired.

2. Use a peel
A peel is a wooden or metal long-handled, thin, flat blade. Slide it under the risen dough or crust and ease it onto the baking stone or oven rack. A peel prevents the raw dough from wrinkling as you slide it into the oven and protects your fingers, preventing burns from the hot oven surfaces or the baking stone.

3. Cut with a pizza wheel
A pizza wheel has a sharpened stainless steel circular wheel anchored to a handle. Use it to cut dough for breadsticks, pizza or toasties.

4. Pre-bake pizza crusts
Bake shaped pizza crusts in a 450°F (220°C) oven for 12 to 15 minutes before adding the toppings. The crust will not become soggy and will bake without burning.

Sausage-Stuffed Stromboli
(page 160)

Red Onion Focaccia

• *Two 8-inch (20 cm) round baking pans, lightly greased*

*Everyone's favorite
for take-out lunches,
this focaccia is easily
prepared in your
bread machine.*

1 tbsp	olive oil	15 mL
1 cup	chopped red onions	250 mL
2	cloves garlic, crushed	2
1 1/2 cups	water	375 mL
1 1/2 tsp	salt	7 mL
1 tsp	granulated sugar	5 mL
1 tbsp	olive oil	15 mL
4 1/4 cups	all-purpose flour or bread flour	1050 mL
1 1/2 tsp	bread machine yeast	7 mL

Tips

Put a few slices of deli
meats and cheese into
a split focaccia and
grill until warmed
through. Add roasted
yellow peppers, sliced
tomatoes and alfalfa
sprouts.

For instructions on
sweating vegetables,
see Techniques
Glossary (page 370).

Variation

Form the dough into
two 9- to 10-inch
(23 to 25 cm) round
focaccia, about 1 inch
(2.5 cm) thick. Brush
with olive oil and
dried herbs or add
your favorite topping
before baking.

1. In a frying pan, heat oil over medium heat. Add
   red onions and garlic; cook until tender but not
   browned. Place in machine's baking pan. Measure
   remaining ingredients into baking pan in the order
   recommended by the manufacturer. Insert pan into
   the oven chamber. Select **Dough Cycle**.

2. Remove dough to a lightly floured surface. Cover
   with a large bowl and let rest for 10 to 15 minutes.
   Divide the dough in half. Stretch each into
   prepared pans. Dimple with flour-coated fingers.
   Cover and let rise in a warm, draft-free place for
   30 minutes, or until not quite doubled in volume.
   Meanwhile, preheat oven to 400°F (200°C).

3. Re-dimple dough and bake in preheated oven on
   lowest rack for 20 to 30 minutes, or until focaccia
   sounds hollow when tapped on the bottom.

Spinach Feta Twist
(page 164)

Herb Pizza Crust

• Two 12-inch (30 cm) pizza pans, lightly greased

According to the topping chosen, select different herbs: oregano for vegetarian, basil for Mediterranean, or fresh rosemary for the milder-flavored leek and mushroom.

1 cup	water	250 mL
1 tsp	salt	5 mL
1 tbsp	granulated sugar	15 mL
2¾ cups	all-purpose flour or bread flour	675 mL
1 tsp	dried basil	5 mL
1 tsp	dried oregano	5 mL
1¼ tsp	bread machine yeast	6 mL

Variation

Instead of dividing the dough, you could prepare one thicker 20- by 8-inch (50 by 20 cm) pizza.

1. Measure ingredients into baking pan in the order recommended by the manufacturer. Insert pan into the oven chamber. Select **Dough Cycle**.
2. Remove dough to a lightly floured board; cover with a large bowl and let rest for 10 to 15 minutes. Divide the dough in half. Meanwhile, preheat oven to 400°F (200°C).
3. Roll out dough or press into the pans. To partially bake the pizza crusts, bake in the preheated oven for 10 to 12 minutes. Spread with your choice of topping (recipes follow).

Mediterranean Topping

This pizza zings with the flavors of the Mediterranean.

Tip

Drain the feta well before using.

3 tbsp	tomato pasta sauce	45 mL
1 cup	grilled zucchini slices	250 mL
3 to 4	grilled eggplant slices	3 to 4
1 cup	grilled shiitake mushrooms	250 mL
½ cup	chopped roasted red pepper	125 mL
3	chopped fresh basil leaves	3
1 cup	shredded mozzarella cheese	250 mL
¼ cup	crumbled feta cheese	50 mL

1. Spread the pasta sauce onto the partially baked pizza crust. Top with the vegetables, basil and cheeses. Bake at 400°F (200°C) for 15 to 20 minutes, or until firm.

Leek and Mushroom Topping with Asiago Cheese

Tips
Use only the white part of the leeks. Slice lengthwise and hold under cold running water to clean out any dirt.

The pan and oil must be hot before adding the mushrooms to sauté.

Variation
Select a meatier-textured variety of mushroom such as cremini, portobello or shiitake.

3 tbsp	olive oil	45 mL
1	clove garlic, minced	1
4 cups	sliced cremini mushrooms	1000 mL
5 cups	sliced leeks	1250 mL
2/3 cup	shredded Asiago cheese	150 mL
2/3 cup	shredded old Cheddar cheese	150 mL

1. In a saucepan, heat oil over medium heat. Add garlic, mushrooms and leeks; cook until tender.
2. Spread vegetables over partially baked pizza crust. Top with the cheeses. Bake at 400°F (200°C) for 15 to 20 minutes, or until firm.

Vegetarian Topping

Here's a great way to use up leftover vegetables! Try mushrooms, broccoli, onions, snow peas, artichokes, tomatoes and roasted peppers.

Tip
Add a bit of crumbled firm tofu or tofu cheese in place of the mozzarella.

Variation
For a new treat, try topping the pizza with blanched green beans or asparagus, sliced cooked potatoes and Spanish onions.

3 tbsp	olive oil	45 mL
1 tbsp	minced garlic	15 mL
2	tomatoes, sliced	2
1/2 cup	thinly sliced onions	125 mL
1 1/2 cups	sliced cremini mushrooms	375 mL
1	red bell pepper, thinly sliced	1
1 cup	broccoli florets	250 mL
1 cup	shredded mozzarella cheese	250 mL
1/2 cup	freshly grated Parmesan cheese	125 mL

1. Brush partially baked pizza crust with olive oil. Sprinkle with garlic. Arrange tomatoes, onions, mushrooms, red pepper and broccoli over top. Sprinkle with cheeses. Bake at 400°F (200°C) for 15 to 20 minutes, or until firm.

Beer Pizza Crust

This tender, thin crust has an extra tang from the beer.

Variations

Instead of dividing the dough, you could prepare one thicker 20- by 8-inch (50 by 20 cm) pizza.

Replace beer with an equal amount of "lite" beer.

• *Two 12-inch (30 cm) pizza pans, lightly greased*

1 cup	beer	250 mL
1 tsp	salt	5 mL
2 tsp	granulated sugar	10 mL
3 cups	all-purpose flour or bread flour	750 mL
2 tsp	dried basil	10 mL
1 1/2 tsp	bread machine yeast	7 mL

1. Measure ingredients into baking pan in the order recommended by the manufacturer. Insert pan into the oven chamber. Select **Dough Cycle**.

2. Remove dough to a lightly floured board; cover with a large bowl and let rest for 10 to 15 minutes. Divide dough in half. Meanwhile, preheat oven to 400°F (200°C).

3. Roll out dough or press into the pans. To partially bake the pizza crusts, bake in preheated oven for 10 to 12 minutes. Spread with your choice of topping (see suggestions, pages 146–147).

Storing Dough

Have you ever prepared a dough recipe and then run out of time to shape, proof and bake it? No need to throw it out. It can be placed in the refrigerator or freezer to finish later.

As soon as you remove the dough from the bread machine, divide it into the amounts the recipe suggests. Flatten each into a circle about 1 inch (2.5 cm) thick. Wrap airtight in plastic wrap or aluminum foil. Place in a self-sealing bag.

To refrigerate: Refrigerate for up to 3 days, remembering to press out air 2 to 3 times. Return to room temperature before shaping.

To freeze: Wrap airtight in a self-sealing bag and freeze for up to 4 weeks.

To thaw: Refrigerate in the original wrapper overnight. Thawing at room temperature will result in uneven thawing and a less-than-perfect product. Once the dough is at room temperature, follow recipe instructions for shaping, proofing and baking.

Greek-Style Pita

• *Baking sheet or preheated baking stone*

1¼ cups	water	300 mL
1	egg	1
1½ tsp	salt	7 mL
2 tsp	granulated sugar	10 mL
2 tbsp	shortening or vegetable oil	25 mL
3¾ cups	all-purpose flour or bread flour	925 mL
½ cup	buttermilk powder	125 mL
1½ tsp	bread machine yeast	7 mL

Greek–style pitas do not puff up to form a pocket. Spread with your favorite filling and roll for a quick portable lunch.

Tips

Steam finished pitas in foil to warm and soften before filling.

See Equipment Glossary, page 357, for instructions on preheating the baking stone.

Variation

Form into large 8-inch (20 cm) circles and bake for 3 minutes. Spread with cream cheese and thinly sliced deli meats. Roll tightly, slice diagonally and serve as hors d'oeuvres.

1. Measure ingredients into baking pan in the order recommended by the manufacturer. Insert pan into the oven chamber. Select **Dough Cycle**.

2. Remove dough to a lightly floured surface; cover with a large bowl and let rest for 10 to 15 minutes. Meanwhile, preheat oven to 450°F (230°C).

3. Divide dough into 12 equal pieces and form into balls. Flatten each ball with your fingertips, working in as much flour as possible. Roll out into 7-inch (18 cm) circles, about ⅛ inch (2 mm) thick.

4. Quickly place 4 pitas on the baking sheet or preheated baking stone. Bake in preheated oven for 3 minutes. For soft pitas, do not brown. Stack the pitas and immediately wrap in a lint-free towel to cool.

Pita Pockets

Watch these pitas puff up in the oven right before your eyes.

Tips

Timing is critical in this recipe. Remove pitas from the oven before they begin to brown.

Work in as much flour as possible with your hand as you form these pitas. This gives the typical texture and makes separating them into pockets easier.

See Equipment Glossary, page 357, for instructions on preheating the baking stone.

Variation

Try making pita crisps. Separate pita layers by cutting or pulling apart. Cut both circles into 4 or 8 wedges. (The number depends on the size of each pita.) Bake, turning once, at 350°F (180°C) for 10 to 15 minutes or until lightly browned and crisp, or broil 2 to 4 minutes until golden and crisp.

• Baking sheet or preheated baking stone

1¼ cups	water	300 mL
1½ tsp	salt	7 mL
1 tbsp	granulated sugar	15 mL
¼ cup	shortening or vegetable oil	50 mL
2¼ cups	all-purpose flour or bread flour	550 mL
1 cup	rye flour	250 mL
½ cup	buttermilk powder	125 mL
2½ tsp	bread machine yeast	12 mL

1. Measure ingredients into baking pan in the order recommended by the manufacturer. Insert pan into the oven chamber. Select **Dough Cycle**.

2. Remove dough to a lightly floured board; cover with a large bowl and let rest for 10 to 15 minutes. Meanwhile, preheat oven to 450°F (230°C)

3. Divide the dough into 16 portions. Form into balls; flatten each with your fingertips, working in as much flour as possible. Roll out into 5-inch (12.5 cm) circles, ⅛ inch (2 mm) thick.

4. Quickly place 3 or 4 pitas on the baking sheet or preheated baking stone. Bake for 3 minutes. For soft pitas, do not brown. Immediately upon removing from the oven, stack the puffed pitas. Wrap in a towel while cooling. If the pitas are too thick, they may not form a pocket.

Spinach Pitas

• Baking sheet or preheated baking stone

Who can resist these savory, green-flecked pita pockets? Whether filled for sandwiches or used as a base for pizza snacks, they're delicious.

1¼ cups	water	300 mL
¼ cup	thawed, chopped frozen spinach	50 mL
1	egg	1
1½ tsp	salt	7 mL
2 tsp	granulated sugar	10 mL
2 tbsp	shortening or vegetable oil	25 mL
1 cup	whole wheat flour	250 mL
3 cups	all-purpose flour or bread flour	750 mL
½ cup	buttermilk powder	125 mL
1½ tsp	bread machine yeast	7 mL

Tips

Don't make the pitas too thick or a pocket won't form.

Be sure to squeeze the moisture out of the spinach before measuring.

See Equipment Glossary, page 357, for instructions on preheating the baking stone.

Variations

Enjoy warm pitas packed with exotic grains and roasted vegetables.

Divide dough into smaller portions for mini-pitas (children love them) or use for hors d'oeuvres.

1. Measure ingredients into machine's baking pan in the order recommended by the manufacturer. Insert pan into the oven chamber. Select **Dough Cycle**.

2. Remove dough to a lightly floured surface. Cover with a large bowl and let rest for 10 to 15 minutes. Meanwhile, preheat oven to 450°F (230°C).

3. Divide the dough into 20 portions. Form each into a ball and then flatten with your fingertips, working in as much flour as possible. Roll out into 4- to 5-inch (10 to 12.5 cm) circles, ⅛ inch (2 mm) thick.

4. Place 3 to 4 pitas on baking sheet or preheated baking stone. Bake in preheated oven for 3 to 4 minutes. For soft pitas, do not allow to brown. Immediately upon removing from the oven, stack the puffed pitas. Wrap in a towel while cooling. If the pitas are too thick, they may not form a pocket.

Calzone

• *Baking sheet, lightly greased*

1½ cups	water	375 mL
¼ cup	skim milk powder	50 mL
1½ tsp	salt	7 mL
2 tbsp	granulated sugar	25 mL
3 tbsp	shortening or vegetable oil	45 mL
3⅔ cups	all-purpose flour or bread flour	875 mL
1 tsp	bread machine yeast	5 mL

Tip

Make ahead, wrap individually and store in an airtight container in the refrigerator for a few days or in the freezer for up to one month.

1. Measure ingredients into baking pan in the order recommended by the manufacturer. Insert pan into the oven chamber. Select **Dough Cycle**.

2. Remove the dough to a lightly floured board. Cover with a large bowl and let the dough rest for 10 to 15 minutes. Divide the dough into 10 portions. Roll out each into a 6-inch (15 cm) circle.

Variation

For smaller cocktail-size calzone, divide dough into 20 portions and roll out each into a 3-inch (7.5 cm) circle. Use half the amount of filling for each. Bake for 15 to 20 minutes.

3. Prepare filling of your choice (recipes follow). Place filling on one half of each circle. Fold in half, sealing the edges tightly. Cover and let rise in a warm, draft-free place until doubled in volume. Meanwhile, preheat oven to 375°F (180°C).

4. Bake in preheated oven for 20 to 25 minutes, or until the calzone sound hollow when tapped on the bottom.

Ham and Swiss Cheese Filling

We had to include our families' favorite combo of ham and Swiss.

10 oz	sliced cooked ham	300 g
10 oz	sliced Swiss cheese	300 g

1. Cut ham and cheese slices into quarters. Place 4 quarters of each, alternating, on half of each circle of dough.

Tip

Cool slightly before serving; the cheese will be very hot!

Variation

Try leftover turkey and stuffing instead of ham.

Broccoli and Goat Cheese Filling

Perfect as hors d'oeuvres.
Serve piping hot. Your
guests will rave.

2 to 3	tomatoes, thinly sliced	2 to 3
1 cup	broccoli florets	250 mL
3 to 4 oz	goat cheese, sliced	90 to 125 g
2 tbsp	grated Parmesan cheese	25 mL
	Freshly ground pepper	
10	fresh basil leaves	10

Tip

No need to pre-cook
these small florets
of broccoli.

1. Cover half of each calzone with a thin slice of tomato, 2 to 3 broccoli florets, goat cheese, $\frac{1}{2}$ tsp (2 mL) Parmesan cheese, a generous grind of black pepper and a fresh basil leaf.

Variation

Try substituting feta
cheese for the goat
cheese and asparagus
for the broccoli.

Smoked Salmon Filling

1 lb	smoked salmon, thinly sliced	500 g
8 oz	goat cheese or cream cheese	250 g
2 tbsp	finely chopped red onion	25 mL
2 tbsp	capers	25 mL

Decadently delicious,
this updated version of
cream cheese and lox
filling combines goat
cheese and smoked
salmon.

1. Cover half of each calzone with salmon slices. Top with the remaining ingredients, dividing equally.

Tip

Purchase pre-sliced
smoked salmon or
slice as thinly as
possible.

Variation

Any soft unripened
cheese, such as quark
or ricotta, can be
substituted. Don't
forget the chopped
onion and capers.

These stuffed mini-pizzas are great for lunch or snacks.

Tip

To prevent a soggy crust, be sure to drain the filling well before enclosing in dough.

Variation

For a totally different shape, try making roasted vegetable cups. See Techniques Glossary, page 370, for instructions.

Roasted Vegetable–Stuffed Calzone

- Roasting pan
- Baking sheet, lightly greased

1⅓ cups	water	325 mL
1¼ tsp	salt	6 mL
2 tbsp	granulated sugar	25 mL
2 tbsp	shortening or vegetable oil	25 mL
3⅓ cups	all-purpose flour or bread flour	825 mL
1 tsp	bread machine yeast	5 mL

ROASTED VEGETABLE FILLING

1	small Italian eggplant, cut into 1-inch (2.5 cm) pieces	1
1	large onion, cut into 1-inch (2.5 cm) pieces	1
1	large red bell pepper, cut into 1-inch (2.5 cm) pieces	1
1	large yellow pepper, cut into 1-inch (2.5 cm) pieces	1
1	medium zucchini, cut into 1-inch (2.5 cm) pieces	1
1 tbsp	roasted garlic and basil–flavored olive oil	15 mL
6	cloves garlic, minced	6
1 tbsp	dried oregano	15 mL

1. Measure the bread ingredients into machine's baking pan in the order recommended by the manufacturer. Insert pan into the oven chamber. Select **Dough Cycle**.

2. *Filling:* Add eggplant to roasting pan, along with onion, red pepper, yellow pepper and zucchini. Brush with oil and sprinkle with garlic and oregano. Roast vegetables in preheated oven, turning once during cooking, for 20 to 30 minutes or until tender. Do not overcook. Set aside to cool. Reduce oven temperature to 375°F (190°C).

3. Remove dough to a lightly floured surface. Cover with a large bowl and let rest for 10 to 15 minutes. Divide the dough into 12 portions. Roll out each into a 5-inch (12.5 cm) circle. Place an equal amount of filling on one-half of each circle. Fold unfilled half over the filled half, sealing the edges tightly. Place on prepared baking sheet. Cover and let rise in a warm, draft-free place for 30 to 45 minutes, or until doubled in volume. Meanwhile, preheat oven to 425°F (220°C).

4. Bake in preheated oven for 25 to 35 minutes, or until calzone sound hollow when tapped on the bottom.

Tips for Preparing Fillings

- Vegetables for fillings should be cut into pieces large enough to be seen and recognized, but not so large that the filled bread falls apart when eaten.

- Ground-meat fillings must be completely cooked before enclosing in the dough since they do not cook as the bread bakes.

- To minimize the fat in fillings, and to prevent soggy bread crusts, always sauté vegetables or brown meats using a minimum of oil. Drain well before enclosing in dough.

- Quickly cool all fillings to room temperature before enclosing in dough. If the filling is too hot, it may kill the yeast, and the dough immediately surrounding the filling may be gummy.

- Spread the filling right to the ends of the dough so that the first and last slices have the same amount of filling as those in the middle.

- Cool meat- or cheese-filled breads quickly and refrigerate following baking. Refrigerate leftovers. Serve warm or cold.

Crunchy Cheese-Filled Pretzels

A little bit more work than some recipes, but definitely worth it. Your family will request encores of this tangy cheese treat.

Tip

Water can be substituted for beer; and Swiss, Havarti or mozzarella cheese for Cheddar cheese.

Variation

To spice up the filling, use an extra-old sharp Cheddar cheese and a few drops of hot pepper sauce or a pinch of cayenne pepper.

Topping

Brush with 1 egg white beaten with 1 tbsp (15 mL) water. Sprinkle with sea salt, coarse salt or poppy seeds.

• Baking sheet, lightly greased

1 cup	beer	250 mL
1 tsp	salt	5 mL
2 tbsp	granulated sugar	25 mL
1 tbsp	butter	15 mL
2¾ cups	all-purpose flour or bread flour	675 mL
¾ tsp	bread machine yeast	4 mL

CHEESE FILLING

1⅔ cups	shredded Cheddar cheese	400 mL
⅓ cup	chopped fresh parsley	75 mL
2 tbsp	Dijon mustard	25 mL
½ tsp	cracked peppercorns	2 mL

1. Measure ingredients into baking pan in the order recommended by the manufacturer. Insert pan into the oven chamber. Select **Dough Cycle**.

2. *Filling:* In a bowl, combine filling ingredients until crumbly; set aside.

3. Remove dough to a lightly floured board; cover with a large bowl and let rest for 10 to 15 minutes. Roll out the dough to a 10- by 16-inch (25 by 40 cm) rectangle. Cut lengthwise into 8 strips. Brush one long edge of each strip with water. Spread ¼ cup (50 mL) filling down the center of each strip to within ½ inch (1 cm) of the ends and edges. Pinch the dough together. On a floured board, roll into a smooth rope, stretching to 16 inches (40 cm) long. Grasp the ends and twist into a rounded heart, at the same time moving to the greased baking sheet. Lightly press the ends into the curved part.

4. Cover and allow to rise in a warm, draft-free place for 1 hour or until doubled in volume. Meanwhile, preheat oven to 400°F (200°C).

5. Brush on the topping (see note, at left). Bake in preheated oven for 18 to 20 minutes, or until pretzel sounds hollow when tapped on the bottom. Cool for 5 minutes. Remove to a rack to cool.

New Orleans–Style Muffaletta

Tip

Refrigerating the stuffed muffaletta before serving allows the flavors to blend and the interior of the bread to soften.

Variation

Use leftover bread from the muffaletta to make croutons or bread crumbs.

• Baking sheet, lightly greased

1¼ cups	water	300 mL
1½ tsp	salt	7 mL
2 tbsp	packed brown sugar	25 mL
2 tbsp	olive oil	25 mL
2 cups	whole wheat flour	500 mL
1¼ cups	all-purpose flour or bread flour	300 mL
¾ cup	7-grain cereal	175 mL
½ cup	buttermilk powder	125 mL
1¼ tsp	bread machine yeast	6 mL

MUFFALETTA FILLING

1	red bell pepper, seeded and diced	1
1	yellow bell pepper, seeded and diced	1
1	large tomato, diced	1
2	cloves garlic, minced	2
¼ cup	store-bought balsamic and herb vinaigrette	50 mL
12 oz	lean chicken breast, thinly sliced	375 g
6 oz	Monterey Jack cheese, shredded	175 g

1. Measure the bread ingredients into machine's baking pan in the order recommended by the manufacturer. Insert pan into the oven chamber. Select **Dough Cycle**.

2. *Filling:* In a large glass bowl, combine red pepper, yellow pepper, tomato and garlic. Add vinaigrette and toss to coat. Marinate for at least 2 hours in the refrigerator.

3. Remove dough to a lightly floured surface. Cover with a large bowl and let rest for 10 to 15 minutes. Form into one 5-inch (12.5 cm) round loaf with a high-rounded top. Place on prepared baking sheet. Cover and let rise in a warm, draft-free place for 30 to 45 minutes, or until doubled in volume. Meanwhile, preheat oven to 350°F (180°C).

4. Transfer dough to preheated oven and bake for 40 to 50 minutes, or until loaf sounds hollow when tapped on the bottom. Set aside to cool completely. Using a serrated knife, cut 1 inch (2.5 cm) off the top of the bread; set the top aside. Cut out center of loaf, leaving at least 1/2 inch (1 cm) of bread on bottom and sides. Cut out top, leaving 1/4 inch (5 mm) of bread.

5. Spread one-third of the pepper mixture on bottom of muffaletta. Top with one-half chicken and then one-half cheese. Repeat with one more layer of pepper mixture, chicken and cheese. Add remaining pepper mixture. Replace reserved bread top. Wrap tightly in plastic wrap, twisting ends to secure, and refrigerate for at least 8 hours. Cut into 8 wedges.

Sausage-Stuffed Stromboli

Stromboli, a specialty of Philadelphia, is a calzone–like sandwich of meat and cheese, usually pepperoni and mozzarella.

Tip

Prepare ahead for any occasion or quick meal. Tightly wrap the unrisen dough and freeze for up to 4 weeks. Thaw in the refrigerator for 6 to 8 hours. Let rise 20 to 45 minutes in a warm, draft-free place, then bake as directed in recipe.

• Baking sheet, lightly greased

1½ cups	water	375 mL
1½ tsp	salt	7 mL
2 tbsp	granulated sugar	25 mL
3¾ cups	all-purpose flour or bread flour	925 mL
1½ tsp	bread machine yeast	7 mL

SAUSAGE FILLING

1 lb	pork sausage, casings removed, meat crumbled	500 g
3	medium carrots, chopped	3
3	medium leeks, chopped	3
1 tbsp	dry rubbed rosemary	15 mL
¾ cup	sliced mushrooms	175 mL
2 tbsp	dry white wine	25 mL

GLAZE

1	egg yolk	1
1 tbsp	water	15 mL

1. Measure the bread ingredients into machine's baking pan in the order suggested by the manufacturer. Insert baking pan into the oven chamber. Select **Dough Cycle.**

2. *Filling:* In a large frying pan, brown sausage meat; drain well and set aside. In the same frying pan, sauté carrots, leeks, mushrooms and rosemary. Add browned sausage meat and white wine. Mix gently and set aside to cool.

3. Remove dough to a lightly floured surface. Cover with a large bowl and let rest for 10 to 15 minutes. Roll out dough to a 16- by 13-inch (40 by 33 cm) rectangle. Place on prepared baking sheet. Cut 2-inch (5 cm) squares out of each corner. Spread cooled filling down the center 6 inches (15 cm), omitting narrow ends.

4. *Glaze:* In a small bowl, whisk together egg yolk and water until smooth.

5. Brush the glaze around the cut corners. Fold short ends of dough over filling. Brush with glaze. With scissors, make cuts on the long side, 1 inch (2.5 cm) apart, from edge of the dough to within ¾ inch (2 cm) of the filling. Repeat on remaining side. Fold alternately in to the center, crisscrossing strips over the filling, at the same time stretching a little to bring the uncut dough up and over the filling. Cover and let rise in a warm, draft-free place for 20 minutes, but not until doubled in volume. Meanwhile, preheat oven to 375°F (190°C).

6. Brush the risen dough with the remaining glaze. Bake in preheated oven for 40 to 45 minutes, or until the stromboli sounds hollow when tapped on the bottom. Cool for 10 minutes before slicing to serve. Refrigerate leftovers.

Turkey-Filled Cheese Braid

• *Baking sheet, lightly greased*

1¼ cups	water	300 mL
1¼ tsp	salt	6 mL
2 tbsp	granulated sugar	25 mL
1 tbsp	shortening or vegetable oil	15 mL
3½ cups	all-purpose flour or bread flour	875 mL
⅓ cup	buttermilk powder	75 mL
¼ cup	grated Parmesan cheese	50 mL
1½ tsp	bread machine yeast	7 mL

TURKEY FILLING

1 to 2 tbsp	vegetable oil	15 to 25 mL
1 lb	ground turkey, crumbled	500 g
½ cup	chopped onions	125 mL
⅓ cup	snipped fresh summer savory	75 mL
1 cup	shredded old Cheddar cheese	250 mL

1. Measure the bread ingredients into machine's baking pan in the order recommended by the manufacturer. Insert pan into the oven chamber. Select **Dough Cycle**.

2. *Filling:* In a large frying pan, heat oil over medium-high heat. Add turkey and cook until browned. Drain well, reserving drippings, and set turkey aside to cool. Return drippings to pan and add onions. Sauté until translucent; drain well. In a large bowl, combine turkey, onions, summer savory and Cheddar cheese. Mix well; set aside to cool.

3. Remove dough to a lightly floured surface. Cover with a large bowl and let rest for 10 to 15 minutes. Roll out the dough to a 20- by 15-inch (50 by 38 cm) rectangle. Cut into 3 strips, each 5 inches (12.5 cm) wide. Spread one-third of the filling down the center of each strip. Bring the edges together over the filling. Pinch to seal. Braid turkey-filled strips together and secure ends. Place on prepared baking sheet. Cover and let rise in a warm, draft-free place for 45 to 60 minutes, or until doubled in volume. Meanwhile, preheat oven to 375°F (190°C).

4. Bake in preheated oven for 35 to 45 minutes, or until braid sounds hollow when tapped on the bottom. Serve warm or cold.

Spinach Feta Twist

• *Tube pan, lightly greased*

For a Greek luncheon treat, cut this twist into thick wedges, add a fresh salad and the menu is complete.

Tip

Be sure to squeeze the moisture out of the spinach before measuring.

Variation

An equal amount of thawed frozen spinach can be substituted for the fresh.

1 cup	water	250 mL
$\frac{1}{2}$ cup	crumbled feta cheese	125 mL
1	egg	1
$1\frac{1}{2}$ tsp	salt	7 mL
2 tbsp	olive oil	25 mL
$3\frac{3}{4}$ cups	all-purpose flour or bread flour	925 mL
$1\frac{1}{4}$ tsp	bread machine yeast	6 mL

SPINACH FILLING

10 oz	fresh spinach	300 g
1 tbsp	melted butter	15 mL
1	clove garlic, minced	1
$\frac{1}{4}$ cup	grated Parmesan cheese	50 mL
2 tsp	dried oregano	10 mL
$\frac{1}{2}$ cup	crumbled feta cheese	125 mL
$\frac{1}{4}$ cup	sliced Kalamata olives	50 mL

TOPPING

1	egg white	1
1 tbsp	water	15 mL
1 tbsp	grated Parmesan cheese	15 mL

1. Measure ingredients into baking pan in the order recommended by the manufacturer. Insert pan into the oven chamber. Select **Dough Cycle**.

2. *Filling:* Wash spinach, shaking off the excess water. Remove stems. Wilt in microwave, uncovered, at High for 2 to 3 minutes, stirring at half time. Squeeze out the excess moisture and allow to cool.

3. In a medium bowl, gently mix together the spinach, butter, garlic, Parmesan cheese and oregano.

4. Remove dough to a lightly floured board; cover with a large bowl and let rest for 10 to 15 minutes. Roll out to an 18- by 15-inch (45 by 38 cm) rectangle.

5. Spread filling on dough to within ½ inch (1 cm) of the edges. Sprinkle with feta cheese and Kalamata olives. Starting at long side, tightly roll up like a jellyroll. Pinch seams to seal. Cut in half lengthwise, using scissors to prevent crushing. Twist the halves together, keeping cut sides up and filling visible (like twisting 2 strands of rope). Keeping the filling-side up, shape into a ring; place in prepared tube pan.

6. Cover and allow to rise in a warm, draft-free place for 45 to 60 minutes, or until doubled in volume. Meanwhile, preheat oven to 375°F (190°).

7. *Topping:* Combine egg white and water and brush onto dough. Sprinkle with Parmesan cheese.

8. Bake in preheated oven for 45 to 55 minutes, or until the bread sounds hollow when tapped on the bottom.

Orange Braid with Poppy Seed Filling

Glazed with orange and dotted with pockets of poppy seeds, this coffee cake is moist and delicious.

Tip

To grind poppy seeds, place in a blender for 2 to 3 minutes, scraping down sides frequently.

Variation

Purchase a ready-made filling, then add the fruit, nuts and zest.

• Baking sheet, lightly greased

3/4 cup	milk	175 mL
1/2 cup	orange juice	125 mL
1	egg	1
3/4 tsp	salt	3 mL
1/4 cup	packed brown sugar	50 mL
2 tbsp	butter	25 mL
3 3/4 cups	all-purpose flour or bread flour	950 mL
2 tsp	orange zest	10 mL
1 1/4 tsp	bread machine yeast	6 mL

POPPY SEED FILLING

3/4 cup	ground poppy seeds	175 mL
1/2 cup	granulated sugar	125 mL
3/4 cup	milk	175 mL
1 tsp	almond extract	5 mL
1	egg white, slightly beaten	1
1/2 cup	raisins	125 mL
1/2 cup	chopped pecans	125 mL
2 tsp	lemon zest	10 mL

1. Measure ingredients into baking pan in the order recommended by the manufacturer. Insert pan into the oven chamber. Select **Dough Cycle**.

2. *Filling:* In a saucepan over low heat, combine poppy seeds, sugar and milk; cook, stirring, for about 15 minutes or until thick. Cool slightly. Add almond extract and egg white. Stir in raisins, pecans and lemon zest. Set aside and allow to cool.

3. Remove dough to a lightly floured board; cover with a large bowl and let rest for 10 to 15 minutes. Divide dough into thirds. Roll out each into an 18- by 3-inch (45 by 7.5 cm) rectangle.

4. Spread one-third of the filling down center of each portion to within $1/2$ inch (1 cm) of ends and edges. Pinch dough together. On floured board, roll each into a smooth rope. Braid, tucking under the ends. Place on prepared baking sheet.

5. Cover and let rise in a warm, draft-free place for 30 to 45 minutes, or until doubled in volume. Meanwhile, preheat oven to 375°F (190°C).

6. Bake in preheated oven for 35 to 40 minutes, or until braid sounds hollow when tapped on the bottom. If necessary, cover loosely with foil for the last 10 to 15 minutes to prevent excess browning.

Savory Cheese Twist

• *Baking sheet, lightly greased*

Serve this savory twist with a chef's salad for lunch or as a mid-morning treat with a crisp red apple and a glass of cold milk.

Tip

For a better blend of flavors, mix the grated cheeses well.

Variation

Try a combination of Asiago, Monterey Jack and feta — or any other cheese your family enjoys.

1 cup	water	250 mL
1/2 cup	cottage cheese	125 mL
1	egg	1
3/4 tsp	salt	3 mL
2 tbsp	granulated sugar	25 mL
2 tbsp	butter	25 mL
3 1/2 cups	all-purpose flour or bread flour	875 mL
1 1/4 tsp	bread machine yeast	6 mL

CHEESE FILLING

3/4 cup	shredded Havarti cheese	175 mL
3/4 cup	shredded Monterey Jack	175 mL
1/4 cup	grated Parmesan cheese	50 mL

1. Measure ingredients into baking pan in the order recommended by the manufacturer. Insert pan into the oven chamber. Select **Dough Cycle**.

2. *Filling:* In a bowl combine filling ingredients until well mixed; set aside.

3. Remove dough to a lightly floured board; cover with a large bowl and let rest for 10 to 15 minutes. Roll out dough into an 18- by 12-inch (45 by 30 cm) rectangle.

4. Sprinkle filling evenly over dough to within 1/2 inch (1 cm) of edges. Beginning at a long end, roll up tightly. Place seam-side down on prepared baking sheet. With scissors, cut lengthwise down the center of roll, about 1 inch (5 cm) deep and to within 1/2 inch (1 cm) of ends. Keeping cut sides up, form into an "S."

5. Cover and let rise in a warm, draft-free place for 30 to 45 minutes, or until doubled in volume. Meanwhile, preheat oven to 350°F (180°C).

6. Bake in preheated oven for 35 to 40 minutes, or until twist sounds hollow when tapped on the bottom. If necessary, cover loosely with foil for the last 10 to 15 minutes to prevent excess browning.

Sourdough Pumpernickel Raisin Bread (page 193)

Overleaf: (clockwise from upper left) Caramelized Vidalia Onion Focaccia (page 142), Triple-Cheese Focaccia (page 143) and Parmesan Walnut Focaccia (page 143)

Bagels and Sourdough

Bagels and sourdoughs present more of a challenge than basic bread recipes, but the results are well worth the extra effort.

Giant Parmesan Rosemary
Breadsticks (page 208)

Steps to Perfect Bagels

1. Kneading

Use the **Dough Cycle** of your bread machine, but only for the kneading portion of the cycle. Remove the dough as soon as kneading finishes; do not allow it to remain in the bread machine to rise and finish the cycle. By doing this, you will end up with a more bagel-like appearance and texture. To get an idea of how long the kneading portion is, check the user's manual for your bread machine.

2. Proofing

Cover and let dough rise in a warm, draft-free place for 30 to 45 minutes, or until doubled in volume. To test readiness, press two fingers into the dough. The indents should remain.

3. Boiling

Boiling bagels before baking gives them a shiny appearance, thick crust and characteristically chewy texture. Boiling also deactivates the yeast by raising the internal temperature to 130°F (55°C).

Bring a large pot of water plus 1 tbsp (15 mL) sugar to a gentle yet full boil. Immerse bagels in water, one at a time, turning upside down. Hold under water for 20 seconds with a skimmer or large spoon until the dough becomes a little puffy. Be sure that you don't boil longer than this or you will wind up with small, tough bagels. For a crunchy finish, dip bagels quickly into a small bowl of seeds before baking.

4. Baking

For a more authentic bagel, sprinkle baking sheet with cornmeal or semolina flour rather than greasing it. Bake at 400°F (200°C) for 15 minutes or until the bagel sounds hollow when tapped on the bottom. Sweet or seed-topped bagels will brown quickly; tent with foil to prevent burning. Remove the foil for the last 5 minutes to brown the bagels.

Basic Bagels

• Baking sheet, lightly greased, or preheated baking stone

1 1/4 cups	water	300 mL
1 tsp	salt	5 mL
2 tbsp	liquid honey	25 mL
3 3/4 cups	all-purpose flour or bread flour	925 mL
1 3/4 tsp	bread machine yeast	8 mL
1 tbsp	granulated sugar	15 mL

Like most bagels today, these are doughnut-shaped. But the first bagels — thought to have originated from Poland in the late 1600s — were made in the shape of a horse's stirrup.

Tip

There are several methods used to form bagels, but we recommend the "cylinder method" described here. It's almost foolproof!

See Equipment Glossary, page 357, for instructions on preheating the baking stone.

Variation

Use your bagels to make bagel chips. To learn how, see Techniques Glossary, page 368.

1. Measure all ingredients *except granulated sugar* into machine's baking pan in the order recommended by the manufacturer. Insert pan into the oven chamber. Select **Dough Cycle**.

2. Stop bread machine when the kneading portion of the cycle is complete. (Do not allow dough to rise in the machine.) Remove dough to a lightly floured surface. Cover with a large bowl and let rest for 10 to 15 minutes. Shape the dough into a round cylinder 13 1/2 inches (35 cm) long. Cut into 9 equal slices, each 1 1/2 inches (4 cm) thick. Push thumbs through the center of each slice and pull into a bagel shape, rounding all surfaces.

3. Place on prepared baking sheet. Cover and let rise in a warm, draft-free place for 15 to 20 minutes. Meanwhile, preheat oven to 400°F (200°C).

4. Bring a large pot of water to a gentle (but full) boil; add sugar. Immerse bagels one at a time in boiling water, turning upside down. With a skimmer or large spoon, hold bagel under the water for 20 seconds or until the dough becomes a little puffy.

5. Place on prepared baking sheet or preheated baking stone. Bake in preheated oven for 15 to 20 minutes, or until bagels sound hollow when tapped on the bottom.

Whole Wheat Bagels

A whole-grain bread flavor and texture make this a real treat for all bagel lovers.

Tips

Stone-ground whole wheat flour is a coarser grind that makes the texture of the bagel slightly heavier.

See Equipment Glossary, page 357, for instructions on preheating the baking stone.

Variation

Bagel chips are great snacks. Cut bagels in half and slice $\frac{1}{8}$ inch (2 mm) thick. Brush with olive oil and bake at 400°F (200°C) for 12 minutes or until crisp.

● *Baking sheet, lightly greased, or preheated baking stone*

1 $\frac{1}{4}$ cups	water	300 mL
1 tsp	salt	5 mL
$\frac{1}{4}$ cup	packed brown sugar	50 mL
2 $\frac{1}{2}$ cups	whole wheat flour	625 mL
2 tsp	bread machine yeast	10 mL
1 tbsp	granulated sugar	15 mL

1. Measure ingredients into baking pan in the order recommended by the manufacturer. Place pan in the oven chamber. Select **Dough Cycle**.

2. Stop bread machine when the kneading portion of the cycle is complete. (Do not allow dough to rise in the machine.) Remove dough to a lightly floured surface; cover with a large bowl and let rest for 10 to 15 minutes. Shape the dough into a round cylinder 12 inches (30 cm) long. Cut into 8 portions 1 $\frac{1}{2}$ inches (4 cm) wide. Push thumbs through the center of each piece and pull into a bagel shape, rounding all the surfaces.

3. Place dough on prepared baking sheet; cover and let rise in a warm, draft-free place for 30 to 45 minutes, or until doubled in volume. Meanwhile, preheat oven to 400°F (200°C).

4. Bring a large pot of water and 1 tbsp (15 mL) sugar to a gentle yet full boil. Immerse bagels in water one at a time, turning upside down. Hold under the water for 20 seconds with a skimmer or large spoon until the dough becomes a little puffy.

5. Bake on the prepared baking sheet or preheated baking stone in preheated oven for 15 minutes, or until the bagels sound hollow when tapped on the bottom.

Muesli Bagels

There's more crunch in every bite when you add a coat of muesli to the tops of these bagels.

Tips

Muesli is quite perishable, so purchase small quantities and store in the refrigerator.

Prepackaged muesli cereals contain extra fat and sugar and may result in a completely different bagel. Choose lower-fat unsweetened varieties.

See Equipment Glossary, page 357, for instructions on preheating the baking stone.

Variation

Add $1/4$ cup (50 mL) each raisins and sunflower seeds.

● Baking sheet, lightly greased, or preheated baking stone

1 $1/4$ cups	water	300 mL
1 tsp	salt	5 mL
2 tbsp	liquid honey	25 mL
2 $3/4$ cups	all-purpose flour or bread flour	675 mL
1 cup	muesli	250 mL
$1/2$ cup	sunflower seeds, raw, unsalted	125 mL
2 tsp	bread machine yeast	10 mL
1 tbsp	granulated sugar	15 mL

1. Measure ingredients into baking pan in the order recommended by the manufacturer. Place in the oven chamber. Select **Dough Cycle**.

2. Stop bread machine when the kneading portion of the cycle is complete. (Do not allow dough to rise in the machine.) Remove dough to a lightly floured surface; cover with a large bowl and let rest for 10 to 15 minutes. Shape the dough into a round cylinder 12 inches (30 cm) long. Cut into 8 portions $1 1/2$ inch (4 cm) wide. Push thumbs through the center of each piece and pull into a bagel shape, rounding all the surfaces.

3. Place dough on prepared baking sheet; cover and let rise in a warm, draft-free place for 30 to 45 minutes, or until doubled in volume. Meanwhile, preheat oven to 400°F (200°C).

4. Bring a large pot of water and 1 tbsp (15 mL) sugar to a gentle yet full boil. Immerse bagels in water one at a time, turning upside down. Hold under the water for 20 seconds with a skimmer or large spoon until the dough becomes a little puffy.

5. Bake on the prepared baking sheet or preheated baking stone in preheated oven for 15 minutes, or until the bagels sound hollow when tapped on the bottom.

Roasted Garlic Bagels

• *Baking sheet, lightly greased, or preheated baking stone*

1¼ cups	water	300 mL
1 tsp	salt	5 mL
3 tbsp	granulated sugar	45 mL
3¾ cups	all-purpose flour or bread flour	925 mL
4	medium cloves garlic, roasted	4
2 tsp	bread machine yeast	10 mL
1 tbsp	granulated sugar	15 mL

1. Measure ingredients into baking pan in the order recommended by the manufacturer. Place pan in the oven chamber. Select **Dough Cycle**.

2. Stop bread machine when the kneading portion of the cycle is complete. (Do not allow dough to rise in the machine.) Remove dough to a lightly floured surface; cover with a large bowl and let rest for 10 to 15 minutes. Shape the dough into a round cylinder 12 inches (30 cm) long. Cut into 8 portions 1½ inches (4 cm) wide. Push thumbs through the center of each piece and pull into a bagel shape, rounding all the surfaces.

3. Place dough on prepared baking sheet; cover and let rise in a warm, draft-free place for 30 to 45 minutes, or until doubled in volume. Meanwhile, preheat oven to 400°F (200°C).

4. Bring a large pot of water and 1 tbsp (15 mL) sugar to a gentle yet full boil. Immerse bagels in water one at a time, turning upside down. Hold under the water for 20 seconds with a skimmer or large spoon until the dough becomes a little puffy.

5. Bake on the prepared baking sheet or preheated baking stone in preheated oven for 15 minutes, or until the bagels sound hollow when tapped on the bottom.

Cheese Onion Bagels

Roasted onions top this savory cheese bagel.

Tips

Whole onions can be roasted on an outside or inside grill. The charred outer layer is easily removed by squeezing one end.

See Equipment Glossary, page 357, for instructions on preheating the baking stone.

Variation

For a stronger cheese flavor, substitute $1/4$ cup (50 mL) Romano cheese for the Parmesan and add $1/4$ tsp (1 mL) dry mustard.

• *Baking sheet, lightly greased, or preheated baking stone*

$1^1/4$ cups	water	300 mL
1 tsp	salt	5 mL
3 tbsp	granulated sugar	45 mL
$3^1/2$ cups	all-purpose flour or bread flour	875 mL
$1/2$ cup	shredded old Cheddar cheese	125 mL
$1/4$ cup	grated Parmesan cheese	50 mL
2 tbsp	minced dried onion	25 mL
2 tsp	bread machine yeast	10 mL
1 tbsp	granulated sugar	15 mL
2	onions, roasted, sliced	2

1. Measure all ingredients *except sugar and onions* into baking pan in the order recommended by the manufacturer. Place pan in the oven chamber. Select **Dough Cycle**.

2. Stop bread machine when the kneading portion of the cycle is complete. (Do not allow dough to rise in the machine.) Remove dough to a lightly floured surface; cover with a large bowl and let rest for 10 to 15 minutes. Shape the dough into a round cylinder 12 inches (30 cm) long. Cut into 8 portions $1^1/2$ inch (4 cm) wide. Push thumbs through the center of each piece and pull into a bagel shape, rounding all the surfaces.

3. Place dough on prepared baking sheet; cover and let rise in a warm, draft-free place for 30 to 45 minutes, or until doubled in volume. Meanwhile, preheat oven to 400°F (200°C).

4. Bring a large pot of water and 1 tbsp (15 mL) sugar to a gentle yet full boil. Immerse bagels in water one at a time, turning upside down. Hold under the water for 20 seconds with a skimmer or large spoon until the dough becomes a little puffy. Top with roasted onions.

5. Bake on the prepared baking sheet or preheated baking stone in preheated oven for 15 minutes, or until the bagels sound hollow when tapped on the bottom.

Sun-Dried Tomato Basil Bagels

Tips

Snip soft sun-dried tomatoes into large $1/2$-inch (1 cm) pieces for an extra burst of tomato goodness.

See Equipment Glossary, page 357, for instructions on preheating the baking stone.

Variation

Use dried tarragon, thyme or oregano in place of basil.

• Baking sheet, lightly greased, or preheated baking stone

1 cup	tomato-vegetable juice	250 mL
2 tbsp	granulated sugar	25 mL
2½ cups	all-purpose flour or bread flour	625 mL
⅓ cup	snipped sun-dried tomatoes	75 mL
2 tsp	dried basil	10 mL
2 tsp	bread machine yeast	10 mL
1 tbsp	granulated sugar	15 mL

1. Measure ingredients into baking pan in the order recommended by the manufacturer. Place pan in the oven chamber. Select **Dough Cycle**.

2. Stop bread machine when the kneading portion of the cycle is complete. (Do not allow dough to rise in the machine.) Remove dough to a lightly floured surface; cover with a large bowl and let rest for 10 to 15 minutes. Shape the dough into a round cylinder 12 inches (30 cm) long. Cut into 8 portions 1½ inches (4 cm) wide. Push thumbs through the center of each piece and pull into a bagel shape, rounding all the surfaces.

3. Place dough on prepared baking sheet; cover and let rise in a warm, draft-free place for 30 to 45 minutes or until doubled in volume. Meanwhile, preheat oven to 400°F (200°C).

4. Bring a large pot of water and 1 tbsp (15 mL) sugar to a gentle yet full boil. Immerse bagels in water one at a time, turning upside down. Hold under the water for 20 seconds with a skimmer or large spoon until the dough becomes a little puffy.

5. Bake on the prepared baking sheet or preheated baking stone in preheated oven for 15 minutes, or until the bagels sound hollow when tapped on the bottom.

Cinnamon Raisin Bagels

Tips

Turning the bagel upside down during boiling helps to ensure a rounded top.

See Equipment Glossary, page 357, for instructions on preheating the baking stone.

Variation

Substitute dried cranberries for the raisins, and cardamom for the cinnamon.

• Baking sheet, lightly greased, or preheated baking stone

1 1/2 cups	water	375 mL
1 tsp	salt	5 mL
3 tbsp	packed brown sugar	45 mL
1 3/4 cups	whole wheat flour	425 mL
2 cups	all-purpose flour or bread flour	500 mL
1 tsp	ground cinnamon	5 mL
2 tsp	bread machine yeast	10 mL
3/4 cup	raisins	175 mL
1 tbsp	granulated sugar	15 mL

1. Measure all ingredients *except raisins and granulated sugar* into machine's baking pan in the order recommended by the manufacturer. Insert pan into the oven chamber. Select **Dough Cycle**.

2. Stop bread machine when the kneading portion of the cycle is complete. (Do not allow dough to rise in the machine.) Remove dough to a lightly floured surface. Cover with a large bowl and let rest for 10 to 15 minutes. Knead in the raisins. Shape the dough into a round cylinder 13 1/2 inches (35 cm) long. Cut into 9 equal slices, each 1 1/2 inches (4 cm) thick. Push thumbs through the center of each slice and pull into a bagel shape, rounding all surfaces. Place on prepared baking sheet. Cover and let rise in a warm, draft-free place for 15 to 20 minutes. Meanwhile, preheat oven to 400°F (200°C).

3. Bring a large pot of water to a gentle (but full) boil; add sugar. Immerse bagels one at a time in water, turning upside down. With a skimmer or large spoon, hold bagel under the water for 20 seconds or until dough becomes a little puffy. Place on prepared baking sheet or preheated baking stone. Bake in preheated oven for 15 to 20 minutes, or until bagels sound hollow when tapped on the bottom.

Butter Pecan Bagels

A pleasantly sweet butterscotch flavor combines with a nutty crunch in this lower-fat dessert bagel.

Tips

To economize, purchase pecan pieces from the bulk store.

See Equipment Glossary, page 357, for instructions on preheating the baking stone.

Variation

Substitute white or semi-sweet chocolate chips for butterscotch chips.

• *Baking sheet, lightly greased, or preheated baking stone*

1 1/4 cups	water	300 mL
1 tsp	salt	5 mL
1/4 cup	packed brown sugar	50 mL
3 1/2 cups	all-purpose flour or bread flour	875 mL
1/2 cup	butterscotch chips	125 mL
1/2 cup	chopped pecans	125 mL
2 tsp	bread machine yeast	10 mL
1 tbsp	granulated sugar	15 mL

1. Measure ingredients into baking pan in the order recommended by the manufacturer. Place pan into the oven chamber. Select **Dough Cycle**.

2. Stop bread machine when the kneading portion of the cycle is complete. (Do not allow dough to rise in the machine.) Remove dough to a lightly floured surface; cover with a large bowl and let rest for 10 to 15 minutes. Shape the dough into a round cylinder 12 inches (30 cm) long. Cut into 8 portions 1 1/2 inches (4 cm) wide. Push thumbs through the center of each piece and pull into a bagel shape, rounding all the surfaces.

3. Place dough on prepared baking sheet; cover and let rise in a warm, draft-free place for 30 to 45 minutes or until doubled in volume. Meanwhile, preheat oven to 400°F (200°C).

4. Bring a large pot of water and 1 tbsp (15 mL) sugar to a gentle yet full boil. Immerse the bagels in water one at a time, turning upside down. Hold under the water for 20 seconds with a skimmer or large spoon until the dough becomes a little puffy.

5. Bake on the prepared baking sheet or preheated baking stone in preheated oven for 15 minutes, or until the bagels sound hollow when tapped on the bottom.

Mocha Bagels

Chocolate and coffee team together in this delicious treat.

Tips

An equal amount of cold leftover coffee can be substituted for the water and instant coffee granules.

See Equipment Glossary, page 357, for instructions on preheating the baking stone.

Variation

Try your favorite flavored coffee, such as Irish Cream or French Vanilla, for a personalized treat.

• Baking sheet, lightly greased, or preheated baking stone

1¼ cups	water	300 mL
1 tsp	salt	5 mL
¼ cup	packed brown sugar	50 mL
3½ cups	all-purpose flour or bread flour	875 mL
½ cup	chocolate chips	125 mL
1 tsp	instant coffee granules	5 mL
2 tsp	bread machine yeast	10 mL
1 tbsp	granulated sugar	15 mL

1. Measure ingredients into baking pan in the order recommended by the manufacturer. Place pan in the oven chamber. Select **Dough Cycle**.

2. Stop bread machine when the kneading portion of the cycle is complete. (Do not allow dough to rise in the machine.) Remove dough to a lightly floured surface; cover with a large bowl and let rest for 10 to 15 minutes. Shape the dough into a round cylinder 12 inches (30 cm) long. Cut into 8 portions 1½ inch (4 cm) wide. Push thumbs through the center of each piece and pull into a bagel shape, rounding all the surfaces.

3. Place dough on prepared baking sheet; cover and let rise in a warm, draft-free place for 30 to 45 minutes, or until doubled in volume. Meanwhile, preheat oven to 400°F (200°C).

4. Bring a large pot of water and 1 tbsp (15 mL) sugar to a gentle yet full boil. Immerse bagels in water one at a time, turning upside down. Hold under the water for 20 seconds with a skimmer or large spoon until the dough becomes a little puffy.

5. Bake on the prepared baking sheet or preheated baking stone in preheated oven for 15 minutes, or until the bagels sound hollow when tapped on the bottom.

New Beginnings for Sourdoughs: Starters vs. Sours

From the time of the early settlers, sourdough breads have required a starter — essentially, a fermented mix of yeast, water, flour and sugar. Traditional starters were maintained for years (often many generations) with periodic "feedings" of sugar, as well as additions of flour and water, to replenish any starter used for making sourdough. While the traditional starter method has a certain charm, and makes wonderfully tangy breads and rolls, it is time-consuming and, with variations in temperature and humidity, can produce inconsistent results.

In recent years, a new type of product has been introduced as an alternative to sourdough starters. These are called "dry active sourdough cultures." Sold under brand names such as lalvain du jour® and SAF Levain, these don't require all the time and care that starters do. Simply make up a "sour," then use it for baking. When finished, make a fresh batch of sour from a new package. The results are more consistent.

Purchasing lalvain du jour®
- Visit www.lallemand.com or phone 1-877-fermipan.
- Visit www.KingArthurFlour.com or phone 1-800-827-6836.
- Visit www.bestbreadrecipes.com or phone 1-613-923-2116.

Using sours
- Prepared *Basic Sour Mix* (see recipe, facing page) should be measured and used directly from the refrigerator.
- Stir well before each use. It is normal for a sour to separate. The liquid rises to the top, while a very white, thick part settles to the bottom of the storage container.
- A fresh sour is less gassy and therefore bakes a loaf with finer texture.

Storing sour and dry active sourdough cultures
- Store prepared sour in refrigerator, covered, for up to 4 weeks. For longer storage, measure the amount called for in the recipe, wrap and over-wrap; freeze for up to 3 months. Thaw in the refrigerator before using. Use cold from the refrigerator.
- Store unopened and opened dry active sourdough culture packages in the refrigerator.

Basic Sour Mix

28 cups	water, 98°F (37°C)	7 L
1 tbsp	granulated sugar	15 mL
5 lbs	unbleached all-purpose flour or bread flour	2.5 kg
1	package (0.17 oz/5 g) dry active sourdough culture	1

For many generations, artisan bakers have used traditional starter to make their sourdough. Today we can duplicate their techniques and results with dry active sourdough culture and a bread machine.

Tips

Sours must be made ahead, allowed to ferment at room temperature, stored, then used as the "starter" in a recipe.

5 lbs (2.5 kg) of flour is equal to about 20 cups (5 L).

This recipe can be halved or quartered. Mix the contents of the dry active sourdough culture package well before measuring.

1. In a large plastic storage container, combine water, sugar, flour and dry active sourdough culture; mix until well blended. Any remaining lumps of flour will disappear as the sour develops.

2. Cover tightly and let stand in a warm, draft-free place for 18 to 24 hours. Refrigerate overnight before using.

Choosing a Bakery Starter

There are four common varieties of bakery starters available:

La1
Mild, almost creamy aroma and taste. It is ideal for pastries and croissants.

La2
Fermented aroma with a buttery cheese note. It makes a great French bread.

La3
Aromatic sour aroma and taste. This is the one for French sourdough bread.

La4
The strongest, sourest San Francisco–style sourdough.

Tips for Working with Sourdough

Sourdough loaves have a crisper crust, a more open interior and a "tuggier" texture than traditional loaves.

1. Preparing
Although traditional artisan breads do not contain sugar or fat, adding a small amount of sugar may result in a more open texture. The dough should be sticky. Resist the temptation to add more flour, since this will make the loaf tougher.

2. Resting
Place dough on the generously floured lid of a large plastic storage container. Dust the top of the dough with flour, cover with the container and tightly seal. Let the dough rest, at room temperature, for 45 minutes to 1 hour before forming. Do not grease the storage container or the dough.

3. Forming
On a floured surface, flatten the dough into a rectangle with the heel of your hand. Fold one-third of the dough over. With the heel of your hand, seal the seam. Repeat with the remaining third from the opposite side. Seal the seam. Rotate the dough by one quarter turn. Roll into a log shape, sealing the seam well. Place the formed dough, seam-side down, on the generously floured lid of a large plastic storage container. Dust the top of the dough with rice flour, cover with the container and tightly seal. (Rice flour stays white during baking, unlike wheat flour, which browns.)

4. Proofing
Proof dough in the refrigerator for at least 14 hours. This slow cool-rise produces the bread's open texture.

5. Slashing
Slash the risen dough with a lame or a sharp knife. (For instructions on this procedure, see Techniques Glossary, page 370.) For long, narrow loaves, make 3 to 5 diagonal slashes; round-shaped loaves can be slashed with an "X" pattern. Dust again with rice flour before baking.

6. Baking
Remove the dough from the refrigerator 30 minutes before baking. Slide the risen dough onto a baking sheet, a baguette pan or a preheated baking stone. Bake in preheated oven.

For a crispy crust, steam the dough immediately after putting it in the oven. See Techniques Glossary, page 370, for instructions.

Sourdough Baguettes

- *Large plastic storage container, lid generously floured*
- *Baguette pan or baking sheet, sprinkled with cornmeal*

*Spread baguettes with
Brie cheese or chèvre
and top with roasted
vegetables for a
delicious light lunch.*

Tip

For information about
baguette pans, see
Equipment Glossary,
page 357.

Variation

Use the dough to
make 1 large loaf.

1¾ cups	cold Basic Sour Mix (see recipe, page 181)	425 mL
1½ tsp	salt	7 mL
1 tsp	granulated sugar	5 mL
3¼ cups	unbleached all-purpose flour or bread flour	800 mL
2 tsp	bread machine yeast	10 mL

1. Measure ingredients into baking pan in the order recommended by the manufacturer. Insert pan into the oven chamber. Select **Dough Cycle**.

2. Stop bread machine when the kneading portion of the cycle is complete. (Do not allow dough to rise in the machine.) Place the dough on prepared storage container lid. Lightly flour top of dough. Cover and tightly seal with inverted storage container base. Let rise for 45 minutes to 1 hour in a warm, draft-free place.

3. Divide dough in half. Form each half into a thin stick 14 inches (35 cm) long, tapering at both ends. Place both on the re-floured lid and dust with flour. Cover tightly and refrigerate for at least 14 hours or overnight.

4. Remove the dough from the refrigerator 30 minutes before baking. Preheat oven to 450°F (220°C). Place the dough on prepared baguette pan or baking sheet. (For crispier crust, steam dough using technique described in Techniques Glossary, page 370). Bake in preheated oven for 10 minutes. Reduce oven temperature to 400°F (200°C) and bake for 8 to 10 minutes if using a baguette pan and 15 to 20 minutes if using a baking sheet, until baguettes sound hollow when tapped on the bottom.

Sourdough Boule

This boule rises high and round. Tear off pieces to serve with split-pea soup.

Tip

For instructions on injecting steam, see Techniques Glossary, page 370.

Variation

For a professional finish, use a banneton (see Equipment Glossary, page 357) or a generously floured wicker basket that is twice the size of the unrisen dough. Place dough in basket, then in large plastic container; cover tightly and refrigerate as in step 3. Gently tip it out of the basket upside down onto a prepared baking sheet. Bake as directed in step 4.

• Large plastic storage container, lid generously floured
• Banneton (optional, see note at left)
• Baking sheet, sprinkled with cornmeal

1⅓ cups	cold Basic Sour Mix (see recipe, page 181)	325 mL
1¼ tsp	salt	6 mL
1 tbsp	liquid honey	15 mL
2 cups	unbleached all-purpose flour or bread flour	500 mL
½ cup	rye flour	125 mL
1½ tsp	bread machine yeast	7 mL

1. Measure ingredients into baking pan in the order recommended by the manufacturer. Insert pan into the oven chamber. Select **Dough Cycle**.

2. Stop bread machine when the kneading portion of the cycle is complete. (Do not allow dough to rise in the machine.) Remove dough to a lightly floured surface. Cover with a large bowl and let rest for 10 to 15 minutes. Place the dough on prepared storage container lid. Lightly flour top of dough and cover and tightly seal with inverted storage container base. Let rise for 45 minutes to 1 hour in a warm, draft-free place.

3. Form into a high rounded ball. Place dough on the re-floured lid and dust with flour (or in banneton, if using) and seal in the storage container. Cover tightly and refrigerate for at least 14 hours or overnight.

4. Remove the dough from the refrigerator 30 minutes before baking. Preheat oven to 400°F (200°C). Place the dough on prepared baking sheet. Inject steam (see Techniques Glossary, page 370). Bake in preheated oven for 10 minutes. Reduce oven temperature to 350°F (180°C) and bake for 20 to 25 minutes, or until boule sounds hollow when tapped on the bottom.

These aren't your average hamburger buns! The flavor trio of cheese, onion and sourdough is sensational.

Tip

Sourdough will be sticky. Flour your fingers for easier handling.

Variation

This recipe can also be used to make 4 submarine buns.

Onion Cheddar Sourdough Hamburger Buns

• *Large plastic storage container, lid generously floured*
• *Baking sheet, dusted with cornmeal*

1¾ cups	cold Basic Sour Mix (see recipe, page 181)	425 mL
1 tsp	salt	5 mL
3 cups	unbleached all-purpose flour or bread flour	750 mL
¾ cup	shredded old Cheddar cheese	175 mL
2 tbsp	minced dry onion	25 mL
1¾ tsp	bread machine yeast	8 mL

1. Measure ingredients into baking pan in the order recommended by the manufacturer. Insert pan into the oven chamber. Select **Dough Cycle**.

2. Stop bread machine when the kneading portion of the cycle is complete. (Do not allow dough to rise in the machine.) Place the dough on prepared storage container lid. Lightly flour the dough. Cover and tightly seal with inverted storage container base. Let rise for 45 minutes to 1 hour in a warm, draft-free place.

3. Divide dough into 8 portions. Form each into a hamburger bun, flattening tops slightly. Place on re-floured lid and cover tightly. Refrigerate for at least 14 hours or overnight.

4. Remove the dough from the refrigerator 30 minutes before baking. Preheat oven to 375°F (190°C). Place buns on prepared baking sheet. Bake in preheated oven for 25 to 35 minutes, or until buns sound hollow when tapped on the bottom.

French Walnut Raisin Sourdough

Tempt your palate with the flavor of this tangy sourdough, with its combination of raisins, rye and walnuts.

Tips

See Tips for Working with Sourdough on page 182.

See Equipment Glossary, page 357, for instructions on preheating the baking stone.

See Techniques Glossary, page 370, for instructions on injecting steam.

- Large plastic storage container, lid generously floured
- Baking sheet, sprinkled with cornmeal, or preheated baking stone

1 1/2 cups	cold Basic Sour Mix (see recipe, page 181)	375 mL
1 1/4 tsp	salt	6 mL
3/4 cup	whole wheat bread flour	175 mL
1 cup	unbleached all-purpose flour or bread flour	250 mL
1/2 cup	rye flour	125 mL
3/4 cup	chopped walnuts	175 mL
1/2 cup	raisins	125 mL
1 tbsp	bread machine yeast	15 mL

1. Measure ingredients into baking pan in the order recommended by the manufacturer. Insert baking pan into oven chamber. Select **Dough Cycle**.

2. Stop bread machine when the kneading portion of the cycle is complete. (Do not allow dough to rise in the machine.) Place the dough on prepared storage container lid. Lightly flour the dough. Cover and tightly seal with inverted storage container base. Let rise for 45 minutes to 1 hour in a warm, draft-free place.

3. Divide risen dough in half. Form each half into a round loaf. Place each on the re-floured lid. Cover tightly and refrigerate for at least 14 hours or overnight.

4. Remove the dough from the refrigerator 30 minutes before baking. Preheat oven to 400°F (200°C). Place loaves on prepared baking sheets or preheated baking stone. (For crispier crust, steam dough using technique described in Techniques Glossary, page 370). Bake in preheated oven for 10 minutes. Reduce the oven temperature to 350°F (180°C) and bake for 20 to 25 minutes, or until loaves sound hollow when tapped on the bottom.

Tips for Successful Starters

1. Using the starter
The starter should have the consistency of thin pancake batter. If too thick, add a small amount of water before measuring. If your bread machine does not have a 20- to 30-minute delay to preheat before mixing, bring the starter to room temperature or place in a bowl of warm water for 15 minutes before measuring. Until the starter becomes established and is working well, remove only 1 cup (250 mL) at a time.

2. Feeding the starter
To replace each 1 cup (250 mL) of starter used in preparing a recipe, add $3/4$ cup (175 mL) water, $3/4$ cup (175 mL) flour and 1 tsp (5 mL) sugar. Stir well, using a wooden spoon, and let stand at room temperature for at least 24 hours, or until bubbly.

3. Storing the starter
Refrigerate, loosely covered, until needed. If not used regularly, stir in 1 tsp (5 mL) sugar every 10 days. The starter can be kept for years, shared with friends, or even passed from generation to generation!

Sourdough Starter

1¼ tsp	yeast	6 mL
2¾ cups	warm water, divided	675 mL
1 tbsp	granulated sugar	15 mL
2 cups	all-purpose flour or bread flour	500 mL

Prepare the starter at least 7 to 10 days before you plan to bake the sourdough bread.

Tips

If the starter liquid is green, pink or orange — or develops mold — throw it out and begin again.

Store prepared starter in a glass jar covered loosely with aluminum foil or a lid partially screwed on to allow gases to escape.

1. In a large glass bowl, sprinkle yeast over ½ cup (125 mL) warm water. Let stand for 10 minutes. Add remaining 2¼ cups (550 mL) warm water, sugar and flour; beat until smooth.

2. Cover bowl with a layer of cheesecloth and let stand at room temperature for 5 to 10 days, stirring with a wooden spoon 2 or 3 times a day. When ready to use, the starter has a sour smell with small bubbles on (or rising to) the surface.

Sourdough Rustic White Bread

Here's a definitive San Francisco-style sourdough. It has that characteristic tangy flavor and tuggy texture.

Tip

For a change in color and flavor, try making and/or feeding the starter with whole wheat rather than bread flour.

Variation

For a rustic brown bread, try using half whole wheat flour.

1 cup	Sourdough Starter (see recipe, page 189)	250 mL
1/2 cup	water	125 mL
1/4 cup	skim milk powder	50 mL
1 1/4 tsp	salt	6 mL
2 tbsp	granulated sugar	25 mL
2 tbsp	shortening or vegetable oil	25 mL
3 cups	all-purpose flour or bread flour	750 mL
1 1/4 tsp	bread machine yeast	6 mL

1. Measure ingredients into baking pan in the order recommended by the manufacturer. Insert pan into the oven chamber.

2. Select **Basic Cycle**.

Sourdough Cracked Wheat Bread

This delightfully tangy loaf has the crunchy texture and natural whole-grain goodness of cracked wheat.

Tip

Be sure the cracked wheat is not touching water or the loaf may be short and heavy.

Variation

Bulgur can be substituted for the cracked wheat.

1 cup	Sourdough Starter (see recipe, page 189)	250 mL
3/4 cup	water	175 mL
1/4 cup	skim milk powder	50 mL
1 1/2 tsp	salt	7 mL
3 tbsp	liquid honey	45 mL
3 tbsp	shortening or vegetable oil	45 mL
1 1/4 cups	whole wheat flour	300 mL
2 cups	all-purpose flour or bread flour	500 mL
3/4 cup	cracked wheat	175 mL
1 3/4 tsp	bread machine yeast	8 mL

1. Measure ingredients into baking pan in the order recommended by the manufacturer. Insert pan into the oven chamber.
2. Select **Whole Wheat Cycle**.

Sourdough Cornmeal Bread

A good old Southern favorite, this bread has a tangy flavor and tuggy texture.

Tip

Because of the egg and the starter in this loaf, you should not use the timer on your machine.

Variation

We use a medium-grind yellow cornmeal; however, blue or white can be substituted.

1 cup	Sourdough Starter (see recipe, page 189)	250 mL
1/2 cup	water	125 mL
1	egg	1
1/4 cup	skim milk powder	50 mL
1 1/2 tsp	salt	8 mL
2 tbsp	liquid honey	25 mL
2 tbsp	shortening or vegetable oil	25 mL
3 1/4 cups	all-purpose flour or bread flour	800 mL
1/3 cup	cornmeal	75 mL
1 tsp	bread machine yeast	5 mL

1. Measure ingredients into baking pan in the order recommended by the manufacturer. Insert pan into the oven chamber.
2. Select **Basic Cycle**.

Sourdough Pumpernickel Raisin Bread

Your taste buds won't know what hit them when they experience the tang of sourdough combined with the sweetness of raisins and the savory flavor of pumpernickel.

Tip

Prepare this loaf for weekend lunches featuring grilled cheese sandwiches.

Variation

Add 2 tsp (10 mL) orange zest and $\frac{1}{2}$ tsp (2 mL) ground anise seed for a more pronounced Scandinavian taste.

1 cup	Sourdough Starter (see recipe, page 189)	250 mL
¾ cup	water	175 mL
¼ cup	skim milk powder	50 mL
1 tsp	salt	5 mL
2 tbsp	liquid honey	25 mL
2 tbsp	molasses	25 mL
2 tbsp	shortening or vegetable oil	25 mL
¾ cup	whole wheat flour	175 mL
1¾ cups	all-purpose flour or bread flour	425 mL
½ cup	rye flour	125 mL
2 tsp	unsweetened cocoa powder	10 mL
1 tsp	instant coffee granules	5 mL
1¼ tsp	bread machine yeast	6 mL
⅓ cup	raisins	75 mL

1. Measure all ingredients *except raisins* into baking pan in the order recommended by the manufacturer. Insert pan into the oven chamber.

2. Select **Basic Cycle**.

3. Add raisins at the "add ingredient" signal.

Sourdough Submarine Buns

A touch of "sour" in these submarine buns complements spicy deli meats.

Tip

Younger children love these buns made in a smaller size — perfect for the lunch box (see below).

Variation

To make a smaller version, suitable for hot dog buns, roll dough into 12 buns, each 6 inches (15 cm) in length. Finish recipe as given.

• Baking sheet, sprinkled with 1 to 2 tbsp (15 to 25 mL) cornmeal

1 cup	Sourdough Starter (see recipe, page 189)	250 mL
3/4 cup	water	175 mL
1	egg	1
1 1/4 tsp	salt	6 mL
1 tbsp	granulated sugar	15 mL
3 1/2 cups	all-purpose flour or bread flour	875 mL
1 1/4 tsp	bread machine yeast	6 mL

TOPPING

| 1 | egg white | 1 |
| 1 tbsp | water | 15 mL |

1. Measure ingredients into baking pan in the order recommended by the manufacturer. Insert pan into the oven chamber. Select **Dough Cycle**.

2. Remove dough to a lightly floured board; cover with a large bowl and let rest for 10 to 15 minutes. Divide into 6 portions. Shape into 12-inch (30 cm) long buns. Place on the prepared baking sheet.

3. Cover and let the dough rise in a warm, draft-free place for 30 to 45 minutes, or until doubled in volume. Meanwhile, preheat oven to 350°F (180°C).

4. *Topping:* Brush with the egg white combined with water.

5. Bake in preheated oven for 15 to 20 minutes, or until the buns sound hollow when tapped on the bottom.

Rolls by the Basketful

Here are the recipes that will have your bread baskets brimming with a magical assortment of rolls. The shapes vary from perfectly round globes to triangular wedges to narrow sticks. Sizes vary from dainty to enormous, satisfying every appetite. Bake and freeze an assortment to enjoy later.

Tips for Forming, Finishing and Baking Rolls

1. Forming
Cover dough with a large bowl and allow to rest for 10 to 15 minutes before forming. This allows the gluten in the warm dough to relax, making the dough less sticky and easier to handle.

Handle the dough as little as possible for more tender rolls. Too much flour added to a slightly sticky dough results in tough, heavy, dense rolls.

2. Choosing the shape
Choose any shape you like — whether from those given in the recipe or those described at the end of the chapter. For example, *Alpine Muesli Rolls* (see recipe, page 199) can become muesli "flower pots" using the technique described for *Pumpernickel Flower Pots* (see recipe, page 210). The possible variations are endless. Follow the recipe directions carefully for size and thickness so that your bread will look as appetizing as it tastes.

3. Finishing
Lightly grease the tops of the dough with a cooking spray or shortening. Choose any finish listed under any recipe. Brush the finish on gently so the dough does not deflate.

4. Proofing
Cover the dough with waxed paper and a lint-free towel to keep it warm and protected from drafts as it rises. To test for readiness, press two fingers into the dough; the indentations should remain.

5. Baking
To ensure even browning when baking two pans at the same time, switch their position in the oven halfway through cooking time.

6. Testing for Doneness
There are two methods. The most common is to tap on the bottom — if the sound is hollow, the bread is baked. If you have an instant-read thermometer, insert into bread at least 2 inches (5 cm). The thermometer should register 190°F (93°C).

Rich White Dinner Rolls

Delight your family with these cloverleaf rolls. Young children love them when formed into four-leaf clovers.

Tip

For easy removal of baked rolls, spray the inside and bottom of muffin tins with cooking spray.

Variation

To make basic pan rolls, divide the dough into 12 portions and place, just touching, in an 8-inch (2 L) square baking pan.

1⅓ cups	milk	325 mL
1¼ tsp	salt	6 mL
2 tbsp	granulated sugar	25 mL
2 tbsp	butter	25 mL
3¼ cups	all-purpose flour or bread flour	800 mL
1¼ tsp	bread machine yeast	6 mL

1. Measure ingredients into baking pan in the order recommended by the manufacturer. Insert pan into the oven chamber. Select **Dough Cycle**.

2. Remove dough to a lightly floured surface; cover with a large bowl and let rest for 10 to 15 minutes.

3. Use the shaping and finishing method described below, or choose from any roll recipe in this chapter.

Cloverleaf Rolls

Divide the dough into 12 portions. Divide each into 3 pieces. Roll into balls. Place 3 in each cup of a lightly greased muffin tin. Cover and let rise in a warm, draft-free place for 30 to 45 minutes, or until doubled in volume. Bake in oven preheated to 375°F (190°C) for 15 to 20 minutes, or until rolls sound hollow when tapped on the bottom.

Golden Glaze

Brush freshly baked rolls with 1 to 2 tbsp (15 to 25 mL) melted butter.

Twelve-Grain Rolls

• *Baking sheets, lightly greased*

1⅓ cups	water	325 mL
1¼ tsp	salt	6 mL
2 tbsp	liquid honey	25 mL
2 tbsp	shortening or vegetable oil	25 mL
2 cups	whole wheat flour	500 mL
1½ cups	all-purpose flour or bread flour	375 mL
¾ cup	12-grain cereal	175 mL
2 tbsp	wheat germ	25 mL
2 tsp	bread machine yeast	10 mL

If you love hearty dinner rolls, try these tonight.

Tip

If you've got some extra wheat germ on hand, try adding 1 to 2 tbsp (15 to 25 mL) to any bread, reducing the flour by an equal amount. This won't affect the shape of the loaf, and it's a great way to add nutrients — especially B-vitamins.

Variation

Substitute cracked wheat for the 12-grain cereal.

1. Measure ingredients into machine's baking pan in the order recommended by the manufacturer. Insert pan into the oven chamber. Select **Dough Cycle**.

2. Remove dough to a lightly floured surface. Cover with a large bowl and let rest for 10 to 15 minutes. Divide the dough in 12 portions. Roll into balls. Place balls on prepared baking sheets, setting them 3 inches (7.5 cm) apart. Cover and let rise in a warm, draft-free place for 30 to 45 minutes, or until doubled in volume. Meanwhile, preheat oven to 375°F (190°C).

3. Bake in preheated oven for 15 to 20 minutes, or until rolls sound hollow when tapped on the bottom.

Pan Rolls

For a different kind of shape, place the 12 balls of dough in a lightly greased 8-inch (2 L) square baking pan. Cover and let rise in a warm, draft-free place for 30 to 45 minutes, or until doubled in volume. Bake in oven preheated to 375°F (190°C) for 30 to 45 minutes, or until rolls sound hollow when tapped on the bottom.

Alpine Muesli Rolls

1¼ cups	water	300 mL
¼ cup	skim milk powder	50 mL
1½ tsp	salt	7 mL
2 tbsp	liquid honey	25 mL
1 tbsp	shortening or vegetable oil	15 mL
2¾ cups	all-purpose flour or bread flour	675 mL
1 cup	muesli	250 mL
1½ tsp	bread machine yeast	7 mL
¼ cup	raisins	50 mL
¼ cup	sunflower seeds, raw, unsalted	50 mL

With 8 different nuts and grains — providing tastes ranging from salty to sweet — every bite is a treat.

Tips

Muesli can be purchased at bulk food stores. It becomes rancid quickly, so keep in the refrigerator and check for freshness before adding to the baking pan.

Prepackaged muesli cereals contain extra fat and sugar and may result in a completely different roll. Choose lower-fat unsweetened products.

Variation

Form dough into 4 mini-loaves, bake and slice thinly. They're ideal bases for hors d'oeuvres.

1. Measure all ingredients *except raisins and sunflower seeds* into baking pan in the order recommended by the manufacturer. Insert pan into the oven chamber. Select **Dough Cycle**.

2. Add raisins and sunflower seeds at the "add ingredient" signal or gently knead into dough at end of cycle.

3. Remove dough to a lightly floured surface; cover with a large bowl and allow to rest for 10 to 15 minutes.

4. Use the shaping and finishing method described below, or choose from any roll recipe in this chapter.

Toasties
Roll out dough to a 12-inch (30 cm) circle. Place on a lightly greased 12-inch (30 cm) pizza pan. Using a pizza wheel, cut into 8 wedges. Cover and let rise in a warm, draft-free place for 30 to 45 minutes or until doubled in volume. Bake in oven preheated to 375°F (190°C) for 25 to 30 minutes, or until toasties sound hollow when tapped on the bottom. Cool completely. Slice each triangle in half crosswise and fill with your favorite deli meats.

Seeds and More Seeds
Gently brush the risen dough with cooled melted butter or milk. Sprinkle with muesli.

These versatile buns can be made as large or small as your family likes.

Variation

Here's a personal favorite: Prepare *Cheddar Beer Bread* (see recipe, page 45) using the **Dough Cycle** and finish as hamburger and hot dog buns.

Hamburger and Hot Dog Buns

1¼ cups	water	300 mL
1	egg	1
1¼ tsp	salt	6 mL
2 tbsp	granulated sugar	25 mL
2 tbsp	shortening or vegetable oil	25 mL
1½ cups	whole wheat flour	375 mL
2½ cups	all-purpose flour or bread flour	625 mL
⅓ cup	buttermilk powder	75 mL
1¼ tsp	bread machine yeast	6 mL

1. Measure ingredients into baking pan in the order recommended by the manufacturer. Insert pan into the oven chamber. Select **Dough Cycle**.

2. Remove dough to a lightly floured surface; cover with a large bowl and let rest for 10 to 15 minutes.

3. Use the shaping and finishing method described below, or choose from any roll recipe in this chapter.

Hot Dog Buns

Divide the dough into 12 equal portions. Form into 5-inch (12.5 cm) hot dog–shaped buns. Place the buns on a lightly greased baking sheet. Cover and let rise in a warm, draft-free place for 30 to 45 minutes, or until doubled in volume. Bake in oven preheated to 375°F (190°C) for 15 to 18 minutes, or until buns sound hollow when tapped on the bottom.

Hamburger Buns

Divide the dough into 9 to 12 portions. Roll each into a ball. Form into a flattened hamburger bun shape between 3 and 3½ inches (7.5 and 9 cm) in diameter. Place buns on a lightly greased baking sheet. Cover and let rise in a warm, draft-free place for 30 to 45 minutes, or until doubled in volume. Bake in oven preheated to 375°F (190°C) for 15 to 20 minutes, or until buns sound hollow when tapped on the bottom.

Submarine Buns

1 cup	water	250 mL
1	egg	1
1 tsp	salt	5 mL
2 tsp	granulated sugar	10 mL
3 1/3 cups	all-purpose flour or bread flour	825 mL
1 1/2 tsp	bread machine yeast	7 mL

This bun is also known as a hero, hoagie, grinder or, in New Orleans, a muffaletta.

Variation

Choose a size to suit individual tastes, making either six 12-inch (30 cm) or twelve 6-inch (15 cm) buns.

1. Measure ingredients into baking pan in the order recommended by the manufacturer. Insert pan into the oven chamber. Select **Dough Cycle**.

2. Remove dough to a lightly floured surface; cover with a large bowl and let rest for 10 to 15 minutes.

3. Use the shaping and finishing method described below, or choose from any roll recipe in this chapter.

Submarine Buns

Divide the dough into 6 equal portions. Form into slightly flattened 12-inch (30 cm) long buns. Place on a baking sheet sprinkled with cornmeal. Cover and let rise in a warm, draft-free place for 30 to 45 minutes, until doubled in volume. Brush with topping. Bake in oven preheated to 350°F (180°C) for 15 minutes, or until buns sound hollow when tapped on the bottom.

Toasted Sesame Seed Topping

Brush the risen dough with 1 to 2 tbsp (15 to 25 mL) melted butter. Sprinkle with 1 to 2 tbsp (15 to 25 mL) sesame seeds. The seeds will toast as the buns bake.

Mustard Rye Mini-Submarines

These submarine-shaped rolls are delicious split in half and piled high with Black Forest ham and Swiss cheese or served with bratwurst sausage.

Tip

Add 1/2 tsp (2 mL) mustard seeds to enhance the flavor.

Variation

For a slightly milder flavor and lighter color, substitute light rye flour.

1 1/4 cups	water	300 mL
2 tbsp	prepared mustard	25 mL
1/2 tsp	salt	2 mL
1 tbsp	packed brown sugar	15 mL
2 tbsp	olive oil	25 mL
3/4 cup	whole wheat flour	175 mL
2 cups	all-purpose flour or bread flour	500 mL
3/4 cup	rye flour	175 mL
1 1/4 tsp	bread machine yeast	6 mL

1. Measure ingredients into baking pan in the order recommended by the manufacturer. Insert pan into the oven chamber. Select **Dough Cycle**.

2. Remove dough to a lightly floured surface; cover with a large bowl and let rest for 10 to 15 minutes.

3. Use the shaping and finishing method described below, or choose from any roll recipe in this chapter.

Mini-Submarine Buns

Divide the dough into 8 portions. Form into 8 submarine-shaped buns, 4 inches (10 cm) long. Place on a lightly greased baking sheet. Cover and let rise in a warm, draft-free place for 30 to 45 minutes, or until doubled in volume. Finish as desired. Bake in oven preheated to 375°F (190°C) for 15 to 20 minutes, or until mini-submarines sound hollow when tapped on the bottom.

Center-Slash Tops

Gently cut one long, deep slash 1/2 inch (1 cm) lengthwise down the center of the risen roll.

Whole Wheat Kaisers

1 1/4 cups	water	300 mL
2	eggs	2
1 1/2 tsp	salt	7 mL
2 tbsp	granulated sugar	25 mL
4 cups	whole wheat flour	1000 mL
1 1/2 tsp	bread machine yeast	7 mL

Impress your family with Kaisers just like those from the bakeshop. It takes a little practice, but before long you will become an expert.

Tip

Turning the Kaisers upside down to rise and then turning them right-side up just before baking helps to prevent the folds from springing open during baking.

Variation

Dust the baking sheet with semolina flour instead of cornmeal.

1. Measure ingredients into baking pan in the order recommended by the manufacturer. Insert pan into the oven chamber. Select **Dough Cycle**.

2. Remove dough to a lightly floured surface; cover with a large bowl and let rest for 10 to 15 minutes.

3. Use the shaping and finishing method described below, or choose from any roll recipe in this chapter.

Kaisers

Divide the dough into 9 portions. Roll each into a ball. With a rolling pin, roll out into a 5-inch (12.5 cm) circle. Place the thumb of your left hand at an edge of the circle; fold approximately one-fifth of the circle over your thumb in toward the center. Press firmly into the dough at the center. Repeat four more times, tucking the end of the fifth fold under the first fold in the space left when thumb is removed. Place the buns upside down on a baking sheet. Cover and let rise in a warm, draft-free place for 30 to 45 minutes, or until doubled in volume. Turn right-side up on a baking sheet sprinkled with 1 to 2 tbsp (15 to 25 mL) of cornmeal. Bake in oven preheated to 350°F (180°C) for 15 to 20 minutes, or until Kaisers sound hollow when tapped on the bottom.

Double Cheese Dill Rolls with Dijon Mustard Glaze

What a flavor combination — cheese, dill and a honey mustard glaze!

Tip

Use fresh dill when available.

Variation

Try the glaze used here on any cheese bread, rye hearth bread or roll.

1¼ cups	water	300 mL
1 tsp	salt	5 mL
1 tbsp	granulated sugar	15 mL
3¼ cups	all-purpose or bread flour	800 mL
⅓ cup	buttermilk powder	75 mL
¾ cup	grated old Cheddar cheese	175 mL
2 tbsp	grated Parmesan cheese	25 mL
½ tsp	dill seeds	2 mL
1 tsp	bread machine yeast	5 mL

1. Measure ingredients into baking pan in the order recommended by the manufacturer. Insert pan into the oven chamber. Select **Dough Cycle**.

2. Remove the dough to a lightly floured surface; cover with a large bowl and let rest for 10 to 15 minutes.

3. Use the shaping and finishing method described below, or choose from any roll recipe in this chapter.

Fan Tans

Divide the dough into 3 portions. Roll out each into a 9-inch (23 cm) square. Brush with 1 tbsp (15 mL) cooled melted butter. With a sharp knife, cut each square into 6 strips. Make 3 stacks of 6 strips each. Cut each stack into six 1½-inch (4 cm) pieces. Place fan tans cut-side up into 18 lightly greased muffin tin cups. Cover and let rise in a warm, draft-free place for 30 to 45 minutes, or until doubled in volume. Finish as desired. Bake in oven preheated to 375°F (190°C) for 15 to 20 minutes, or until rolls sound hollow when tapped on the bottom.

Dijon Mustard Glaze

Combine 1 egg and 1 tbsp (15 mL) Dijon mustard. Lightly brush over the risen rolls just before baking.

Potato Cloverleaf Rolls

● *Muffin tins, lightly greased*

1⅓ cups	water	325 mL
¼ cup	skim milk powder	50 mL
1½ tsp	salt	7 mL
1 tbsp	packed brown sugar	15 mL
2 tbsp	butter	25 mL
4¼ cups	all-purpose flour or bread flour	1000 mL
¾ cup	mashed baked potato	175 mL
1 tsp	dried thyme	5 mL
1	clove garlic, minced	1
2 tsp	bread machine yeast	10 mL

The fluffy texture of these rolls will remind you of childhood family dinners.

Tip

Bake an extra potato or use leftover baked potatoes. Simply peel and mash quickly with a fork. No need to add any butter or salt. One large potato makes ¾ cup (175 mL) mashed.

Variation

To make this recipe as a loaf, select the 2 lb (1 kg) **Basic Cycle** rather than the **Dough Cycle**.

1. Measure ingredients into machine's baking pan in the order recommended by the manufacturer. Insert pan into the oven chamber. Select **Dough Cycle**.

2. Remove dough to a lightly floured surface. Cover with a large bowl and let rest for 10 to 15 minutes.

3. Use the shaping and finishing method described below, or choose from any roll recipe in this chapter.

Cloverleaf Rolls
Divide the dough into 54 portions. Roll into balls. Place 3 balls in each cup of prepared muffin tins. Cover and let rise in a warm, draft-free place for 30 to 45 minutes, or until doubled in volume. Meanwhile, preheat oven to 350°F (180°C). Bake in preheated oven for 15 to 20 minutes, or until rolls sound hollow when tapped on the bottom.

Crunchy Seed Mini-Loaves

Finish these rolls with seeded toppings for added crunch using a mixture of flax, sunflower, sesame, poppy and pumpkin seeds.

Tip

Brush risen dough lightly with a mixture of 1 egg white and 1 tbsp (15 mL) water to ensure that the seeds will stick.

Variation

Vary the proportions of seeds used, but keep the total amount the same as called for in the recipe.

1 1/4 cups	water	300 mL
1/4 cup	skim milk powder	50 mL
1 1/4 tsp	salt	6 mL
2 tbsp	liquid honey	25 mL
2 tbsp	shortening or vegetable oil	25 mL
1 cup	whole wheat flour	250 mL
2 1/4 cups	all-purpose flour or bread flour	550 mL
1/4 cup	pumpkin seeds	50 mL
1/4 cup	sesame seeds	50 mL
1/4 cup	sunflower seeds, raw, unsalted	50 mL
1 1/2 tsp	bread machine yeast	7 mL

1. Measure ingredients into baking pan in the order recommended by the manufacturer. Insert pan into the oven chamber. Select **Dough Cycle**.

2. Remove dough to a lightly floured surface; cover with a large bowl and allow to rest for 10 to 15 minutes.

3. Use the shaping and finishing method described below, or choose from any roll recipe in this chapter.

Mini-Loaves

Divide the dough into 8 portions. Form into small loaves. Place in lightly greased mini-loaf pans. Cover and let rise in a warm, draft-free place for 30 to 45 minutes, or until doubled in volume. Finish as desired. Bake in oven preheated to 375°F (190°C) for 20 to 25 minutes, or until rolls sound hollow when tapped on the bottom.

Extra Crunch

Gently brush the risen dough with water. Sprinkle sesame, pumpkin or sunflower seeds on the tops of the loaves just before baking. The seeds will toast to a crunchy texture.

Crusty French Onion Mini-Sticks

Tear apart these savory mini-sticks and enjoy the flaky crust.

1 1/4 cups	water	300 mL
1 1/4 tsp	salt	6 mL
2 tsp	granulated sugar	10 mL
3 1/2 cups	all-purpose flour or bread flour	875 mL
1/2 cup	minced dried onion	125 mL
1 1/4 tsp	bread machine yeast	7 mL

Tips

Dried onion flakes are more convenient than fresh and give a stronger flavor.

Fresh onions are not recommended here as they contain too much water.

Don't add onion salt to enhance the onion flavor.

Variation

Cut mini-sticks into thick slices or large cubes and use to top French onion soup.

1. Measure ingredients into baking pan in the order recommended by the manufacturer. Insert pan into the oven chamber. Select **Dough Cycle**.

2. Remove dough to a lightly floured surface; cover with a large bowl and allow to rest for 10 to 15 minutes.

3. Use the shaping and finishing method described below, or choose from any roll recipe in this chapter.

Mini French Sticks

Divide the dough into 12 portions. Form into small loaves, tapering the ends slightly. Place at least 2 inches (5 cm) apart on a baking sheet sprinkled with 2 tbsp (25 mL) cornmeal. Cover and let rise in a warm, draft-free place for 30 to 45 minutes, or until doubled in volume. Bake in oven preheated to 400°F (200°C) for 15 to 20 minutes, or until the mini-sticks sound hollow when tapped on the bottom.

Crisp and Flaky

Place a metal pan containing 12 ice cubes on the bottom rack of the oven. Before baking, let cubes melt. Brush risen dough with cold water. Spritz with cold water every 5 minutes during baking.

Giant Parmesan Rosemary Breadsticks

As tasty as they are fun to make, these thin, crunchy sticks are as long as your baking sheet.

Tip

Stretch the ends of the bread sticks as you place them on the baking sheet.

Variations

For a spicy treat, add 1 tbsp (15 mL) cracked black peppercorns.

Make these breadsticks in the shape of a focaccia (see recipe, page 142); brush with olive oil and coarse salt.

1 1/2 cups	water	375 mL
1/4 cup	skim milk powder	50 mL
1 1/2 tsp	salt	7 mL
1 tbsp	granulated sugar	15 mL
1 tbsp	olive oil	15 mL
3 3/4 cups	all-purpose flour or bread flour	925 mL
1 1/4 tsp	bread machine yeast	6 mL

1. Measure ingredients into baking pan in the order recommended by the manufacturer. Insert pan into the oven chamber. Select **Dough Cycle**.

2. Remove dough to a lightly floured surface; cover with a large bowl and let rest for 10 to 15 minutes.

3. Use the shaping and finishing method described below, or choose from any roll recipe in this chapter.

Giant Breadsticks

Roll out the dough into a 16- by 6-inch (40 by 15 cm) rectangle. Finish with topping. Cut into 12 strips, 16 inches (40 cm) long and 1/2 inch (1 cm) wide. If shorter breadsticks are preferred, cut into 32 strips, 6 inches (15 cm) long and 1/2 inch (1 cm) wide. Finish with topping. Bake on a lightly greased baking sheet in oven preheated to 400°F (200°C) for 15 to 18 minutes, or until breadsticks sound hollow when tapped on the bottom.

Parmesan Rosemary Topping

Brush dough with a mixture of 1 tbsp (15 mL) minced garlic and 1 tbsp (15 mL) olive oil. Sprinkle with 2 tbsp (25 mL) grated Parmesan cheese and 2 tsp (10 mL) dried rosemary.

Multigrain Bow Knots

1 1/4 cups	water	300 mL
1/4 cup	skim milk powder	50 mL
1 1/2 tsp	salt	7 mL
3 tbsp	granulated sugar	45 mL
2 tbsp	shortening or vegetable oil	25 mL
3 cups	all-purpose flour or bread flour	750 mL
1/4 cup	cracked wheat	50 mL
1/4 cup	flaxseed, cracked	50 mL
1/4 cup	7-grain cereal	50 mL
2 tbsp	oat bran	25 mL
2 tbsp	wheat germ	25 mL
1 1/2 tsp	bread machine yeast	7 mL

These rolls are a crunchy, nutty treat and go perfectly with a Caesar salad.

Tip

For more uniform ropes, roll pieces of dough on the breadboard — not in the air between your hands.

Variation

Make one large free-form bun 10 inches (25 cm) in diameter. Cut in half crosswise, pile on the veggies and cold cuts, and cut into wedges for a nutritious lunch dish.

1. Measure ingredients into baking pan in the order recommended by the manufacturer. Insert pan into the oven chamber. Select **Dough Cycle**.

2. Remove dough to a lightly floured surface; cover with a large bowl and let rest for 10 to 15 minutes.

3. Use the shaping and finishing method described below, or choose from any roll recipe in this chapter.

Bow Knots
Divide the dough into 24 equal portions. Roll out each into a 9-inch (23 cm) rope. Tie ropes to make a knot at the center. (Don't pull too tightly.) Place on a lightly greased baking sheet, 2 inches (5 cm) apart. Cover and let rise in a warm, draft-free place for 30 to 45 minutes, or until doubled in volume. Finish as desired. Bake in oven preheated to 375°F (190°C) for 15 to 20 minutes, or until rolls sound hollow when tapped on the bottom.

Shiny Egg Yolk Glaze
Combine 1 egg yolk and 1 tbsp (15 mL) water. Lightly brush over rolls before baking. Sprinkle with 1 tbsp (15 mL) sesame seeds.

Puffed up like little ice cream cones, these rolls make an interesting conversation piece.

Tip

Fill the flower pots only half full with dough. They will double in size during rising and will bake to the perfect size.

Variation

Add 1/2 cup (125 mL) raisins at the "add ingredient" signal.

Pumpernickel Flower Pots

1¼ cups	cold coffee	300 mL
2 tbsp	white vinegar	25 mL
1 tsp	salt	5 mL
3 tbsp	molasses	45 mL
3 tbsp	shortening or vegetable oil	45 mL
3¼ cups	all-purpose flour or bread flour	800 mL
¾ cup	rye flour	175 mL
2 tbsp	unsweetened cocoa powder	25 mL
2 tsp	caraway seeds	10 mL
1½ tsp	bread machine yeast	7 mL

1. Measure ingredients into baking pan in the order recommended by the manufacturer. Insert pan into the oven chamber. Select **Dough Cycle**.

2. Remove dough to a lightly floured surface; cover with a large bowl and let rest for 10 to 15 minutes.

3. Use the shaping and finishing method described below, or choose from any roll recipe in this chapter.

Flower Pots

Divide the dough into 3 or 4 portions, depending on the flower pot size. (The dough should only fill the pots halfway). Shape into a cone. Place into well-greased, glazed baking pots. Cover and let rise in a warm, draft-free place for 30 to 45 minutes, or until doubled in volume. Finish as desired. Bake in oven preheated to 375°F (190°C) for 18 to 25 minutes, or until flower pots sound hollow when tapped on the bottom.

Glossy Finish

With a fork, combine 1 slightly beaten egg white and 1 tbsp (15 mL) water. Lightly brush on the risen dough just before baking.

Saffron Currant Bath Buns with Lemon Glaze

This traditional British favorite originated in the city of Bath. The bun's light, soft texture has the sweet taste of saffron.

Tips

To enhance the flavor of saffron, soak individual strands in boiling water before adding. Allow soaking water to cool to room temperature, then use to make up part of the ³/₄ cup (175 mL) water called for in the recipe.

Currants discolor the dough when added at the "add ingredient" signal.

Variation

For crispier buns, bake the dough in individual muffin cups.

³/₄ cup	water	175 mL
1 tsp	saffron strands	5 mL
2	eggs	2
1 tsp	salt	5 mL
2 tbsp	granulated sugar	25 mL
2 tbsp	butter	25 mL
2³/₄ cups	all-purpose flour or bread flour	675 mL
¹/₄ cup	buttermilk powder	50 mL
1 tsp	bread machine yeast	5 mL
1 cup	dried currants	250 mL

1. Measure all ingredients *except currants* into baking pan in the order recommended by the manufacturer. Insert pan into the oven chamber. Select **Dough Cycle**.

2. Remove dough to a lightly floured surface; cover with a large bowl and let rest for 10 to 15 minutes. Knead in currants.

3. Use the shaping method for Round Buns (see page 212) and the finishing method below, or choose from any roll recipe in this chapter.

Lemon Glaze
Brush risen dough with a mixture of 1 tbsp (15 mL) lemon juice and 1 slightly beaten egg white. If desired, sprinkle with 2 tsp (10 mL) coarse granulated sugar.

Additional Shapes for Rolls

Prepare any roll recipe from this chapter. Select a shape from below. Proof and bake according to the recipe directions.

Braided Wreaths

Divide any roll dough recipe into 12 equal portions. Divide each portion into thirds. Roll out each piece into a 10-inch (25 cm) rope. Braid the three ropes together, pinching the ends to seal. Place on a lightly greased baking sheet and attach the ends to form a wreath.

Crescent Rolls

Roll out the dough into a rectangle 10 inches (25 cm) wide and $1/8$ inch (2 mm) thick. (The length will depend on the amount of dough you are working with.) Cut the dough into triangles with a sharp pizza cutter or knife. Stretch the corners of the long side outward slightly. Roll up the dough to the point. Stretch the point slightly as you roll. Bend into a crescent shape. Be sure the point faces inside and is tucked under so it won't pop up during baking. Any dough recipe can be made into crescents.

> *OR*

Divide the dough in half. Roll each half into a circle $1/8$ inch (2 mm) thick (or desired thickness). Cut into 8 to 12 wedges. Follow the shaping instructions described above.

Pistolet

Divide any roll dough recipe into 18 portions. Form each into a ball. Dust the tops with rice flour, and press the handle of a wooden spoon into the center of each dough circle to almost split in half. Pull gently to lengthen the roll; the sides will almost come together.

Round Buns

Divide the dough into 12 portions. Roll into balls, flattening slightly. Place on a lightly greased baking sheet, almost touching. Cover and let rise in a warm, draft-free place for 30 to 45 minutes, or until doubled in volume. Bake in oven preheated to 375°F (190°C) for 15 to 20 minutes, or until buns sound hollow when tapped on the bottom.

From the Hearth

Traditionally, dough was formed into round loaves and placed on the hearth to rise. The tops were quickly scored, brushed with butter, then baked. The aroma greeted the family as they gathered for meals. You can continue this custom with the recipes in this chapter.

Tips for Making Hearth Breads

1. Forming

Cover with a large bowl, and allow dough to rest for 10 to 15 minutes before forming. If the dough is sticky, flour your hands and add a small amount to the board. Too much flour added at this stage will result in a tough, heavy texture.

Choose any forming method from any hearth bread recipe. Follow the instructions carefully. If the dough keeps shrinking back when rolled, cover and let it rest for 10 to 15 minutes, then try again. The length of loaves is geared to the common sizes of baking sheets available.

2. Proofing

Cover dough and let rise in a warm, draft-free place until doubled in volume. To test for readiness, press two fingers into the dough; the indents made should remain.

3. Finishing

Choose any finishing method from any hearth bread recipe. Deep cuts, made before or after proofing, will open wider than shallow cuts.

Company Country Grain Bread

This granary-style loaf of wheat, oats and rye is shaped, slashed, then baked.

Tip

Slash the top of the dough with a lame or sharp knife just before baking. Deeper slashes produce wider cuts.

Variation

Make personal mini-buns 3 inches (7.5 cm) long and 1 inch (2.5 cm) high; taper at the ends and slash lengthwise down the center.

1 1/4 cups	water	300 mL
1/4 cup	skim milk powder	50 mL
1 1/2 tsp	salt	7 mL
3 tbsp	packed brown sugar	45 mL
2 tbsp	shortening or vegetable oil	25 mL
1 cup	whole wheat flour	250 mL
2 cups	all-purpose flour or bread flour	500 mL
1/4 cup	cracked wheat	50 mL
1/4 cup	7-grain cereal	50 mL
2 tbsp	flaxseed, cracked	25 mL
2 tbsp	oat bran	25 mL
2 tbsp	wheat germ	25 mL
2 tsp	bread machine yeast	10 mL

1. Measure ingredients into baking pan in the order recommended by the manufacturer. Insert pan into the oven chamber. Select **Dough Cycle**.

2. Remove dough to a lightly floured surface; cover with a large bowl and let rest for 10 to 15 minutes.

3. Refer to facing page for tips on forming, proofing and finishing hearth breads.

Oval

Form the dough into a large oval with a high rounded top. Place on a lightly greased baking sheet; cover and let rise in a warm, draft-free place for 30 to 45 minutes, or until doubled in volume. Finish as desired. Bake in oven preheated to 375°F (190°C) for 35 to 45 minutes, or until loaf sounds hollow when tapped on the bottom.

Triple Slashed

With a lame or sharp knife, gently cut 3 diagonal slashes 1/2 inch (1 cm) deep on top of the risen loaf.

Prairie Bread

Here's a favorite recipe that combines 3 popular bread flours.

Tip

To make a traditional loaf with puréed raisins, soak large Muscat raisins in water for a few minutes before preparing this recipe. They will purée during the kneading cycle.

Variation

Vary the color of this loaf by choosing different types of rye flour.

1⅓ cups	water	325 mL
¼ cup	skim milk powder	50 mL
1 tsp	salt	5 mL
⅓ cup	packed brown sugar	75 mL
3 tbsp	vegetable oil	45 mL
1¼ cups	whole wheat flour	300 mL
2 cups	all-purpose flour or bread flour	500 mL
¾ cup	rye flour	175 mL
1¾ tsp	bread machine yeast	8 mL

1. Measure ingredients into baking pan in the order recommended by the manufacturer. Insert pan into the oven chamber. Select **Dough Cycle**.

2. Remove dough to a lightly floured surface; cover with a large bowl and let rest for 10 to 15 minutes.

3. Refer to page 214 for tips on forming, proofing and finishing hearth breads.

Fit for a King

Divide dough into four pieces. Form each into a 6-inch (15 cm) round loaf. Place on a lightly greased baking sheet; cover and let rise in a warm, draft-free place for 30 to 45 minutes, or until doubled in volume. Score top to form the crown. Bake in oven preheated to 375°F (190°C) for 20 to 25 minutes, or until loaves sound hollow when tapped on the bottom.

Eight-Point Crown

Cut 4 intersecting slashes, ¼ inch (5 mm) deep, on the top of each loaf. Slashes made before the dough rises will open wider than slashes made on the risen dough. Your choice!

Tuscan Walnut Toasties (page 226)

Overleaf: An assortment of Montreal–style bagels (pages 169–79)

Settler's Cracked Wheat Braid

Midwesterners like to place this braid on a large wooden board to slice and serve at the table.

Tip

This is another good loaf to bake on a preheated baking stone placed on the bottom rack of the oven.

Variation

For added variety in flavor and texture, try substituting one of the many types of wheat blend flours that are available.

1 1/4 cups	water	300 mL
1 1/4 tsp	salt	6 mL
2 tbsp	packed brown sugar	25 mL
2 tbsp	shortening or vegetable oil	25 mL
1 1/4 cups	whole wheat flour	300 mL
2 cups	all-purpose flour or bread flour	500 mL
1/2 cup	cracked wheat	125 mL
1/3 cup	buttermilk powder	75 mL
1 1/2 tsp	bread machine yeast	7 mL

1. Measure ingredients into baking pan in the order recommended by the manufacturer. Insert pan into the oven chamber. Select **Dough Cycle**.

2. Remove dough to a lightly floured surface; cover with a large bowl and let rest for 10 to 15 minutes.

3. Refer to page 214 for tips on forming, proofing and finishing hearth breads.

Braid

Form the dough into three 12-inch (30 cm) ropes of equal diameter. Braid, tucking the ends under the loaf. Place on a lightly greased baking sheet; cover and let rise in a warm, draft-free place for 30 to 45 minutes, or until doubled in volume. Finish as desired. Bake in oven preheated to 375°F (190°C) for 40 to 45 minutes, or until braid sounds hollow when tapped on the bottom.

Shiny with a Crunch

Gently brush the risen dough with cooled melted butter or milk. Sprinkle with cracked wheat or bulgur.

Sunny Rye Loaf (page 230)

Canadian Maple Leaf Walnut Loaf

What a way to celebrate Canada Day! Take this loaf to your family picnic and listen to the raves.

Tip

To make a leaf pattern for dusting: Draw one half of a maple leaf on a folded piece of paper, cut it out and unfold for a symmetrical leaf. Make your pattern the size just to fit the flat top of the loaf. Be sure to dust with rice flour, since it does not brown during baking.

Variation

To bake this dough in your machine, prepare on a 2 lb (1 kg) **Basic Cycle**.

• Baking sheet, lightly greased

1 1/4 cups	water	300 mL
2 tsp	maple flavoring	10 mL
1/4 cup	skim milk powder	50 mL
1 1/2 tsp	salt	7 mL
2 tbsp	maple syrup	25 mL
2 tbsp	packed brown sugar	25 mL
2 tbsp	butter	25 mL
3 1/2 cups	all-purpose flour or bread flour	875 mL
1 cup	chopped walnuts	250 mL
1 1/2 tsp	bread machine yeast	7 mL
	Rice flour	

1. Measure ingredients *except rice flour* into machine's baking pan in the order recommended by the manufacturer. Insert pan into the oven chamber. Select **Dough Cycle**.

2. Remove dough to a lightly floured surface. Cover with a large bowl and let rest for 10 to 15 minutes.

3. Form dough into a large oval or round, flattening the top slightly. Place on prepared baking sheet. Gently place a real maple leaf or maple leaf pattern on top of the center of the loaf. Dust around the leaf generously with rice flour. Remove leaf, being careful not to get flour on the center of the loaf. Cover and let rise in a warm, draft-free place for 30 to 45 minutes, or until doubled in volume. Meanwhile, preheat oven to 350°F (180°C).

4. Bake in preheated oven for 35 to 40 minutes, or until loaf sounds hollow when tapped on the bottom.

Batarde

1 1/2 cups	water	375 mL
1 1/2 tsp	salt	7 mL
1 tbsp	granulated sugar	15 mL
3 3/4 cups	all-purpose flour or bread flour	950 mL
1 1/2 tsp	bread machine yeast	7 mL

These long, slender sticks are called pain ordinaire, *or "everyday bread," in France. They are served freshly made with every course, from soup to dessert.*

Tip

Crisp with a spritz of water during baking. Bake over a pan of hot water.

Variations

Slice leftover loaf into 1-inch (2.5 cm) thick slices to use for French onion soup.

Make mini French loaves. Remember the baked loaf will be double the size of the dough when placed in the pan.

Form into one large round for a *boule*.

1. Measure ingredients into baking pan in the order recommended by the manufacturer. Insert pan into the oven chamber. Select **Dough Cycle**.

2. Remove dough to a lightly floured surface; cover with a large bowl and let rest for 10 to 15 minutes.

3. Refer to page 214 for tips on forming, proofing and finishing hearth breads.

Traditional French

Form dough into a 14-inch (36 cm) stick with a slightly flattened top, tapering at both ends. Place on a baking sheet sprinkled with cornmeal or semolina flour; cover and let rise in a warm, draft-free place for 30 to 45 minutes, or until doubled in volume. Finish the loaf as desired. Bake in oven preheated to 425°F (220°C) for 20 to 25 minutes, or until loaf sounds hollow when tapped on the bottom.

French Crusty

With a lame or sharp knife, gently cut 5 long parallel diagonal slashes, approximately 1/2 inch (1 cm) deep, across the top of the risen loaf. Spritz with cold water just before baking. Repeat frequently during the first 10 minutes of baking.

Country French Stick

1⅓ cups	water	325 mL
1½ tsp	salt	7 mL
1 tbsp	granulated sugar	15 mL
3½ cups	all-purpose flour or bread flour	875 mL
1¼ tsp	bread machine yeast	6 mL

More crust than bread, this long, flat stick is narrow and tuggy-textured. It should be thickly sliced on the bias.

Tip

To keep the crust nice and crisp, store the loaf loosely covered in a paper bag.

Variation

For a crispier crust, place a pan of hot water on the bottom rack of the oven during preheating and spritz with water every 3 to 5 minutes during baking.

1. Measure ingredients into baking pan in the order recommended by the manufacturer. Insert pan into the oven chamber. Select **Dough Cycle**.

2. Remove dough to a lightly floured surface; cover with a large bowl and let rest for 10 to 15 minutes.

3. Refer to page 214 for tips on forming, proofing and finishing hearth breads.

French Stick

Form the dough into a long, thin stick, 14 inches (36 cm) long. Place on a baking sheet sprinkled with cornmeal; cover and let rise in a warm, draft-free place for 30 to 45 minutes, or until doubled in volume. Finish as desired. Bake in oven preheated to 375°F (190°C) for 20 to 25 minutes, or until loaf sounds hollow when tapped on the bottom.

Chewy and Crusty

Place a metal pan containing 12 ice cubes on the bottom rack of the oven. Let melt before baking dough. Spritz loaves with water just before baking.

Crusty Italian Bread

Tip

Make 3 parallel cuts $1/4$ inch (5 mm) deep across the top of the loaf just before baking.

Variation

To turn into a crunchy *grissini* (Italian breadstick), form into 18-inch (45 cm) long, thin ropes and bake at 375°F (190°C) for 15 minutes.

$1^1/_3$ cups	water	325 mL
$1^1/_2$ tsp	salt	7 mL
1 tbsp	granulated sugar	15 mL
1 tbsp	shortening or vegetable oil	15 mL
$3^1/_3$ cups	all-purpose flour or bread flour	825 mL
$1^1/_4$ tsp	bread machine yeast	6 mL

1. Measure ingredients into baking pan in the order recommended by the manufacturer. Insert pan into the oven chamber. Select **Dough Cycle**.

2. Remove dough to a lightly floured surface; cover with a large bowl and let rest for 10 to 15 minutes.

3. Refer to page 214 for tips on forming, proofing and finishing hearth breads.

Viva Italian

Divide the dough in half. Form each half into a loaf measuring 10 by 4 by 2 inches (25 by 10 by 5 cm) with a slightly flattened top. Place on a baking sheet dusted with cornmeal; cover and let rise in a warm, draft-free place for 30 to 45 minutes, or until doubled in volume. Bake in oven preheated to 375°F (190°C) for 20 to 25 minutes, or until loaves sound hollow when tapped on the bottom.

Slash and Dust

With a lame or sharp knife, gently cut 3 diagonal slashes $1/2$ inch (1 cm) deep on top of the risen dough. Dust with rice flour as soon as it is baked. Do not use with any other wash or glaze.

Russian Black Bread

1 1/2 cups	cold coffee	375 mL
3 tbsp	white vinegar	45 mL
1 1/4 tsp	salt	6 mL
1/4 cup	molasses	50 mL
2 tbsp	shortening or vegetable oil	25 mL
3 1/2 cups	all-purpose flour or bread flour	875 mL
1 cup	rye flour	250 mL
1/2 cup	buttermilk powder	125 mL
1/4 cup	wheat berries, cooked	50 mL
2 tbsp	unsweetened cocoa powder	25 mL
1 tbsp	caraway seeds	15 mL
1 1/2 tsp	bread machine yeast	7 mL

Company coming? Hollow out and fill this round loaf with the ever-popular spinach dip. (See facing page.)

Tips

Use fancy molasses rather than the blackstrap variety, which contains extra sulphur (not a good mix with yeast).

To cook wheat berries, cover with water and allow to stand overnight. Drain and cover with fresh water. Simmer for 30 to 45 minutes or until tender. Drain and cool completely.

Variation

For a dinner party, make personal-sized loaves for each of your guests.

1. Measure ingredients into baking pan in the order recommended by the manufacturer. Insert pan into the oven chamber. Select **Dough Cycle**.
2. Remove dough to a lightly floured surface; cover with a large bowl and let rest for 10 to 15 minutes.
3. Refer to page 214 for tips on forming, proofing and finishing hearth breads.

Hearth

Shape dough into a 9-inch (22.5 cm) round loaf, leaving it higher in the center than at the edges. Place on a lightly greased baking sheet; cover and let rise in a warm, draft-free place for 30 to 45 minutes, or until doubled in volume. Finish as desired. Bake in oven preheated to 375°F (190°C) for 35 to 45 minutes, or until loaf sounds hollow when tapped on the bottom.

Child's "X and O" Board

With a sharp knife, cut 5 parallel slashes 1/4 inch (5 mm) deep both lengthwise and crosswise to form squares on the surface of the risen dough. Dust the freshly baked loaf with bread flour for an added color contrast.

Combine all dip
ingredients at least
2 or 3 hours ahead;
refrigerate to allow
the flavors to blend.
Just before serving,
fill the loaf and serve
with cubed bread
for dipping.

Spinach Dip

10 oz	thawed chopped spinach, well drained	300 g
8 oz	softened cream cheese	250 g
1 cup	plain yogurt or sour cream	250 mL
1	small chopped onion	1
1	package (4 oz/125 g) vegetable soup mix	1

1. In a large bowl, combine all dip ingredients until well mixed.

Large Bowl

Form the dough into a large ball, with a high, rounded top. Place on a lightly greased baking sheet; cover and let rise in a warm, draft-free place for 35 to 45 minutes, or until doubled in volume. Bake in oven preheated to 375°F (190°C) for 35 to 45 minutes, or until loaf sounds hollow when tapped on the bottom. When cool, cut out the center, leaving at least a 1-inch (2.5 cm) thickness of bread on the bottom and sides. Fill with Spinach Dip (see recipe, above).

Swedish Limpa Mini-Hearth

The traditional Scandinavian trio of anise, caraway and fennel seeds give this orange-scented rye loaf a unique flavor.

Tip

For a smoother texture, use a food mill to grind the caraway, fennel and anise seeds.

Variations

To heighten the orange flavor, add $1/2$ tsp (2 mL) orange extract to the liquid.

Select the **Basic Cycle** if you are in a hurry; it makes a beautiful loaf.

1$^1/_3$ cups	water	325 mL
1$^1/_2$ tsp	salt	7 mL
$^1/_4$ cup	dark corn syrup	50 mL
2 tbsp	butter	25 mL
1$^1/_4$ cups	whole wheat flour	300 mL
1$^1/_2$ cups	all-purpose flour or bread flour	375 mL
1 cup	rye flour	250 mL
2 tsp	anise seeds	10 mL
2 tsp	caraway seeds	10 mL
2 tsp	fennel seeds	10 mL
2 tsp	orange zest	10 mL
1$^1/_2$ tsp	bread machine yeast	7 mL

1. Measure ingredients into baking pan in the order recommended by the manufacturer. Insert pan into the oven chamber. Select **Dough Cycle**.

2. Remove dough to a lightly floured surface; cover with a large bowl and let dough rest for 10 to 15 minutes.

3. Refer to page 214 for tips on forming, proofing and finishing hearth breads.

Mini-Hearths

Divide dough into 4 portions. Form each into a 2$^1/_2$-inch (6 cm) round loaf, leaving it higher in the center. Place on a lightly greased baking sheet; cover and let rise in a warm, draft-free place for 30 to 45 minutes, or until doubled in volume. Finish as desired. Bake in oven preheated to 375°F (190°C) for 15 to 20 minutes, or until loaves sound hollow when tapped on the bottom.

"X" Marks the Spot

With a sharp knife or a lame, make 2 intersecting cuts $^3/_4$ inch (2 cm) deep, in the shape of an "X".

Bonnie's Après-Ski Loaf

The perfect end to a day of skiing, serve this crunchy loaf with a bowl of spicy chili.

Tip

Substitute large-flake oatmeal or rye flakes for the barley flakes.

Variation

Instead of a single loaf, form dough into two narrow baguettes, each 14 inches (35 cm) long. Bake at 375°F (190°C) for 20 to 30 minutes. Slice on an angle.

● *Baking sheet, lightly greased*

1 1/4 cups	water	300 mL
1/4 cup	skim milk powder	50 mL
1 1/2 tsp	salt	7 mL
3 tbsp	packed brown sugar	45 mL
2 tbsp	olive oil	25 mL
3 cups	all-purpose flour or bread flour	750 mL
2/3 cup	cracked wheat	150 mL
2/3 cup	barley flakes	150 mL
1/2 cup	sunflower seeds, raw, unsalted	125 mL
1 1/2 tsp	bread machine yeast	7 mL

1. Measure the bread ingredients into machine's baking pan in the order recommended by the manufacturer. Insert pan into the oven chamber. Select **Dough Cycle**.

2. Remove dough to a lightly floured surface. Cover with a large bowl and let rest for 10 to 15 minutes. Form into an Italian-style loaf, 12 by 4 inches (30 by 10 cm). Place on prepared baking sheet. Cover and let rise in a warm, draft-free place for 30 to 45 minutes, or until doubled in volume. Meanwhile, preheat oven to 375°F (190°C).

3. Bake in preheated oven for 30 to 35 minutes, or until loaf sounds hollow when tapped on the bottom.

Topping
Slash dough lengthwise, from end to end, 3/4 inch (2 cm) deep, with a lame or sharp knife. Brush with 2 tbsp (25 mL) water and sprinkle with 2 to 3 tbsp (25 to 45 mL) barley flakes.

Tuscan Walnut Toasties

Tip

Feel free to use your own favorite sandwich fillings.

● Baking sheet, lightly greased

1½ cups	water	375 mL
1 tsp	orange zest	5 mL
1½ tsp	salt	7 mL
1 tbsp	granulated sugar	15 mL
3¾ cups	all-purpose flour or bread flour	950 mL
⅓ cup	buttermilk powder	75 mL
⅔ cup	chopped walnuts	150 mL
2 tsp	bread machine yeast	10 mL

SANDWICH FILLING

	Lean prosciutto, thinly sliced	
	Genoa salami, thinly sliced	
	Provolone or Monterey Jack cheese, thinly sliced	
½ cup	alfalfa sprouts	125 mL
2 tbsp	extra virgin olive oil	25 mL

1. Measure the bread ingredients into machine's baking pan in the order recommended by the manufacturer. Insert pan into the oven chamber. Select **Dough Cycle**.

2. Remove dough to a lightly floured surface. Cover with a large bowl and let rest for 10 to 15 minutes. Form into one 9-inch (22.5 cm) round or two 6-inch (15 cm) round loaves with slightly flattened tops. Place on prepared baking sheet. Using a pizza wheel, cut into 6 or 8 wedges. Cover and let rise in a warm, draft-free place for 30 to 45 minutes, or until doubled in volume. Meanwhile, preheat oven to 375°F (190°C).

3. Bake in preheated oven for 25 to 40 minutes, or until loaves sound hollow when tapped on the bottom. Set aside to cool completely.

Barbecue Sandwiches

Preheat barbecue or grill. Slice each baked toastie in half horizontally. On the bottom half, arrange prosciutto, salami, cheese and alfalfa sprouts. Top with other half of toastie and press together. Brush both sides of sandwiches with a thin layer of oil before placing on hot barbecue or grill. Cook, turning once, until the sandwich is browned and crisp and the cheese is melted. Cut into wedges. Serve hot.

New-Fashioned Oatmeal Loaf

Here's an oatmeal loaf updated for the new millennium with oat bran.

Tip

Use small- or medium-flake oatmeal but not the "instant cooking" variety.

Variation

Toasting the oats will give a nuttier flavor. Spread in a shallow pan. Bake at 350°F (180°C), stirring frequently, for 10 to 15 minutes, or until brown.

1⅓ cups	milk	325 mL
1¼ tsp	salt	6 mL
3 tbsp	packed brown sugar	45 mL
2 tbsp	shortening or vegetable oil	25 mL
1 cup	whole wheat flour	250 mL
2 cups	all-purpose flour or bread flour	500 mL
½ cup	quick-cooking oats	125 mL
¼ cup	oat bran	50 mL
1½ tsp	bread machine yeast	7 mL

1. Measure ingredients into baking pan in the order recommended by the manufacturer. Insert pan into the oven chamber. Select **Dough Cycle**.

2. Remove dough to a lightly floured surface; cover with a large bowl and let rest for 10 to 15 minutes.

3. Refer to page 214 for tips on forming, proofing and finishing hearth breads.

Free-Formed Hearth

Form the dough into a loaf 10 by 3 inches (25 by 7.5 cm) with a slightly flattened top. Place on a lightly greased baking sheet; cover and let rise in a warm, draft-free place for 30 to 45 minutes, or until doubled in volume. Bake in oven preheated to 375°F (190°C) for 35 to 40 minutes, or until loaf sounds hollow when tapped on the bottom.

The Granary Touch

Gently brush the risen loaf with either milk or water. Sprinkle large-flake oatmeal on the top of the loaf just before baking. It will toast to a nutty sweetness.

Beer Rye Bread

1 1/4 cups	beer	300 mL
1 1/2 tsp	salt	7 mL
2 tbsp	packed brown sugar	25 mL
1 tbsp	molasses	15 mL
2 tbsp	shortening or vegetable oil	25 mL
3/4 cup	whole wheat flour	200 mL
1 1/2 cups	all-purpose flour or bread flour	375 mL
1 cup	rye flour	250 mL
2 tsp	caraway seeds	10 mL
1 1/4 tsp	bread machine yeast	6 mL

What a combination!
The robust flavor of
beer complements
a dark rye.

Tip

Make this loaf with
your choice of either
a full-bodied ale or a
lighter-flavored lager.

Variation

Substituting water for
beer will result in a
milder, less tangy bread.

1. Measure ingredients into baking pan in the order
   recommended by the manufacturer. Insert pan into
   the oven chamber. Select **Dough Cycle**.

2. Remove dough to a lightly floured surface; cover
   with a large bowl and let rest for 10 to 15 minutes.

3. Refer to page 214 for tips on forming, proofing and
   finishing hearth breads.

Hearth

Shape dough into a 9-inch (22.5 cm) round loaf,
leaving it higher in the center than at the edges. Place
on a lightly greased baking sheet; cover and let rise in
a warm, draft-free place for 30 to 45 minutes, or until
doubled in volume. Finish as desired. Bake in oven
preheated to 375°F (190°C) for 35 to 45 minutes, or
until loaf sounds hollow when tapped on the bottom.

Triple Slashed

With a sharp knife or a lame, make 3 long parallel
slashes 3/4 inch (2 cm) deep from side to side across
the top of the risen loaf. These will open during
baking, resulting in a football-shaped loaf.

Sunny Rye Loaf

1 1/4 cups	water	300 mL
1/4 cup	skim milk powder	50 mL
1 1/4 tsp	salt	6 mL
1 tbsp	liquid honey	15 mL
1 tbsp	molasses	15 mL
2 tbsp	shortening or vegetable oil	25 mL
1 1/4 cups	whole wheat flour	300 mL
1 1/4 cups	all-purpose flour or bread flour	300 mL
1/2 cup	rye flour	125 mL
1/2 cup	sunflower seeds, raw, unsalted	125 mL
2 tsp	orange zest	10 mL
1 1/4 tsp	bread machine yeast	6 mL

1. Measure ingredients into baking pan in the order recommended by the manufacturer. Insert pan into the oven chamber. Select **Dough Cycle**.

2. Remove dough to a lightly floured surface; cover with a large bowl and let rest for 10 to 15 minutes.

3. Refer to page 214 for tips on forming, proofing and finishing hearth breads.

Long Oval
Form dough into a log measuring 14 by 4 by 2 inches (36 by 10 by 5 cm) with a slightly flattened top. Place on a lightly greased baking sheet; cover and let rise in a warm, draft-free place for 30 to 45 minutes, or until doubled in volume. Finish as desired. Bake in oven preheated to 375°F (190°C) for 30 to 35 minutes, or until loaf sounds hollow when tapped on the bottom.

Crunchy with Sunflower Seeds
Gently brush the risen loaf with cooled melted butter or milk. Sprinkle with sunflower seeds.

Multi-Seed Baguettes

• Baking sheet, lightly greased

With its hearty
combination of cracked
wheat, flaxseed and
sunflower seeds, this
loaf is equally good
with a comforting
winter stew or a
crisp summer salad.

1½ cups	water	375 mL
1½ tsp	salt	7 mL
1 tbsp	packed brown sugar	15 mL
2 tbsp	shortening or vegetable oil	25 mL
1½ cups	whole wheat flour	375 mL
1¾ cups	all-purpose flour or bread flour	425 mL
½ cup	cracked wheat	125 mL
¼ cup	flaxseed, cracked	50 mL
¼ cup	sunflower seeds, raw, unsalted	50 mL
2¼ tsp	bread machine yeast	11 mL

Tip

Be patient! This
heavier-textured loaf
may take a little longer
to double in volume.

Variation

Seed Glaze: Before
rising and baking,
brush the top of the
baguettes with water
and roll in sunflower
seeds or a mixture of
flaxseed and sunflower
seeds. The flavor of
the roasted seeds is
delicious, and the top
crust turns a crispy,
golden brown.

1. Measure ingredients into machine's baking pan in the order recommended by the manufacturer. Insert pan into the oven chamber. Select **Dough Cycle**.

2. Remove dough to a lightly floured surface. Cover with a large bowl and let rest for 10 to 15 minutes. Divide dough in half. Form each half into a 16-inch (40 cm) stick, 1 inch (2.5 cm) in diameter. Place on prepared baking sheet. Cover and let rise in a warm, draft-free place for 30 to 45 minutes, or until doubled in volume. Meanwhile, preheat oven to 400°F (200°C).

3. With a lame or a sharp knife, gently cut 5 long parallel diagonal slashes approximately ½ inch (1 cm) deep across the top of risen loaves. Spritz with cold water just before baking. Spritz 3 to 4 times during first 15 minutes of baking. Bake in preheated oven for 20 to 25 minutes, or until baguettes sound hollow when tapped on the bottom.

Pumpernickel Turban

• *Baking sheet, lightly greased*

Our inspiration for this seed-studded turban shape originally came from King Arthur's "Baker's Store" in Norwich, Vermont. Outstanding visual appeal makes this a perfect centerpiece for a gourmet dinner.

Tip

Use the seeds and grains as given in the recipe, or choose others to provide a variety of different colors and textures.

Variation

To bake as a hearth bread without the seeds, let the dough double in volume before baking. Cut into wedges and serve.

1 1/4 cups	coffee (room temperature)	300 mL
2 tbsp	vinegar	25 mL
1 tsp	salt	5 mL
1/4 cup	molasses	50 mL
2 tbsp	shortening or vegetable oil	25 mL
1 1/3 cups	whole wheat flour	325 mL
1 cup	all-purpose flour or bread flour	250 mL
2/3 cup	rye flour	150 mL
1/3 cup	buttermilk powder	75 mL
2 tbsp	unsweetened cocoa powder	25 mL
1 1/4 tsp	bread machine yeast	6 mL

SEED TOPPING

3	egg yolks	3
1/4 cup	sunflower seeds, raw, unsalted	50 mL
1/4 cup	caraway seeds	50 mL
1/4 cup	sesame seeds	50 mL
1/4 cup	fennel seeds	50 mL
1/4 cup	millet meal	50 mL
1/4 cup	flaxseed, cracked	50 mL
1/4 cup	12-grain cereal	50 mL
1/4 cup	poppy seeds	50 mL
1/4 cup	oat bran	50 mL
1/4 cup	pumpkin seeds	50 mL
1/4 cup	anise seeds	50 mL
1/4 cup	millet	50 mL

1. Measure bread ingredients into machine's baking pan in the order recommended by the manufacturer. Insert pan into the oven chamber. Select **Dough Cycle.**

2. Remove dough to a lightly floured surface. Cover with a large bowl and let rest for 10 to 15 minutes. Form into an 8-inch (20 cm) dome, 2 to $2^1/_2$ inches (5 to 6 cm) high in the center. Preheat oven to 375°F (190°C).

3. From a piece of paper, cut out a 7-inch (18 cm) circle. Fold the paper to form 12 equal sections. Gently set on the center of dome. With scissors, make $^1/_4$-inch (5 mm) cuts at the edge of the dough to mark each fold. With a pastry wheel and using a ruler as a guide, connect the cuts, making 6 intersecting lines, each $^1/_8$ inch (2 mm) deep. Cut out one wedge from the pattern. Use the "open" wedge of the pattern as the guide to keep the seeds in the correct location.

4. *Topping:* Brush exposed wedges of dough with egg yolk and sprinkle with sunflower seeds, covering exposed area completely. Move the pattern to the next wedge and repeat with the next seed or grain. Continue until the entire dome is covered with topping.

5. Bake in preheated oven for 30 to 35 minutes, or until turban sounds hollow when tapped on the bottom.

Twisted Breadsticks

● *Baking sheet, lightly greased*

Tip

For thinner, crunchier breadsticks, do not let the dough rise; bake immediately.

Variation

Brush with an egg white glaze and sprinkle with freshly grated Parmesan (or your favorite dried herbs) just before baking.

1^1/$_3$ cups	water	325 mL
1^1/$_2$ tsp	salt	7 mL
1 tbsp	granulated sugar	15 mL
1 tbsp	extra virgin olive oil	15 mL
3^1/$_2$ cups	all-purpose flour or bread flour	875 mL
^{1}/$_3$ cup	buttermilk powder	75 mL
1^1/$_4$ tsp	bread machine yeast	6 mL

1. Measure ingredients into machine's baking pan in the order recommended by the manufacturer. Insert pan into the oven chamber. Select **Dough Cycle**.

2. Remove dough to a lightly floured surface. Cover with a large bowl and let rest for 10 to 15 minutes. Roll out dough into a 16- by 6-inch (40 by 15 cm) rectangle. Cut into 12 strips, each 16 inches (40 cm) long and ^{1}/$_2$ inch (1 cm) wide. Fold strips in half lengthwise to 8 inches (20 cm) in length.

3. Place one strip crosswise on the surface in front of you. With the palm of your hands, roll one end toward you and the other end away from you so that the strip twists. Stretch the strip slightly as you twist it. Repeat with remaining strips. Place on prepared baking sheet. Cover and let rise in a warm, draft-free place for 30 to 45 minutes, or until doubled in volume. Meanwhile, preheat oven to 400°F (200°C).

4. Bake in preheated oven for 15 to 18 minutes, or until breadsticks sound hollow when tapped.

Pepperoni Wheat Stick

Chunks of salty pepperoni dot this loaf for a taste treat in every bite.

Tip

This large loaf can be baked on a preheated baking stone placed on the bottom rack of the oven.

Variation

Substitute Black Forest ham, prosciutto or any spicy or smoked meat for the pepperoni.

1 1/3 cups	water	325 mL
3/4 tsp	salt	4 mL
2 tsp	granulated sugar	10 mL
1 cup	whole wheat flour	250 mL
2 1/2 cups	all-purpose flour or bread flour	625 mL
2/3 cup	diced pepperoni	150 mL
1/4 cup	snipped fresh parsley	50 mL
1 tsp	cracked peppercorns	5 mL
1 1/2 tsp	bread machine yeast	7 mL

HONEY MUSTARD GLAZE

1 tbsp	liquid honey	15 mL
1 tbsp	prepared mustard	15 mL

1. Measure the bread ingredients into baking pan in the order recommended by the manufacturer. Insert pan into the oven chamber. Select **Dough Cycle**.

2. Remove dough to a lightly floured surface; cover with a large bowl and let rest for 10 to 15 minutes.

3. Refer to page 214 for tips on forming, proofing and finishing hearth breads.

4. *Glaze:* In a small bowl, mix together honey and mustard; brush on top of baked loaf.

A Big Stick

Form the dough into a 14- by 3-inch (36 by 7.5 cm) log. Flatten the top slightly and gently taper the ends. Place on a lightly greased baking sheet; cover and let rise in a warm, draft-free place for 30 to 45 minutes, or until doubled in volume. Bake in oven preheated to 375°F (190°C) for 20 to 30 minutes, or until stick sounds hollow when tapped on the bottom. Apply honey mustard glaze as soon as the stick is baked.

Wheat Berry Crown

Here's flavor fit for a king (or queen). The cooked wheat berries and sunflower seeds add extra crunch.

Tips

Make cuts deep enough to get the full effect of the crown shape.

For instructions on cooking wheat berries, see Techniques Glossary, page 370.

Variation

Substitute cooked rye groats or bulgur for the wheat berries.

• Baking sheet, lightly greased

1⅓ cups	water	325 mL
1½ tsp	salt	7 mL
3 tbsp	packed brown sugar	45 mL
2 tbsp	vegetable oil	25 mL
2½ cups	whole wheat flour	625 mL
1 cup	all-purpose flour or bread flour	250 mL
⅓ cup	buttermilk powder	75 mL
½ cup	sunflower seeds, raw, unsalted	125 mL
⅓ cup	cooked wheat berries	75 mL
1½ tsp	bread machine yeast	7 mL

1. Measure ingredients into machine's baking pan in the order recommended by the manufacturer. Insert pan into the oven chamber. Select **Dough Cycle**.

2. Remove dough to a lightly floured surface. Cover with a large bowl and let rest for 10 to 15 minutes. Form into a high, round ball. Place on prepared baking sheet. Cover and let rise in a warm, draft-free place for 30 to 45 minutes, or until doubled in volume. Meanwhile, set oven rack to lowest position in oven. Preheat oven to 425°F (220°C).

3. With a sharp knife or lame, gently cut 4 intersecting slashes, each ¾ inch (2 cm) deep, across top of ball. Bake in preheated oven for 10 minutes. Reduce oven temperature to 375°F (190°C) and bake for 30 to 40 minutes, or until crown sounds hollow when tapped on the bottom.

Braided Squash Crescent

Beautiful on the outside, golden on the inside, this bread complements every autumn menu.

Tips

Use butternut or Hubbard squash for this recipe. Scoop out seeds from one half squash and cook the squash in the microwave on High for 3 to 4 minutes per pound (500 g), or until tender, without adding butter or sugar.

For a light-textured loaf, mashed squash should be at room temperature before adding to baking pan.

Variation

Add ²⁄₃ cup (150 mL) chopped pecans at the "add ingredient" signal or knead into the dough after resting, before forming into ropes.

• Baking sheet, lightly greased

1/2 cup	water	125 mL
1 cup	mashed cooked squash	250 mL
1	egg	1
1/4 cup	skim milk powder	50 mL
1 1/2 tsp	salt	7 mL
3 tbsp	packed brown sugar	45 mL
2 tbsp	butter	25 mL
3 1/2 cups	all-purpose flour or bread flour	875 mL
1/2 tsp	ground nutmeg	2 mL
1 1/2 tsp	bread machine yeast	7 mL

SEED GLAZE

1	egg yolk	1
1 tbsp	water	15 mL
2 tbsp	sunflower or sesame seeds	25 mL

1. Measure the bread ingredients into machine's baking pan in the order recommended by the manufacturer. Insert pan into the oven chamber. Select **Dough Cycle**.

2. Remove dough to a lightly floured surface. Cover with a large bowl and let rest for 10 to 15 minutes. Divide dough into 3 portions. Roll each, with the palm of your hand, into a long, smooth rope, 1 inch (2.5 cm) in diameter. Taper at ends, leaving the middle thicker. Braid the 3 ropes and place on prepared baking sheet, curving to form a crescent. Cover and let rise in a warm, draft-free place for 30 to 45 minutes, or until doubled in volume. Meanwhile, preheat oven to 350°F (180°C).

3. *Glaze:* In a small bowl, whisk together egg yolk and water until smooth. Brush the risen dough lightly with glaze and sprinkle with seeds. Bake in preheated oven for 25 to 30 minutes, or until crescent sounds hollow when tapped on the bottom.

Soup-in-a-Bread-Bowl

Hate to do the dishes? Then this is the recipe for you. After enjoying the hearty soup, just eat the bowl!

Tip

To ensure the bowls are deep enough to hold the soup, form the dough into high, well-rounded balls. Each bowl should hold ²/₃ to ³/₄ cup (150 to 175 mL) of soup.

Variation

Our *German Lentil Soup* (recipe follows) is ideal for filling these bowls. But any hearty soup will do.

• *Baking sheet, lightly greased*

1¹/₂ cups	water	375 mL
1¹/₂ tsp	salt	7 mL
3 tbsp	packed brown sugar	45 mL
3 tbsp	shortening or vegetable oil	45 mL
3 cups	whole wheat flour	750 mL
1 cup	all-purpose flour or bread flour	250 mL
³/₄ cup	cracked wheat	175 mL
¹/₂ cup	buttermilk powder	125 mL
1¹/₄ tsp	bread machine yeast	6 mL

1. Measure ingredients into baking pan in the order recommended by the manufacturer. Insert pan into the oven chamber. Select **Dough Cycle**.

2. Remove dough to a lightly floured surface. Cover with a large bowl and let rest for 10 to 15 minutes. Divide into 4 portions. Form into balls 3¹/₂ inches (9 cm) in diameter and at least 2¹/₂ inches (6 cm) high. Cover and let rise in a warm, draft-free place for 30 to 45 minutes, or until doubled in volume. Meanwhile, preheat oven to 375°F (190°C).

3. Bake in preheated oven for 20 to 25 minutes. When cool, cut out the center, leaving at least a 1-inch (2.5 cm) thickness of bread on the bottom and the sides. Fill with hot soup (see recipe on facing page) and serve.

This recipe makes more than twice the amount of soup needed to fill 4 bowls. If you don't want the extra soup, just halve the recipe.

German Lentil Soup

5	slices bacon, diced	5
2	onions, sliced	2
2	carrots, sliced	2
2	stalks celery, sliced	2
1	ham bone (optional)	1
1 lb	lentils	500 g
1/2 tsp	freshly ground black pepper	2 mL
1/2 tsp	dried thyme	2 mL
2	bay leaves	2
10 cups	chicken stock	2.5 L
2 cups	chopped ham	500 mL
1 to 2 tbsp	lemon juice	15 to 25 mL

1. In a large frying pan over medium-high heat, cook bacon; remove with a slotted spoon and set aside. Return pan to heat and add onions, carrots and celery; sauté until tender but not browned.

2. In a large pot over medium heat, combine bacon, sautéed vegetables, ham bone, if using, lentils, pepper, thyme, bay leaves and stock. Simmer for 1 hour or until lentils are tender. Remove bone and bay leaves. Add chopped ham. Add lemon juice just before serving.

Sour Cream Pansies

A rich, creamy crust and an interesting shape. These pansies are delicious — and fun, too!

Tip

Be sure to make the cuts deep enough, or the shape of the petals will be lost when the dough rises.

Variation

Think of any large-petalled flower and make the number of cuts needed to recreate the appearance you want.

● *Baking sheet, lightly greased*

1/2 cup	water	125 mL
1/2 cup	sour cream	125 mL
2	eggs	2
1 1/4 tsp	salt	6 mL
2 tbsp	granulated sugar	25 mL
2 tbsp	butter	25 mL
3 1/4 cups	all-purpose flour or bread flour	800 mL
1 1/2 tsp	bread machine yeast	7 mL

GLAZE

1	egg yolk	1
1 tbsp	water	15 mL
2 tbsp	sesame or poppy seeds	25 mL

1. Measure bread ingredients into machine's baking pan in the order recommended by the manufacturer. Insert pan into the oven chamber. Select **Dough Cycle**.

2. Remove dough to a lightly floured surface. Cover with a large bowl and let rest for 10 to 15 minutes. Divide the dough into 16 portions. Roll into balls and place on prepared baking sheet; flatten tops slightly. Using kitchen shears, make 5 cuts, each 1/2 inch (1 cm) long, all the way through the dough, equally spaced around the outside. Cover and let rise in a warm, draft-free place for 30 to 45 minutes, or until doubled in volume. Meanwhile, preheat oven to 375°F (190°C).

3. *Glaze:* In a small bowl, whisk together egg yolk and water until smooth. Brush the risen dough with the glaze. Sprinkle the center of each pansy with seeds.

4. Bake in preheated oven for 15 to 20 minutes, or until pansies sound hollow when tapped on the bottom.

Braided Squash Crescent (page 237)

Holiday Celebration Breads

Ours is a multicultural nation. Our traditions live on through the passing of knowledge, food and customs from one generation to the next. We have adapted special holiday recipes for use in the bread machine. Serve these to your guests with pride.

Soup-in-a-Bread-Bowl (page 238)

Hints for Perfect Holiday Breads

- If your bread machine does not have an "add ingredient" signal on the **Dough Cycle**, gently knead the fruit into the dough after it has been removed from the bread machine. Handle the dough as little as possible.

- Carefully follow the measurements for size and thickness as given in the recipes. The rising and baking times are based on them.

- Measure with a steel or a plastic (not a wooden) ruler. Sanitize it in the dishwasher.

- Make cuts with sharp scissors; a knife will often crush the filling and flatten the shape.

- To ensure even browning when baking two pans of dough at the same time, switch their oven position at half time.

- Sweet dough recipes brown quickly during baking because of the high sugar and fat content. If getting too dark on the top, tent with foil.

- Use a long flat metal spatula to loosen baked shapes from the baking sheet. Slide, rather than lift, the bread onto a cooling rack.

Baba au Rhum

• *Bundt or tube pan, well-greased and floured*

1¼ cups	milk (room temperature)	300 mL
2	eggs	2
1½ tsp	salt	7 mL
3 tbsp	granulated sugar	45 mL
2 tbsp	butter	25 mL
3 cups	all-purpose flour or bread flour	750 mL
1½ tsp	bread machine yeast	7 mL

RUM SYRUP

1 cup	granulated sugar	250 mL
½ cup	water	125 mL
¾ cup	orange juice	175 mL
⅓ cup	dark rum	75 mL

Named after Ali Baba (the storybook hero) and invented by Polish King Lesczyinski in the 1600s, this rum-soaked cake is perfect for any festive occasion.

Tips

More like a stiff batter, this dough will be too sticky to handle; resist the urge to add flour.

The rum syrup can also be prepared in the microwave.

Variation

For a "Baba au Orange," replace rum with additional orange juice. Melt orange marmalade and brush over top of the cake.

1. Measure cake ingredients into machine's baking pan in the order recommended by the manufacturer. Insert pan into the oven chamber. Select **Dough Cycle**.

2. With floured hands or with a rubber spatula, remove dough from baking pan and place directly into prepared pan. Cover and let rise in a warm, draft-free place for 45 to 60 minutes, or until bubbly. Meanwhile, preheat oven to 350°F (180°C).

3. *Rum syrup:* In a small saucepan over medium-high heat, combine sugar and water. Bring to a boil and cook for 1 minute. Remove from heat and stir in orange juice and rum; set aside.

4. Bake cake in preheated oven for 30 to 35 minutes. Tip the baba from the pan onto a large plate. Leave upside down. Immediately, with a long wooden skewer, poke numerous holes into the cake. Slowly spoon the rum syrup over the cake, letting it soak in. Let stand for at least 2 hours before serving.

Valentine Chocolate Sweetheart Bread

This rich, chocolatey heart is the perfect treat for Valentine's Day. But don't let that stop you from enjoying it any time of the year.

Tips

Looking at the fudge-like consistency of this dough, it's hard to imagine that it will ever rise. But be patient — while the dough will take more time to double in volume, it's worth the wait.

Use regular (not spreadable) cream cheese for the filling.

Variation

Canned pears, well-drained and chopped, can be substituted for the fresh.

• Baking sheet, lightly greased

½ cup	milk (room temperature)	125 mL
¼ cup	instant chocolate syrup	50 mL
2	eggs	2
1 tsp	salt	5 mL
¼ cup	granulated sugar	50 mL
3 tbsp	butter	45 mL
3 cups	all-purpose flour or bread flour	750 mL
3 tbsp	unsweetened cocoa powder	45 mL
1½ tsp	bread machine yeast	7 mL

PEAR AND CREAM CHEESE FILLING

1	package (8 oz/250 g) cream cheese, softened	1
3 or 4	fresh pears, chopped	3 or 4
2 to 3 tbsp	instant chocolate syrup	25 to 45 mL

1. Measure bread ingredients into baking pan in the order recommended by the manufacturer. Insert pan into the oven chamber. Select **Dough Cycle**.

2. *Filling:* In a small bowl, cream softened cream cheese. Set aside.

3. Remove dough to a lightly floured surface. Cover with a large bowl and let rest for 10 to 15 minutes. Roll out dough into a 22- by 8-inch (55 by 20 cm) rectangle. Spread with the cream cheese. Add chopped pears and drizzle with chocolate syrup.

4. Beginning at the long side, roll jellyroll-style. Pinch to seal seam. Place on prepared baking sheet, seam-side down, shaping into a heart. Pinch ends together. With scissors, along each side of the heart shape, cut down the center of dough, leaving 3 to 4 inches (7.5 to 10 cm) uncut at the top and bottom of the heart. Open the cut sections to show filling. Cover and let rise in a warm, draft-free place for 1 to 2 hours, or until doubled in volume. Meanwhile, preheat oven to 350°F (180°C).

5. Bake in preheated oven for 35 to 40 minutes, or until heart sounds hollow when tapped on the bottom.

Baltic Birthday Bread

In the Baltic countries of Latvia, Lithuania and Estonia, this saffron-flavored fruit bread is traditionally served at birthday celebrations. But you can enjoy it anytime.

Tip

Soaking the saffron threads in boiling water ensures a strong saffron flavor and a deep yellow color.

Variation

To personalize this bread, form the dough into the celebrant's initial — or number of years.

• Baking sheet, lightly greased

¼ cup	boiling water	50 mL
1 tsp	saffron threads	5 mL
1 cup	milk (room temperature)	250 mL
1½ tsp	salt	7 mL
3 tbsp	honey	45 mL
2 tbsp	butter	25 mL
3¼ cups	all-purpose flour or bread flour	800 mL
½ cup	raisins	125 mL
½ cup	slivered almonds	125 mL
¼ cup	candied mixed peel	50 mL
1½ tsp	bread machine yeast	7 mL

ALMOND FINISH

1	egg yolk	1
1 tbsp	water	15 mL
¼ cup	sliced almonds	50 mL

1. In a bowl, combine boiling water and saffron; cool to room temperature. Place in bread machine baking pan. Measure remaining ingredients into baking pan in the order recommended by the manufacturer. Insert pan into the oven chamber. Select **Dough Cycle**.

2. Remove dough to a lightly floured surface. Cover with a large bowl and let rest for 10 to 15 minutes. Form into a 30-inch (75 cm) rope. Place on prepared baking sheet, shaping into a figure 8. Tuck the ends under at the point of intersection. Cover and let rise in a warm, draft-free place for 30 to 45 minutes, or until doubled in volume. Meanwhile, preheat oven to 375°F (190°C).

3. *Almond finish:* In a small bowl, whisk together egg yolk and water until smooth. Brush the risen dough with the glaze and sprinkle with sliced almonds.

4. Bake in preheated oven for 35 to 40 minutes, or until bread sounds hollow when tapped on the bottom.

Greek Trinity Easter Bread

Three small loaves join in a cloverleaf design for this traditional Greek Easter bread representing the Holy Trinity.

Tip

Remove from pan carefully to prevent the three sections from separating. Slice sections individually.

Variation

Prepare as one large circular hearth bread. Dust with confectioner's (icing) sugar and serve warm with hot chocolate.

• Large baking sheet, lightly greased

1 cup	water	250 mL
1/4 cup	skim milk powder	50 mL
1 tsp	salt	5 mL
2 tbsp	butter	25 mL
2 3/4 cups	all-purpose flour or bread flour	675 mL
1/2 cup	chopped dried apricots	125 mL
1/2 cup	chopped glacé cherries	125 mL
1 tsp	orange zest	5 mL
1 3/4 tsp	bread machine yeast	8 mL

1. Measure ingredients into baking pan in the order recommended by the manufacturer. Insert pan into the oven chamber. Select **Dough Cycle**.

2. Remove dough to a lightly floured board; cover with a large bowl and let rest for 10 to 15 minutes.

3. Divide dough into thirds. Form each piece into a smooth ball. Arrange balls so they are just touching, in the shape of a cloverleaf, on prepared baking sheet. Cover and let rise in a warm, draft-free place for 30 to 45 minutes, or until doubled in volume. Meanwhile, preheat oven to 375°F (190°C).

5. Bake in preheated oven for 30 to 35 minutes, or until bread sounds hollow when tapped on the bottom.

Dove-Shaped Columba Bun

Similar to an Italian panettone, but with the addition of almonds, this Easter bread is from Lombardy, Italy. The dove shape signifies the divine protection that Milanese soldiers were thought to have received during battle in 1176.

Tips

If your bread machine doesn't have an "add ingredient" signal on **Dough Cycle**, gently knead the fruit into the dough as soon as the cycle finishes. Don't add extra flour or over-knead the dough; otherwise, it will toughen.

This bread makes an attractive centerpiece for your Easter celebration. The almond paste glaze adds a festive appearance.

• Large baking sheet, lightly greased

1 cup	milk (room temperature)	250 mL
1	egg	1
1 tsp	salt	5 mL
¼ cup	granulated sugar	50 mL
2 tbsp	butter	25 mL
3¼ cups	all-purpose flour or bread flour	800 mL
¾ tsp	crushed anise seeds	3 mL
¼ tsp	lemon zest	1 mL
2 tsp	bread machine yeast	10 mL
¼ cup	dried currants	50 mL
¼ cup	raisins	50 mL
¼ cup	dried candied fruit	50 mL
¼ cup	toasted slivered almonds	50 mL
GLAZE		
¼ cup	almond paste	50 mL
2 tbsp	granulated sugar	25 mL
1	egg white, slightly beaten	1
2 tbsp	slivered almonds	25 mL

1. Measure all ingredients *except currants, raisins, fruit and almonds* into baking pan in the order recommended by the manufacturer. Insert pan into the oven chamber. Select **Dough Cycle**. Add currants, raisins, fruit and almonds at "add ingredient" signal.

2. *Glaze:* In a bowl, combine almond paste and sugar until smooth; set aside.

3. Remove dough to a lightly floured board; cover with a large bowl and let rest for 10 to 15 minutes. Divide dough in half.

4. *Wings of the dove:* Roll out half the dough to a 4- by 9-inch (10 by 23 cm) oval. Place crosswise on a large prepared baking sheet.

5. *Body of the dove:* Roll out remaining dough into a triangle with a 4-inch (10 cm) base for tail, and 9 inches (23 cm) in length. Place across and on top of the wings. Hold at center, twist head one half turn clockwise, press 9-inch (23 cm) base down for tail. Squeeze head to form a beak. Cut slits $\frac{1}{4}$ inch (5 cm) deep and $\frac{1}{4}$ inch (5 cm) apart to form tail and wing feathers.

6. Cover and let rise in a warm, draft-free place for 30 to 45 minutes, or until doubled in volume. Meanwhile, preheat oven to 350°F (180°C).

7. Brush entire dove with slightly beaten egg white. Spread glaze over wings and tail. Sprinkle almonds over the glaze.

8. Bake in preheated oven for 45 to 50 minutes, or until bun sounds hollow when tapped on the bottom.

Easter Egg Twist

This simple braided wreath has scarlet-colored hard-cooked eggs embedded in the rich cardamom-flavored dough.

Tip

Fruit juices, cake decorating colors or food coloring can be used as dyes for eggs.

Variation

For a crust with a shiny appearance, brush the risen dough with egg yolk before baking.

• Baking sheet, lightly greased

1 cup	water	250 mL
2	eggs	2
1¼ tsp	salt	6 mL
3 tbsp	granulated sugar	45 mL
3 tbsp	shortening	45 mL
3⅔ cups	all-purpose flour or bread flour	900 mL
1 tbsp	lemon zest	15 mL
1½ tsp	ground cardamom	7 mL
1 tsp	bread machine yeast	5 mL

TO DYE EASTER EGGS

1 tbsp	white vinegar	15 mL
	Food coloring	
3, 5 or 7	hard-cooked eggs	3, 5 or 7

GLAZE

1	egg white, slightly beaten	1
1 tbsp	water	15 mL

1. Measure the dough ingredients into baking pan in the order recommended by the manufacturer. Insert pan into the oven chamber. Select **Dough Cycle**.

2. *To dye eggs:* In a saucepan, bring to a boil vinegar, food coloring and enough water to cover eggs. Remove from heat and dip eggs until desired color is reached. (Amounts will vary with time and intensity of color desired.) Place eggs on a rack and allow to dry thoroughly.

3. Remove dough to a lightly floured board; cover with a large bowl and let rest for 10 to 15 minutes.

4. Divide dough into thirds. Roll each piece into a 24-inch (60 cm) rope. Braid all three together. Form braid into a circle. Pinch ends to seal. Place on prepared baking sheet.

5. Press eggs into the dough at evenly spaced intervals, tucking them deep under the braids so they won't be pushed out during rising.

6. Cover and let rise in a warm, draft-free place for 30 to 45 minutes, or until doubled in volume. Meanwhile, preheat oven to 375°F (190°C).

7. *Glaze:* In a bowl, beat together egg white and water. Brush the glaze over the braid.

8. Bake in preheated oven for 25 to 35 minutes, or until twist sounds hollow when tapped on the bottom.

Hot Cross Buns

- *Baking sheet, lightly greased*

1 cup	milk	250 mL
1	egg	1
1 1/4 tsp	salt	6 mL
1/4 cup	honey	50 mL
1/4 cup	butter	50 mL
3 3/4 cups	all-purpose flour or bread flour	950 mL
1 tsp	ground cinnamon	5 mL
1/2 tsp	ground cloves	2 mL
1/4 tsp	ground nutmeg	1 mL
1 1/4 tsp	bread machine yeast	6 mL
3/4 cup	raisins	175 mL

GLAZE

1	egg white	1
1 tbsp	water	15 mL

Before its significance for Christians, the cross symbolized the four quarters of the lunar cycle. So ancient Aztecs, Egyptians and Saxons all enjoyed hot cross buns. They have been served on Easter since the early days of the church.

Tip

Use a pastry bag and tip to pipe on icing.

Variation

To prepare California-style buns, add mixed candied peel and dates.

1. Measure all dough ingredients *except raisins* into baking pan in the order recommended by the manufacturer. Insert pan into the oven chamber. Select **Dough Cycle**. Add raisins at the "add ingredient" signal.

2. Remove dough to a lightly floured board; cover with a large bowl and let rest for 10 to 15 minutes.

3. Divide dough into 12 portions. Roll each into a ball. Place buns at least 2 inches (5 cm) apart on prepared baking sheet and flatten slightly. Cover and let rise in a warm, draft-free place for 30 to 45 minutes, or until doubled in volume. Meanwhile, preheat oven to 375°F (190°C).

4. *Glaze:* In a bowl, beat together glaze ingredients; brush on dough. Make two 1/4-inch (5 mm) deep cuts in the shape of a cross on the top of each bun.

5. Bake in preheated oven for 15 to 20 minutes, or until buns sound hollow when tapped on the bottom.

Italian Panettone

Tips

Anise gives this loaf a subtle licorice flavor. Double the amount in the recipe — or leave it out entirely to suit your family's taste.

To plump raisins, see Techniques Glossary, page 369.

Variations

Prepare this loaf using the **Dough Cycle**; place in a traditional high, round can, let rise and bake. The domed loaf has a soft, open texture.

Decorate the shiny crust with blanched almonds and candied cherries.

1.5 LB (750 G)		
¾ cup	milk (room temperature)	175 mL
1	egg	1
1 tsp	salt	5 mL
2 tbsp	honey	25 mL
2 tbsp	butter	25 mL
2½ cups	all-purpose flour or bread flour	625 mL
¾ tsp	crushed anise seeds	4 mL
1½ tsp	bread machine yeast	7 mL
⅓ cup	dried currants	75 mL
⅓ cup	raisins, plumped in 2 tbsp (25 mL) brandy	75 mL
¼ cup	candied citron	50 mL

2 LB (1 KG)		
1 cup	milk (room temperature)	250 mL
1	egg	1
1 tsp	salt	5 mL
2 tbsp	honey	25 mL
2 tbsp	butter	25 mL
3¼ cups	all-purpose flour or bread flour	800 mL
¾ tsp	crushed anise seeds	3 mL
2 tsp	bread machine yeast	10 mL
½ cup	dried currants	125 mL
½ cup	raisins, plumped in 3 tbsp (40 mL) brandy	125 mL
⅓ cup	candied citron	75 mL

1. Measure all ingredients *except currants, raisins and citron* into baking pan in the order recommended by the manufacturer. Insert pan into the oven chamber.

2. Select **Sweet Cycle**.

3. Add currants, raisins and citron at the "add ingredient" signal.

Thanksgiving Harvest Twist

The sweetness of the apple contrasts with the tang of apricots and prunes in this twisted bread.

Tip

Instead of one large twist, divide all amounts in half and make two smaller ones. Keep one and give the other one as a gift.

Variation

Filling may be made of other readily available dried fruit such as dried apples, cranberries, blueberries or cherries.

• *Baking sheet, lightly greased*

1/2 cup	milk	125 mL
1/4 cup	water	50 mL
2	egg yolks	2
1/2 tsp	salt	2 mL
2 tbsp	granulated sugar	25 mL
2 cups	all-purpose flour or bread flour	500 mL
3/4 tsp	bread machine yeast	3 mL

FRUIT FILLING

4	Golden Delicious apples, diced	4
1 tbsp	butter	15 mL
2 tbsp	granulated sugar	25 mL
1/3 cup	coarsely chopped prunes	75 mL
1/3 cup	coarsely chopped dried apricots	75 mL

LEMON GLAZE

2 tsp	soft butter	10 mL
1 tsp	lemon juice	5 mL
3/4 cup	sifted icing sugar	175 mL

1. Measure dough ingredients into baking pan in the order recommended by the manufacturer. Insert pan into the oven chamber. Select **Dough Cycle**.

2. *Filling:* In a large frying pan cook apples, butter and sugar over medium heat, just until tender. Add prunes and apricots. Heat until warmed through. Set aside to cool before using.

3. Remove dough to a lightly floured board. Cover with a large bowl and let rest for 10 to 15 minutes.

4. Roll out the dough into a 28- by 9-inch (75 by 23 cm) rectangle. Spread filling to within $\frac{1}{2}$ inch (1 cm) of edge. Beginning at long side, roll up jellyroll-style. Pinch to seal seam. Shape into large circular twist. Place on prepared baking sheet.

5. Cover and let rise in a warm, draft-free place for 30 to 45 minutes, or until doubled in volume. Meanwhile, preheat oven to 350°F (180°C).

6. Bake in preheated oven for 40 to 50 minutes, or until twist sounds hollow when tapped on the bottom.

7. *Glaze:* In a bowl, beat together glaze ingredients. Drizzle over warm bread.

Circle of Light

- *Baking sheet, lightly greased*
- *3 or 5 dripless candles*

Let flickering candlelight cast a warm glow over your family gathering this Thanksgiving. Revive an old custom and decorate your table with this braided centerpiece.

1 1/2 cups	water	375 mL
1 1/4 tsp	salt	6 mL
1 tbsp	granulated sugar	15 mL
2 tbsp	shortening	25 mL
4 1/4 cups	all-purpose flour or bread flour	1050 mL
1 1/4 tsp	bread machine yeast	6 mL

Tips

Check indents in the bread after 15 minutes of baking. If holes have closed, quickly enlarge to the correct size with the base of the candle. Continue baking.

Air-drying may take up to 2 weeks in hot, humid climates.

To preserve centerpiece, apply 2 coats of shellac, allowing to dry completely between coats.

Variation

Taper each rope slightly at the ends before braiding, then leave the braid in a long loaf resembling a Challah.

1. Measure ingredients into baking pan in the order recommended by the manufacturer. Insert pan into the oven chamber. Select **Dough Cycle**.

2. Remove dough to a lightly floured surface. Cover with a large bowl and let rest for 10 to 15 minutes.

3. Divide dough into 3 portions. Roll each with the palm of your hand into a long, smooth rope 1 inch (2.5 cm) in diameter. Braid all three together. Form braid into a circle. Pinch ends to seal. Place on prepared baking sheet.

4. Wrap a square of foil around the base of each candle. Push the candles in between the ropes of the dough, at evenly spaced intervals, tucking them deep so they won't be pushed out when the dough rises. Cover and let rise in a warm, draft-free place for 30 to 40 minutes, or until doubled in volume. Meanwhile, preheat oven to 350°F (180°C).

5. Remove candles, leaving the foil in the dough. Bake in preheated oven for 40 to 45 minutes, or until the braid sounds hollow when tapped on the bottom. Air-dry completely on a cooling rack before using as a centerpiece.

Challah Braid

The Jewish Sabbath meal is not complete without this egg-rich, fine-textured bread. Serve as two braids nestled in silk or satin on a silver platter.

Tip

The easiest braid is a simple three-strand type, similar to that used for a child's hair.

Variation

Form dough into a 30-inch (75 cm) rope and, holding one end in place, wrap the remaining rope around to form a tight coil, higher in the center. This is traditional for the Jewish New Year.

● *Baking sheet, lightly greased*

1 cup	water	250 mL
2	eggs	2
1 1/4 tsp	salt	6 mL
3 tbsp	granulated sugar	45 mL
3 tbsp	shortening	45 mL
3 2/3 cups	all-purpose flour or bread flour	900 mL
1 tsp	bread machine yeast	5 mL
GLAZE		
1	egg yolk	1
1 tbsp	water	15 mL
1 tbsp	sesame seeds (optional)	15 mL

1. Measure bread ingredients into baking pan in the order recommended by the manufacturer. Insert pan into the oven chamber. Select **Dough Cycle**.

2. Remove dough to a lightly floured board; cover with a large bowl and let rest for 10 to 15 minutes.

3. Divide dough into 5 portions. Roll each with the palm of your hand into long, smooth ropes 1 inch (2.5 cm) in diameter. Taper at ends, leaving the middle thicker. Braid the three ropes and place on prepared baking sheet. Twist the remaining 2 ropes, pinching ends together. Center on the top of braid. Press lightly. Cover and let rise in a warm, draft-free place for 30 to 45 minutes, or until doubled in volume. Meanwhile, preheat oven to 375°F (190°C).

4. *Glaze:* When dough has risen, beat together egg yolk and water. Brush the braid with glaze and, if desired, sprinkle with sesame seeds.

5. Bake in preheated oven for 30 to 35 minutes, or until braid sounds hollow when tapped on the bottom.

Christmas Shapes for Sweet Dough

Prepare a sweet dough recipe such as the *Ladder Loaf* (see page 330). Form using instructions given below to create a variety of Christmas shapes. Proof and bake according to instructions for the ladder loaf.

Poinsettia

Roll out dough into a 16- by 12-inch (40 by 30 cm) rectangle. Spread with your choice of filling to within $1/2$ inch (1 cm) of edge. Roll up as a jellyroll, beginning with narrow end. Cut the roll into twelve 1-inch (2.5 cm) pieces. Divide the end pieces in half. Shape into 4 balls. Center on a lightly greased baking sheet. Arrange the remaining pieces, touching, cut-side down, in a circle around the balls. Pinch the ends to form petals.

Christmas Trees

Prepare as poinsettias. Cut dough into ten 1-inch (2.5 cm) pieces and one 2-inch (5 cm) piece. Arrange, cut-side down, on a lightly greased baking sheet. Center a slice near top. Snugly arrange the slices in three more rows, adding one more slice to each row. Center the 2-inch (5 cm) slice lengthwise under the tree for the trunk.

Swedish Tea Ring

Prepare as poinsettias but do not cut. With the seam-side down, shape into a ring on a lightly greased baking sheet. Pinch the ends together. With scissors, make cuts two-thirds of the way through the ring, $3/4$ inch (2 cm) apart. Turn each section on its side.

Holiday Teddy Bears

Makes 1 large teddy bear

Divide dough in half. Form one half into a large round ball for the body. Place on a large, lightly greased baking sheet; flatten slightly. Divide the remaining piece in half. Break off a $1^1/2$-inch (3.5 cm) piece and shape it into a ball for the nose. Shape the remainder of that piece into a ball for the head. Attach to the body, pinching to seal.

Make 6 balls from the remaining half of dough for the paws and the ears. Use raisins for eyes and buttons. Cover, proof and bake at 350°F (180°C) for 30 to 35 minutes, or until teddy bear sounds hollow when tapped on the bottom.

Makes 2 smaller teddy bears

Divide dough in half. Use one half for each teddy bear. Follow instructions for large teddy bear above. Use $3/4$-inch (2 cm) piece for nose. Repeat with other half of dough to make a second teddy bear. Proof and bake at 350°F (180°C) for 20 to 25 minutes, or until teddy bears sound hollow when tapped on the bottom.

Spicy Gingerbread

With the sweetness of cinnamon, ginger and cloves, every bite will remind you of spice cake and gingerbread people.

Tip

Vary amounts of spices to your taste. A small amount of allspice, nutmeg or mace could be added.

Yes, you're reading it right: The 1.5 lb (750 g) recipe contains *more* yeast than the 2 lb (1 kg).

Variation

Try this recipe with 1 cup (250 mL) raisins added at the "add ingredient" signal.

1.5 LB (750 G)

1 cup	water	250 mL
1	egg	1
1/4 cup	skim milk powder	50 mL
1 tsp	salt	5 mL
2 tbsp	packed brown sugar	25 mL
2 tbsp	molasses	25 mL
1 tbsp	shortening or vegetable oil	15 mL
3 cups	all-purpose flour or bread flour	750 mL
3/4 tsp	ground ginger	4 mL
1/2 tsp	ground cinnamon	3 mL
1/4 tsp	ground cloves	2 mL
1 1/2 tsp	bread machine yeast	8 mL

2 LB (1 KG) • extra large

1 1/4 cups	water	300 mL
1	egg	1
1/4 cup	skim milk powder	50 mL
1 1/4 tsp	salt	6 mL
3 tbsp	packed brown sugar	45 mL
2 tbsp	molasses	25 mL
1 tbsp	shortening or vegetable oil	15 mL
3 2/3 cups	all-purpose flour or bread flour	925 mL
1 tsp	ground ginger	5 mL
1 tsp	ground cinnamon	5 mL
1/2 tsp	ground cloves	2 mL
1 1/4 tsp	bread machine yeast	6 mL

1. Measure ingredients into baking pan in the order recommended by the manufacturer. Insert pan into the oven chamber.
2. Select **Sweet Cycle**.

Almond-Filled Christmas Cranberry Kringle

For an elegant Christmas brunch, place the Kringle on the center of the table. Garnish with holly and fresh cranberries. Serve with clementines and a tray of assorted cheeses.

Tip

To soften almond paste that has dried, place in an airtight plastic bag with a slice of bread. As it softens, break off pieces to allow moisture to soften the remaining block.

Variation

Frozen cranberries can be substituted for the fresh; no need to defrost before adding.

• Baking sheet, lightly greased

1 cup	milk (room temperature)	250 mL
1	egg	1
1¼ tsp	salt	6 mL
3 tbsp	granulated sugar	45 mL
¼ cup	butter	50 mL
3¾ cups	all-purpose flour or bread flour	925 mL
½ cup	fresh cranberries	125 mL
½ tsp	ground cardamom	2 mL
½ tsp	ground cinnamon	2 mL
1½ tsp	bread machine yeast	7 mL

ALMOND FILLING

¼ cup	softened butter	50 mL
¼ cup	almond paste	50 mL
3 tbsp	all-purpose flour	45 mL
1½ tsp	lemon zest	7 mL
¼ cup	packed brown sugar	50 mL
1	egg white	1
1 tsp	vanilla	5 mL
¾ tsp	ground cardamom	4 mL
¾ cup	fresh cranberries	175 mL
½ cup	chopped pecans	125 mL

EGG YOLK GLAZE

1	egg yolk	1
2 tbsp	water	25 mL

1. Measure bread ingredients into machine's baking pan in the order recommended by the manufacturer. Insert pan into the oven chamber. Select **Dough Cycle**.

2. *Filling:* In a large bowl, beat together butter and almond paste until creamy. Add flour, zest, brown sugar, egg white, vanilla and cardamom; whip until smooth and set aside.

3. Remove dough to a lightly floured surface. Cover with a large bowl and let rest for 10 to 15 minutes.

4. Roll out the dough to a 15- by 10-inch (38 by 25 cm) rectangle. Spread with filling. Sprinkle with cranberries and pecans. Beginning at the long side, roll jellyroll-style. Pinch to seal seam. Form into a wreath, pinching ends to seal. Place on prepared baking sheet, seam-side down. Cover and let rise in a warm, draft-free place for 30 to 45 minutes, or until doubled in volume. Meanwhile, preheat oven to 375°F (190°C).

5. *Glaze:* In a small bowl, whisk together egg yolk and water. Brush the risen dough with glaze. Cut 4 slits in the wreath.

6. Bake in preheated oven for 30 to 35 minutes, or until wreath sounds hollow when tapped on the bottom. Serve warm from the oven or cooled to room temperature.

Cranberry Orange Mini-Wreaths

Tips

Marmalade makes an easy filling. Choose a thick, high-quality three-fruit conserve for a great taste treat.

Tuck the ends of the wreaths in tightly or they will pull out during proofing. Leave a large hole in the center of the wreath or it will close in, leaving a bun shape.

Variation

For a decorative holiday table, form dough into one large wreath and place a cranberry-scented pillar candle in the center.

● *Baking sheet, lightly greased*

³⁄₄ cup	water	175 mL
¹⁄₄ cup	cranberry juice	50 mL
¹⁄₄ cup	orange marmalade	50 mL
¹⁄₄ tsp	orange extract	2 mL
¹⁄₄ cup	skim milk powder	50 mL
1¹⁄₂ tsp	salt	7 mL
1 tbsp	granulated sugar	15 mL
2 tbsp	butter	25 mL
2³⁄₄ cups	all-purpose flour or bread flour	675 mL
2 tsp	orange zest	10 mL
1¹⁄₂ tsp	bread machine yeast	7 mL
¹⁄₂ cup	dried cranberries	125 mL

CRANBERRY FILLING

³⁄₄ cup	chopped dried cranberries	175 mL
¹⁄₃ cup	marmalade	75 mL

1. Measure all ingredients *except cranberries* into baking pan in the order recommended by the manufacturer. Insert pan into the oven chamber. Select **Dough Cycle**. Add cranberries at "add ingredient" signal.

2. *Filling:* In a small bowl, combine filling ingredients; set aside.

3. Remove dough to a lightly floured board; cover with a large bowl and let rest for 10 to 15 minutes.

4. Roll out dough to a 15- by 10-inch (38 by 25 cm) rectangle. Spread half of the filling mixture over the middle third of the dough. Fold one side over the filling. Spread with remaining filling. Fold over last side. Cut into ten 1- by 5-inch (2.5 by 12.5 cm) strips. Holding strip at each end, pull gently and twist 3 times. Form into a wreath, pinching ends together. Place on prepared baking sheet. Cover and let rise in a warm, draft-free place for 30 to 45 minutes, or until doubled in volume. Meanwhile, preheat oven to 350°F (180°C).

5. Bake in preheated oven for 12 to 15 minutes, or until wreaths sound hollow when tapped on the bottom.

Friendly Frosty

This jolly fellow isn't made from snow, but light, fluffy dough. What child (or grown-up) can resist?

Tip

After 10 to 15 minutes in the oven, check Frosty to make sure his parts and decorations are still in place. If not, remove from the oven and adjust as necessary.

Variation

After you've finished baking and allowed Frosty to cool, you and your young helpers can add further decorations — such as licorice pipe, a carrot nose and a narrow scarf.

● *Baking sheet, lightly greased*

1 1/2 cups	milk	375 mL
1 tsp	salt	5 mL
1/4 cup	granulated sugar	50 mL
3 tbsp	butter	45 mL
3 1/2 cups	all-purpose flour or bread flour	875 mL
1 1/2 tsp	bread machine yeast	7 mL

FINISHING TOUCHES

2	raisins	2
1	rope licorice	1
4	chocolate chips	4

1. Measure bread ingredients into machine's baking pan in the order recommended by the manufacturer. Insert pan into the oven chamber. Select **Dough Cycle**.

2. Remove dough to a lightly floured surface. Cover with a large bowl and let rest for 10 to 15 minutes.

3. Divide dough into 4 portions, making 2 portions slightly larger.

4. *Body:* Form the 2 larger portions of dough into a 6-inch (15 cm) and a 5-inch (12.5 cm) circle, slightly flattened on one side. Place with flattened sides touching and with larger circle at the bottom of prepared baking sheet. Seal seam.

5. *Head:* Form 1 portion of the dough into a 4-inch (10 cm) slightly rounded circle. Place on baking sheet, touching the 5-inch (12.5 cm) circle, to form the snowman. Seal seam.

6. *Hat:* Roll out remaining portion of the dough into a 5-inch (12.5 cm) square. Cut 1 inch (2.5 cm) off one side and lengthen to 6 inches (15 cm) to form the brim. Place the brim on the head of the snowman on an angle. Place the square over the brim.

7. *Finishing touches:* Add raisins for eyes, rope licorice for a mouth and a row of chocolate chips for buttons. Cover and let rise in a warm, draft-free place for 30 to 45 minutes, or until doubled in volume. Meanwhile, preheat oven to 350°F (180°C).

8. Bake in preheated oven for 30 to 40 minutes, or until Frosty sounds hollow when tapped on the bottom.

Finnish Cardamom Bread

Cardamom, the second most valued spice in the world (after saffron), is a favorite in Scandinavian countries.

Tip

Use cardamom as you would cinnamon — with fruits and desserts.

Variation

Prepare using the **Dough Cycle** and shape into a candy cane or tea ring.

1.5 LB (750 G)		
1 cup	evaporated milk	250 mL
1	egg	1
1¼ tsp	salt	6 mL
2 tbsp	granulated sugar	25 mL
2 tbsp	butter	25 mL
2¼ cups	all-purpose flour or bread flour	550 mL
½ cup	rye flour	125 mL
1 tsp	ground cardamom	5 mL
1 tsp	orange zest	5 mL
½ tsp	lemon zest	2 mL
1¼ tsp	bread machine yeast	6 mL
½ cup	raisins	125 mL
¼ cup	slivered almonds	50 mL

2 LB (1 KG) • extra large		
1¼ cups	evaporated milk	300 mL
2	eggs	2
1¼ tsp	salt	6 mL
2 tbsp	granulated sugar	25 mL
2 tbsp	butter	25 mL
2⅔ cups	all-purpose flour or bread flour	650 mL
⅔ cup	rye flour	150 mL
2 tsp	ground cardamom	10 mL
2 tsp	orange zest	10 mL
1 tsp	lemon zest	5 mL
1½ tsp	bread machine yeast	7 mL
¾ cup	raisins	175 mL
½ cup	slivered almonds	125 mL

1. Measure all ingredients *except raisins and almonds* into baking pan in the order recommended by the manufacturer. Insert pan into the oven chamber.

2. Select **Sweet Cycle**.

3. Add raisins and almonds at the "add ingredient" signal.

German Stollen

- *Baking sheet, lightly greased*

1 cup	water	250 mL
2	eggs	2
1/4 cup	skim milk powder	50 mL
1 1/2 tsp	salt	7 mL
2 tbsp	granulated sugar	25 mL
2 tbsp	butter	25 mL
3 1/2 cups	all-purpose flour or bread flour	875 mL
2 tsp	lemon zest	10 mL
3/4 tsp	ground nutmeg	3 mL
1 1/4 tsp	bread machine yeast	6 mL
1/2 cup	mixed candied fruit	125 mL
1/2 cup	raisins	125 mL
1/4 cup	slivered almonds	50 mL

Stollen is a traditional German Christmas bread. It is served on Christmas Eve when families gather to celebrate before going to church.

Tip

With a sharp knife, make a cut 1/2 inch (1 cm) deep just off center. Fold along this line.

Variation

Stollen is often dusted with icing sugar to resemble a light covering of snow.

1. Measure all ingredients *except fruit, raisins and almonds* into baking pan in the order recommended by the manufacturer. Insert pan into oven chamber. Select **Dough Cycle**. Add fruit, raisins and almonds at the "add ingredient" signal.

2. Remove dough to a lightly floured board; cover with a large bowl and let rest for 10 to 15 minutes.

3. Divide dough in half. Roll out each half into a 9-inch (22.5 cm) circle. Fold one circle almost in half with top layer set back about 1/2 inch (1 cm) from the bottom. Repeat with the other half. Place on prepared baking sheet. Cover and let rise in a warm, draft-free place for 30 to 45 minutes, or until doubled in volume. Meanwhile, preheat oven to 375°F (190°C).

4. Bake in preheated oven for 35 to 40 minutes, or until stollen sound hollow when tapped on the bottom. Dust with icing sugar while warm.

Ukrainian Egg Bread (Kolach)

Kolach (the Ukrainian word for "circle") is shaped into three rings to symbolize the Trinity, and is traditionally served at Holy Night supper.

Tip

Stack baked rings with the largest on the bottom and insert a long taper candle through the center.

Variation

To make one large braid, make only first batch of dough.

● *Two baking sheets, lightly greased*

BREAD (BATCH 1)

¾ cup	water	175 mL
2	eggs	2
1¼ tsp	salt	6 mL
2 tbsp	granulated sugar	25 mL
2 tbsp	butter	25 mL
3 cups	all-purpose flour or bread flour	750 mL
1¼ tsp	bread machine yeast	6 mL
¼ cup	milk	50 mL

BREAD (BATCH 2)

¾ cup	water	175 mL
2	eggs	2
1¼ tsp	salt	6 mL
2 tbsp	granulated sugar	25 mL
2 tbsp	butter	25 mL
3 cups	all-purpose flour or bread flour	750 mL
1¼ tsp	bread machine yeast	6 mL
¼ cup	milk	50 mL

1. Measure Batch 1 ingredients *except milk* into machine's baking pan in the order recommended by the manufacturer. Insert pan into the oven chamber. Select **Dough Cycle**.

2. Remove dough to a lightly floured surface. Cover with a large bowl and let rest for 10 to 15 minutes.

3. Divide dough into 3 portions. Roll each into a 28-inch (72 cm) rope. Braid the 3 ropes. Form into a circle, pinching ends together. Place on prepared baking sheet. Cover and let rise in a warm, draft-free place for 30 to 45 minutes, or until doubled in volume. Meanwhile, preheat oven to 350°F (180°C).

4. Repeat Steps 1 to 3 with Batch 2 ingredients.

5. Brush the ring from Batch 1 with milk. Bake in preheated oven for 10 minutes, then brush with milk a second time. Bake for another 15 to 20 minutes, or until ring sounds hollow when tapped on the bottom.

6. Divide dough from Batch 2 into 2 portions, one twice as large as the other. Using the larger portion, divide dough into 3 portions; roll each into a 21-inch (53 cm) rope. Braid the 3 ropes. Form into a circle, pinching ends together. Divide remaining dough into 3 portions; roll each into a 14-inch (36 cm) rope. Braid the 3 ropes. Form into a circle, pinching ends together. Place circles at least 2 inches (5 cm) apart on prepared baking sheet. Cover and let rise in a warm, draft-free place for 30 to 45 minutes, or until doubled in volume.

7. Brush the rings from Batch 2 with milk. Bake in preheated oven for 10 minutes, then brush with milk a second time. Bake for 10 to 15 minutes, or until rings sound hollow when tapped on the bottom.

8. Stack cooled rings, with the largest ring on the bottom. Insert a long taper candle through the center of the three rings.

Kolaches

• *Two baking sheets, lightly greased*

These traditional East European pastries are great to pack in a lunch or serve as an after-school snack or as a special holiday treat.

1¼ cups	water	300 mL
1	egg	1
1½ tsp	salt	7 mL
3 tbsp	honey	45 mL
2 tbsp	shortening	25 mL
3¾ cups	all-purpose flour or bread flour	925 mL
⅓ cup	buttermilk powder	75 mL
1 tsp	bread machine yeast	5 mL

MINCEMEAT FILLING

1½ cups	prepared mincemeat	375 mL
2 tbsp	dark rum	25 mL

Tips

Make sure the rims of the dough circles are slightly higher than the centers or the filling will spill over.

Just before filling, press the center of each circle flat, using the bottom of a flour-coated glass.

Variations

Try making Kolach Bundles: Roll the dough into 3-inch (7.5 cm) squares. Place 1 tbsp (15 mL) filling in the center of each square. Pull the opposite corners over the dough and tuck in the loose ends.

Try the date filling from the recipe for *Date Orange Bundles* (see page 284).

1. Measure kolach ingredients into baking pan in the order recommended by the manufacturer. Insert pan into the oven chamber. Select **Dough Cycle**.

2. *Filling:* In a small bowl, combine mincemeat and rum; set aside.

3. Remove dough to a lightly floured surface. Cover with a large bowl and let rest for 10 to 15 minutes.

4. Divide dough into 24 portions. Form into balls. Flatten into 2½-inch (6 cm) circles, leaving a ¼-inch (5 mm) rim. Spoon 1 tbsp (15 mL) filling in the center of each. Place kolaches 1 inch (2.5 cm) apart on prepared baking sheets. Cover and let rise in a warm, draft-free place for 30 to 45 minutes, or until doubled in volume. Meanwhile, preheat oven to 350°F (180°C).

5. Bake in preheated oven for 20 to 25 minutes, or until kolaches sound hollow when tapped on the bottom.

Dessert, Anyone?

Sweet bread recipes calling for milk, eggs and butter provide the extra-rich flavor we enjoy for dessert. Their warm, golden crusts and sweet fragrance will greet you as you open the lid of the bread machine.

continued next page...

Daffodil Bread

Tip

Use a zester for long thin strips of citrus peel. Be sure to remove only the outer skin, avoiding the bitter white pith underneath.

Yes, you're reading it right: The 1.5 lb (750 g) recipe contains the *same* amount of yeast as the 2 lb (1 kg).

Variation

Make this into a lemon bread by using all lemon juice and lemon zest or an orange bread with all orange ingredients.

1.5 LB (750 G)		
³⁄₄ cup	water	175 mL
2 tbsp	fresh orange juice	25 mL
1 tbsp	fresh lemon juice	15 mL
1 tbsp	lemon zest	15 mL
1 tbsp	orange zest	15 mL
2	eggs	2
¼ cup	skim milk powder	50 mL
1½ tsp	salt	7 mL
2 tbsp	granulated sugar	25 mL
2 tbsp	butter	25 mL
3 cups	all-purpose flour or bread flour	750 mL
³⁄₄ tsp	bread machine yeast	4 mL

2 LB (1 KG) • extra large		
1 cup	water	250 mL
2 tbsp	fresh orange juice	25 mL
1 tbsp	fresh lemon juice	15 mL
1 tbsp	lemon zest	15 mL
1 tbsp	orange zest	15 mL
2	eggs	2
⅓ cup	skim milk powder	75 mL
1¾ tsp	salt	8 mL
3 tbsp	granulated sugar	45 mL
3 tbsp	butter	45 mL
4 cups	all-purpose flour or bread flour	1000 mL
³⁄₄ tsp	bread machine yeast	4 mL

1. Measure ingredients into baking pan in the order recommended by the manufacturer. Insert pan into the oven chamber.
2. Select **Basic Cycle**.

Apricot Pecan Twists

• Baking sheet, lightly greased

1¼ cups	milk	300 mL
1	egg	1
¾ tsp	salt	3 mL
¼ cup	granulated sugar	50 mL
2 tbsp	butter	25 mL
3¾ cups	all-purpose flour or bread flour	950 mL
1¼ tsp	bread machine yeast	6 mL

APRICOT PECAN FILLING

½ cup	packed brown sugar	125 mL
½ tsp	ground cinnamon	2 mL
⅔ cup	finely chopped dried apricots	150 mL
⅔ cup	finely chopped pecans	150 mL
¼ cup	melted butter	50 mL

ORANGE GLAZE

1 cup	sifted icing sugar	250 mL
4 to 5 tsp	frozen orange juice concentrate, thawed (see Tip on page 283)	20 to 25 mL

Tip

Press the ends flat to prevent them from untwisting on the baking sheet.

Variation

To please the younger lunchbox set, substitute the sweeter flavors of apple or cherry for the apricots.

1. Measure dough ingredients into baking pan in the order recommended by the manufacturer. Insert pan into the oven chamber. Select **Dough Cycle**.

2. *Filling:* In a bowl, combine brown sugar and cinnamon. Toss gently with apricots and pecans; set aside. Let melted butter cool slightly; set aside.

3. Remove dough to a lightly floured board; cover with a large bowl and let rest for 10 to 15 minutes.

4. Divide dough in half. Roll out each half into a 12-inch (30 cm) square. Brush one square with half the melted butter. Sprinkle half the filling over half the dough. Fold over the other half and carefully pinch to seal. Cut crosswise into ten strips, 6 inches (15 cm) long. Twist each strip twice. Place on prepared baking sheet. Repeat procedure with remaining square of dough. Cover and let rise in a warm, draft-free place for 30 to 45 minutes, or until doubled in volume. Meanwhile, preheat oven to 350°F (180°C).

5. Bake in preheated oven for 12 to 15 minutes, or until twists sound hollow when tapped on the bottom.

6. *Glaze:* In a bowl stir together glaze ingredients until smooth. Drizzle over warm twists.

Sugar-Free Apricot Tea Ring

Watching your sugar intake doesn't have to mean giving up dessert. Try this tea ring and see!

Tips

For baking, the best sugar substitute is sucralose, which is made from processed sugar and remains stable at any temperature.

Other sugar-free recipes are *Moroccan Anise Bread* (see recipe, page 133) and *Swiss Rye Loaf* (see recipe, page 90).

Variation

Substitute applesauce or any other sugar-free fruit spread for the apricot spread.

• Baking sheet, lightly greased

1 cup	milk	250 mL
1/4 cup	unsweetened orange juice	50 mL
1	egg	1
3/4 tsp	salt	4 mL
1/4 cup	granulated sugar substitute (see Tip, at left)	50 mL
2 tbsp	butter	25 mL
3 3/4 cups	all-purpose flour or bread flour	925 mL
1 1/4 tsp	bread machine yeast	6 mL

APRICOT FILLING

1/4 to 1/2 cup	dried apricots (optional)	50 to 125 mL
1/3 to 2/3 cup	sugar-free apricot spread	75 to 150 mL

ALMOND TOPPING

2 tbsp	milk	25 mL
2 tbsp	granulated sugar substitute (see Tip, at left)	25 mL
1/2 cup	sliced almonds	125 mL

1. Measure ingredients into baking pan in the order recommended by the manufacturer. Insert pan into the oven chamber. Select **Dough Cycle**.

2. Remove dough to a lightly floured surface. Cover with a large bowl and let rest for 10 to 15 minutes.

3. *Filling:* In a bowl, snip apricots into 6 pieces. Add apricot spread and mix gently; set aside.

4. Divide dough in half. Roll out each half to a 12- by 6-inch (30 by 15 cm) rectangle. Spread each with one-half the filling to within $1/2$ inch (1 cm) of the edges. Beginning at the long side, roll jellyroll-style. Pinch to seal seam. Form into a ring, pinching ends together. Place on prepared baking sheet. With scissors, make cuts two-thirds of the way through the ring, 1 inch (2.5 cm) apart. Repeat with remaining half of dough. Cover and let rise in a warm, draft-free place for 30 to 45 minutes, or until doubled in volume. Meanwhile, preheat oven to 350°F (180°C).

5. *Topping:* Brush risen dough with milk. Sprinkle with sugar substitute and sliced almonds.

6. Bake in preheated oven for 20 to 25 minutes, or until tea rings sound hollow when tapped on the bottom.

Tips for a Terrific Loaf

- For a more tender loaf, use homogenized or 2% milk rather than water.

- Check your bread machine's manual. If it does not have a preheat cycle or requires liquids at room temperature, microwave the milk until just lukewarm; if it's too hot, it will kill the yeast.

- Butter, at room temperature, should be added in little dollops, not one big clump, when adding with the other ingredients to the baking pan.

- Large amounts of pumpkin, sweet potato or applesauce should be warmed to room temperature before adding.

- Eggs should be large and used straight from the refrigerator.

- Loaves containing milk, butter, eggs and other perishables should not be prepared using the timer.

- Add raisins and fruit at the "add ingredient" signal. If your bread machine doesn't have this feature, check your manual to determine the time to add them. The time is important; too early and the fruit breaks up and is puréed; too late and it sits on the outside and could have a burnt taste.

- Nuts, whole dates and chocolate chips can be added with the dry ingredients.

- Keep cinnamon away from yeast; it slows down the rising action.

Blueberry Poppy Loaf

This light-textured
loaf is one of our friend
Patti's favorites. She
loves the unique flavor
and richness it gets
from the sour cream.

Tip

This is an extra-large
loaf. To avoid the top of
the loaf hitting the lid
of the bread machine,
try the 1.5 lb (750 g)
loaf first.

Yes, you're reading it
right: The 1.5 lb
(750 g) recipe contains
more yeast than the
2 lb (1 kg).

Variation

Dried currants can
be substituted for the
blueberries, and orange
zest for the lemon.

1.5 LB (750 G)		
1 1/2 cups	sour cream	375 mL
1 tsp	lemon zest	5 mL
1 tsp	salt	5 mL
2 tbsp	granulated sugar	25 mL
1 tbsp	vegetable oil	15 mL
2 3/4 cups	all-purpose flour or bread flour	675 mL
1/3 cup	poppy seeds	75 mL
1 1/2 tsp	bread machine yeast	7 mL
1/3 cup	dried blueberries	75 mL

2 LB (1 KG) • extra large		
2 cups	sour cream	500 mL
2 tsp	lemon zest	10 mL
1 1/2 tsp	salt	7 mL
3 tbsp	granulated sugar	45 mL
2 tbsp	vegetable oil	25 mL
4 cups	all-purpose flour or bread flour	1000 mL
1/2 cup	poppy seeds	125 mL
1 tsp	bread machine yeast	5 mL
1/2 cup	dried blueberries	125 mL

1. Measure all ingredients *except dried blueberries* into baking pan in the order recommended by the manufacturer. Insert pan into the oven chamber.
2. Select **Sweet Cycle**.
3. Add dried blueberries at "add ingredient" signal.

Blueberry Peach Streusel Cake

Tip

Unwashed blueberries can be frozen for up to 2 months without losing flavor or quality. When ready to use, rinse frozen berries quickly under cold water and dry well. No need to thaw.

Variation

Substitute 4 cups (1000 mL) of sliced apples (or another seasonal fruit) for the peaches. Place in overlapping circles for an attractive design.

• Two 10-inch (3 L) springform pans, bottoms lightly greased

1/2 cup	water	125 mL
1/2 cup	orange juice	125 mL
2 tsp	orange zest	10 mL
1/4 cup	skim milk powder	50 mL
1	egg	1
1 1/2 tsp	salt	7 mL
1/4 cup	packed brown sugar	50 mL
2 tbsp	butter	25 mL
3 cups	all-purpose flour or bread flour	750 mL
1/2 tsp	ground nutmeg	2 mL
1 1/2 tsp	bread machine yeast	7 mL

FRUIT FILLING

4 cups	sliced fresh peaches	1000 mL
2 cups	fresh or frozen blueberries	500 mL

STREUSEL TOPPING

2 cups	packed brown sugar	500 mL
1/2 cup	all-purpose flour	125 mL
4 tsp	orange zest	20 mL
6 tbsp	butter, melted	90 mL
2 cups	sliced almonds	500 mL

1. Measure cake ingredients into machine's baking pan in the order recommended by the manufacturer. Insert pan into the oven chamber. Select **Dough Cycle**.

2. *Filling:* In a large bowl, combine peaches and blueberries; set aside.

3. *Topping:* In a small bowl, combine brown sugar, flour and orange zest. Add melted butter and mix until crumbly; set aside.

4. Remove dough to a lightly floured surface. Cover with a large bowl and let rest for 10 to 15 minutes.

5. Divide dough in half. Press one portion of the dough into one prepared pan. Top with half of the prepared filling. Sprinkle with half of the topping and then half of the sliced almonds. Repeat with the second pan. Cover and let rise in a warm, draft-free place for 45 to 60 minutes, or until doubled in volume. Meanwhile, preheat oven to 350°F (180°C).

6. Bake in preheated oven for 40 to 45 minutes, or until streusel cakes are golden brown. Serve warm from the oven or at room temperature.

Tips for Making Sweet Yeast Breads

- When adding fruit and/or nuts at the "add ingredient" signal, scrape any dry ingredients out of the corners of the baking pan with a rubber spatula.

- Very sweet or rich dough requires more proofing time than standard breads. Be patient! It may take over an hour.

- After baking, remove the loaf immediately from the bread machine or oven and transfer to a wire cooling rack. If set on a plate, the bottom of the loaf will become soggy.

- For maximum freshness, wrap sweet loaves airtight and store at room temperature. (They'll become stale more quickly in the refrigerator.) Watch for the development of mold during hot, humid weather.

- While they shouldn't be refrigerated, sweet yeast breads and coffee cakes freeze well. Allow to cool completely before wrapping airtight for the freezer. It's best to over-wrap the bread. Freeze for up to 6 weeks. When ready to use, thaw the bread, being sure to keep it wrapped so that it doesn't dry out.

- For a fresher, more attractive appearance, glaze the loaf, then decorate it with toasted nuts and fruit wedges.

Orange Pecan Loaf

1.5 LB (750 G)		
1 1/4 cups	water	300 mL
2 tbsp	frozen orange juice concentrate, thawed	25 mL
1/4 tsp	orange extract	1 mL
1 1/4 tsp	salt	6 mL
2 tbsp	granulated sugar	25 mL
2 tbsp	shortening	25 mL
3 1/3 cups	all-purpose flour or bread flour	850 mL
1/2 cup	chopped pecans	125 mL
2 tsp	orange zest	10 mL
1 tsp	ground cinnamon	5 mL
1 tsp	bread machine yeast	5 mL

2 LB (1 KG) • extra large		
1 1/3 cups	water	325 mL
1/4 cup	frozen orange juice concentrate, thawed	50 mL
1/2 tsp	orange extract	2 mL
1 1/2 tsp	salt	7 mL
3 tbsp	granulated sugar	45 mL
2 tbsp	shortening	25 mL
3 3/4 cups	all-purpose flour or bread flour	950 mL
2/3 cup	chopped pecans	150 mL
1 tbsp	orange zest	15 mL
1 tsp	ground cinnamon	5 mL
1 1/4 tsp	bread machine yeast	6 mL

1. Measure ingredients into baking pan in the order recommended by the manufacturer. Insert pan into the oven chamber.
2. Select **Sweet Cycle**.

A triple-orange aroma greets you as you open the bread machine lid. The orange flavor enhances every bite.

Tip

To thaw frozen orange juice, remove lid from container; microwave 20 seconds on High. This way you can scoop out just the juice you need without thawing the whole container.

Variation

For a mixed citrus flavor, substitute lemon extract for the orange extract.

Date Orange Bundles

• Baking sheet, lightly greased

These little date-filled packages not only look irresistible, but taste great, too.

1 cup	milk (room temperature)	250 mL
2 tbsp	frozen orange juice concentrate, thawed (see Tip on page 283)	25 mL
1 tbsp	orange zest	15 mL
1/4 tsp	orange extract	1 mL
1	egg	1
1 1/4 tsp	salt	6 mL
2 tbsp	granulated sugar	25 mL
1/4 cup	butter	50 mL
3 1/2 cups	all-purpose flour or bread flour	875 mL
1 tsp	bread machine yeast	5 mL

DATE FILLING

2 cups	pitted dates	500 mL
1 1/2 cups	water	375 mL

EGG WHITE GLAZE

1	egg white	1
1 tbsp	water	15 mL

Tips

For best appearance, roll circles thinner at the edges than in the center.

A 12-oz (360 g) package yields about 2 cups (500 mL) dates.

Variations

To complete the presentation, tie a licorice ribbon at the point where dough is pinched near the top.

Try adding 1/4 cup (50 mL) raisins to the dates in the filling.

1. Measure dough ingredients into machine's baking pan in the order recommended by the manufacturer. Insert pan into the oven chamber. Select **Dough Cycle.**

2. *Filling:* In a saucepan over low heat, combine pitted dates and water. Cook, stirring occasionally, until the dates are soft and have the consistency of jam. Set aside to cool.

3. Remove dough to a lightly floured surface. Cover with a large bowl and let rest for 10 to 15 minutes.

4. Divide dough into 16 portions. Roll into balls; stretch each into a 5-inch (12.5 cm) circle. Place 2 tbsp (25 mL) filling in the center of each circle. Pull the dough up around the filling, pleating tightly above filling, pinching tightly to seal. Place on prepared baking sheet. Cover and let rise in a warm, draft-free place for 30 to 45 minutes, or until doubled in volume. Meanwhile, preheat oven to 350°F (180°C).

5. *Glaze:* In a small bowl, whisk together egg white and water. Pinch the pleats again in the risen dough and brush with glaze.

6. Bake in preheated oven for 20 to 25 minutes, or until bundles sound hollow when tapped on the bottom.

The Great Divide (How to Portion Accurately)

It seems like every time we work with dough the first thing that has to be done is to divide it into equal portions. It is important to be sure that all portions are the same size, or some will burn while others remain raw. To divide evenly, round the dough into a large, slightly flattened ball. Always cut rather than pull the dough. Use a sharp French-style knife or a pizza wheel.

For 4 portions
Divide the dough ball in half (to get 2), then each piece in half (to get 4).

For 8 portions
Divide the dough ball in half (to get 2), then each piece in half (to get 4), then each in half again (to get 8).

For 9 portions
Divide the dough ball in thirds (to get 3), then each piece in 3 again (to get 9).

For 12 portions
Divide the dough ball in half (to get 2), then each piece in thirds (to get 6), then each piece in half (to get 12).

For 16 portions
Divide the dough ball in half (to get 2), then each piece in half (to get 4), then each piece in fourths (to get 16).
The results will be a lot more even than if you simply hack off small amounts and hope you end up with the right number.

Alternatively, if you have a kitchen scale, you could weigh the dough, divide it into the required number of pieces, then make sure all the pieces weigh the same amount. For example, if your dough weighs 24 oz (750 g), and you are dividing it into 12 pieces, each piece should weigh 2 oz (60 g).

Orange-Glazed Breakfast Cake

• Tube pan, lightly greased

1/2 cup	water	125 mL
1/2 cup	fresh orange juice	125 mL
1/2 cup	cottage cheese	125 mL
1	egg	1
2 tsp	orange zest	10 mL
3/4 tsp	salt	4 mL
2 tbsp	granulated sugar	25 mL
2 tbsp	butter	25 mL
3 1/2 cups	all-purpose flour or bread flour	875 mL
1 1/2 tsp	bread machine yeast	7 mL

ORANGE GLAZE

1 cup	sifted icing sugar	250 mL
1 to 2 tbsp	fresh orange juice	15 to 25 mL

1. Measure the cake ingredients into machine's baking pan in the order recommended by the manufacturer. Insert pan into the oven chamber. Select **Dough Cycle**.

2. Remove dough to a lightly floured surface. Cover with a large bowl and let rest for 10 to 15 minutes.

3. Divide the dough into 3 portions. Roll each into an 18-inch (45 cm) rope. Braid the three ropes. Place in prepared tube pan, pinching ends together to form a ring. Cover and let rise in a warm, draft-free place for 30 to 45 minutes, or until doubled in volume. Preheat oven to 350°F (180°C).

4. Bake in preheated oven for 30 to 35 minutes, or until the breakfast cake sounds hollow when tapped on the bottom.

5. *Glaze:* In a bowl, combine icing sugar and orange juice; mix until smooth. Drizzle over the warm breakfast cake.

Orange Breakfast Danish

Easier to make than traditional Danish, these cream cheese-filled pinwheels will be a hit with your family.

Tip

Roll the ropes tightly but coil them loosely, leaving a small space between each, then flatten as you form the pinwheel. Otherwise the dough will puff up and look more like a snail than a Danish.

Variation

Try different jams or applesauce for the Danish centers.

● *Baking sheet, lightly greased*

1¼ cups	water	300 mL
2 tbsp	frozen orange juice concentrate, thawed	25 mL
1¼ tsp	salt	6 mL
2 tbsp	granulated sugar	25 mL
2 tbsp	shortening	25 mL
3½ cups	all-purpose flour or bread flour	875 mL
2 tsp	orange zest	10 mL
¾ tsp	bread machine yeast	4 mL

FILLING

1	package (8 oz/250 g) cream cheese, softened	1
½ cup	granulated sugar	125 mL
4 tsp	frozen orange juice concentrate, thawed	20 mL
½ cup	raspberry jam	125 mL

1. Measure ingredients into baking pan in the order recommended by the manufacturer. Insert pan into the oven chamber. Select **Dough Cycle**.

2. *Filling:* In a bowl, beat cream cheese together with sugar and juice concentrate until smooth.

3. Remove dough to a lightly floured board; cover with a large bowl and let rest 10 to 15 minutes.

4. Roll out the dough into a 16- by 10-inch (40 by 25 cm) rectangle. Cut into 10 strips, 1 inch (2.5 cm) wide. On the prepared baking sheet, beginning in the center, coil each strip in a circle, keeping the dough ¼ inch (5 mm) apart. Tuck end under. Cover and let rise in a warm, draft-free place for 30 to 45 minutes, or until doubled in volume. Meanwhile, preheat oven to 375°F (190°C).

5. Spread tops with 2 tbsp (25 mL) filling and in the center with 2 tsp (10 mL) jam.

6. Bake in preheated oven for 15 to 20 minutes, or until Danish sound hollow when tapped on the bottom.

Black Forest Loaf

1.5 LB (750 G)

3/4 cup	milk (room temperature)	175 mL
1 tbsp	brandy	15 mL
1	egg	1
1 1/2 tsp	salt	7 mL
2 tbsp	honey	25 mL
2 tbsp	butter	25 mL
2 1/2 cups	all-purpose flour or bread flour	625 mL
1 1/4 tsp	bread machine yeast	6 mL
1/2 cup	semi-sweet chocolate chips	125 mL
1/2 cup	dried cherries	125 mL

2 LB (1 KG)

1 cup	milk (room temperature)	250 mL
2 tbsp	brandy	25 mL
1	egg	1
1 1/2 tsp	salt	7 mL
3 tbsp	honey	45 mL
2 tbsp	butter	25 mL
3 1/2 cups	all-purpose flour or bread flour	875 mL
1 1/2 tsp	bread machine yeast	7 mL
2/3 cup	semi-sweet chocolate chips	150 mL
2/3 cup	dried cherries	150 mL

1. Measure all ingredients *except chocolate chips and cherries* into baking pan in the order recommended by the manufacturer. Insert pan into the oven chamber.

2. Select **Sweet Cycle**.

3. Add chocolate chips and dried cherries at the "add ingredient" signal.

Baltic Birthday Bread (page 246)

Overleaf: An assortment of rolls (pages 195–212)

Chop Suey Loaf

Tip

For a lighter, less-sweet loaf, rinse the candied fruit under cold water and dry well before adding to the baking pan.

Yes, you're reading it right: The 1.5 lb (750 g) recipe contains the *same* amount of yeast as the 2 lb (1 kg).

Variation

This recipe can become a Russian kulich by substituting part of the fruit with the same amount of raisins and toasted almonds.

1.5 LB (750 G)		
³⁄₄ cup	water	175 mL
1	egg	1
¼ cup	skim milk powder	50 mL
1¼ tsp	salt	6 mL
2 tbsp	granulated sugar	25 mL
2 tbsp	butter	25 mL
2¹⁄₃ cups	all-purpose flour or bread flour	575 mL
1¼ tsp	bread machine yeast	6 mL
1 cup	mixed candied fruit	250 mL
¼ cup	raisins	50 mL

2 LB (1 KG)		
1 cup	water	250 mL
2	eggs	2
¼ cup	skim milk powder	50 mL
1½ tsp	salt	7 mL
2 tbsp	granulated sugar	25 mL
2 tbsp	butter	25 mL
3½ cups	all-purpose flour or bread flour	825 mL
1¼ tsp	bread machine yeast	6 mL
1½ cups	mixed candied fruit	375 mL
½ cup	raisins	125 mL

1. Measure all ingredients *except candied fruit and raisins* into baking pan in the order recommended by the manufacturer. Insert pan into the oven chamber.

2. Select **Sweet Cycle**.

3. Add raisins and fruit at the "add ingredient" signal.

Thanksgiving Harvest Twist (page 254)

Tip

Be sure to buy pumpkin purée — not pumpkin pie filling, which is too sweet and contains too much moisture for this recipe.

Yes, you're reading it right: The 1.5 lb (750 g) recipe contains *more* yeast than the 2 lb (1 kg).

Variation

Substitute butterscotch chips for the dried cranberries. Add them with the other ingredients; there's no need to wait for the "add ingredient" signal.

Autumn Pumpkin Loaf

1.5 LB (750 G)		
½ cup	water	125 mL
½ cup	canned pumpkin purée	125 mL
1	egg	1
¼ cup	skim milk powder	50 mL
1¼ tsp	salt	6 mL
¼ cup	granulated sugar	50 mL
2 tbsp	shortening	25 mL
2¾ cups	all-purpose flour or bread flour	675 mL
½ tsp	ground allspice	2 mL
¼ tsp	ground ginger	1 mL
¼ tsp	ground nutmeg	1 mL
1½ tsp	bread machine yeast	7 mL
¼ cup	dried cranberries	50 mL
¼ cup	pumpkin seeds	50 mL

2 LB (1 KG)		
⅔ cup	water	150 mL
⅔ cup	canned pumpkin purée	150 mL
2	eggs	2
⅓ cup	skim milk powder	75 mL
1½ tsp	salt	7 mL
⅓ cup	granulated sugar	75 mL
2 tbsp	shortening	25 mL
3 cups	all-purpose flour or bread flour	750 mL
½ tsp	ground allspice	2 mL
¼ tsp	ground ginger	1 mL
¼ tsp	ground nutmeg	1 mL
1¼ tsp	bread machine yeast	6 mL
⅓ cup	dried cranberries	75 mL
⅓ cup	pumpkin seeds	75 mL

1. Measure all ingredients *except dried cranberries and pumpkin seeds* into baking pan in the order recommended by the manufacturer. Insert pan into the oven chamber.

2. Select **Sweet Cycle**.

3. Add dried cranberries and pumpkin seeds at "add ingredient" signal.

French Cuts Using the Lame

Wondering how to get a perfect slash on the top of a French baguette? The loaf can look professional if you use a lame (pronounced "lahm") — a curved 5-inch (12 cm) extra-sharp blade, held securely in a plastic holder. It looks like a razor blade with a plastic handle and comes with a plastic blade protector.

Most French and hearth breads are slashed across the top just before baking. The cuts open as the loaf expands during baking. If slashes are made before the loaf rises, it may split along the side rather than open at the slashes.

In general, make 4 to 5 bias cuts in each baguette. Each slash should overlap the end of the preceding one by about a third of its length. Make sure the loaf is not over-risen; otherwise, it may collapse as you slash. To make the cuts, hold the lame on a 30- to 40-degree angle off the horizontal, not as you would hold a knife to slice dough, but as you would to shave a bit off the top of a loaf. Using firm, decisive strokes, make long, straight cuts about 1/4-inch (0.5 cm) deep. (Or make deeper cuts; the loaf will open even more.) Once the loaf has baked, examine the cuts to see the results of different stroke lengths and depths. This will help you figure out what works best for next time.

For a round loaf or an oval one (boule), hold the lame at a sharper, almost vertical angle. Rather than forming a lip, this will result in an open, flatter cut. Boules or round loaves may be slashed in a diagonal pattern or in a crisscross pattern.

Remember, practice makes perfect. If you find that the lame is dragging and sticking, just use a quicker, firmer stroke.

Grandma's Cinnamon Raisin Bread

*The aroma of toasted cinnamon bread —
what better way to ensure everyone arrives at the breakfast table with a smile?*

Tip

For a stronger cinnamon flavor, serve with a cinnamon sugar spread. Do not increase the cinnamon called for in the recipe or the loaf will be short.

Variation

For an interesting taste treat, add 1/4 cup (50 mL) chopped walnuts with the raisins.

1.5 LB (750 G)

1 1/4 cups	water	300 mL
1	egg	1
1/4 cup	skim milk powder	50 mL
1 1/4 tsp	salt	6 mL
2 tbsp	packed brown sugar	25 mL
2 tbsp	shortening	25 mL
3 1/2 cups	all-purpose flour or bread flour	875 mL
1 tsp	ground cinnamon	5 mL
3/4 tsp	bread machine yeast	4 mL
3/4 cup	raisins	150 mL

2 LB (1 KG)

1 1/3 cups	water	325 mL
1	egg	1
1/4 cup	skim milk powder	50 mL
1 1/4 tsp	salt	6 mL
1/4 cup	packed brown sugar	50 mL
2 tbsp	shortening	25 mL
3 3/4 cups	all-purpose flour or bread flour	950 mL
1 1/2 tsp	ground cinnamon	7 mL
1 tsp	bread machine yeast	5 mL
1 cup	raisins	250 mL

1. Measure all ingredients *except raisins* into baking pan in the order recommended by the manufacturer. Insert pan into the oven chamber.

2. Select **Sweet Cycle**.

3. Add raisins at "add ingredient" signal.

Cranberry Raisin Loaf

This recipe was inspired by the request of a newsletter subscriber for a raisin bread that is not too sweet.

Tip

Even with less yeast than in the 1.5 lb (750 g) recipe (see below), the 2 lb (1 kg) loaf may hit the lid of some bread machines. To avoid this, try the 1.5 lb (750 g) recipe first.

Yes, you're reading it right: The 1.5 lb (750 g) recipe contains *more* yeast than the 2 lb (1 kg).

Variation

Try substituting chocolate chips for half the raisins.

1.5 LB (750 G)		
1 cup	water	250 mL
1	egg	1
1/4 cup	skim milk powder	50 mL
1 tsp	salt	5 mL
1 tbsp	packed brown sugar	15 mL
2 tbsp	shortening	25 mL
2 3/4 cups	all-purpose flour or bread flour	675 mL
1 1/2 tsp	ground cardamom	7 mL
1 1/2 tsp	bread machine yeast	7 mL
1/3 cup	dried cranberries	75 mL
1/3 cup	raisins	75 mL

2 LB (1 KG) • extra large		
1 1/4 cups	water	300 mL
1	egg	1
1/3 cup	skim milk powder	75 mL
1 1/4 tsp	salt	6 mL
2 tbsp	packed brown sugar	25 mL
2 tbsp	shortening	25 mL
3 1/2 cups	all-purpose flour or bread flour	875 mL
2 tsp	ground cardamom	10 mL
1 1/4 tsp	bread machine yeast	6 mL
1/2 cup	dried cranberries	125 mL
1/2 cup	raisins	125 mL

1. Measure all ingredients *except dried cranberries and raisins* into baking pan in the order recommended by the manufacturer. Insert pan into the oven chamber.

2. Select **Sweet Cycle**.

3. Add dried cranberries and raisins at "add ingredient" signal.

Cran-Raspberry Orange Bread

Bake this tart but sweet loaf at the first sign of fall, when fresh cranberries arrive in the grocery store.

Tip

Choose only unsweetened fruit juices. Fruit drinks or sweetened juices will result in a less-than-perfect loaf.

Yes, you're reading it right: The 1.5 lb (750 g) recipe contains the *same* amount of yeast as the 2 lb (1 kg).

Variation

For a different taste treat, try other cranberry juice combinations.

1.5 LB (750 G)		
$3/4$ cup	water	175 mL
$1/4$ cup	cran-raspberry juice	50 mL
$1/4$ cup	orange marmalade	50 mL
$1/2$ tsp	orange extract	2 mL
$1/4$ cup	skim milk powder	50 mL
$1^1/2$ tsp	salt	7 mL
1 tbsp	granulated sugar	15 mL
2 tbsp	butter	25 mL
$2^3/4$ cups	all-purpose flour or bread flour	675 mL
2 tsp	orange zest	10 mL
$1^3/4$ tsp	bread machine yeast	8 mL
$1/2$ cup	fresh cranberries	125 mL

2 LB (1 KG)		
1 cup	water	250 mL
$1/3$ cup	cran-raspberry juice	75 mL
$1/3$ cup	orange marmalade	75 mL
$1/2$ tsp	orange extract	2 mL
$1/4$ cup	skim milk powder	50 mL
$1^1/2$ tsp	salt	7 mL
2 tbsp	granulated sugar	25 mL
2 tbsp	butter	25 mL
$3^1/2$ cups	all-purpose flour or bread flour	875 mL
1 tbsp	orange zest	15 mL
$1^3/4$ tsp	bread machine yeast	8 mL
$3/4$ cup	fresh cranberries	175 mL

1. Measure all ingredients *except cranberries* into baking pan in the order recommended by the manufacturer. Insert pan into the oven chamber.
2. Select **Sweet Cycle**.
3. Add cranberries at the "add ingredient" signal.

The Scoop on Cranberries

One of the many foods that herald the fall harvest in the northeastern region of North America is the cranberry, named "crane berry" by German and Dutch settlers. Native Americans have long used cranberries for their medicinal properties.

Cranberries have become a part of holiday culture. In fact, it is believed the Pilgrims may have served cranberries at the first Thanksgiving. The annual harvest of this fruit, one of very few native to North America, begins in late September and continues for six weeks.

Availability

The fresh crop starts to appear in grocery stores around the first week of October and usually disappears by the end of December. They can be frozen right in the plastic package, so plan to purchase enough to last until the next harvest. Add straight from the freezer to any recipe calling for fresh cranberries.

Health benefits

These include heart disease prevention, cancer inhibition and maintenance of urinary tract health.

Nutritional value

Cranberries are high in Vitamin C and fiber and low in calories: 1 cup (250 mL) has 50 calories.

Dried cranberries

When fresh cranberries are soaked in a sugar solution and then dried, they are known as dried cranberries or C'raisins®. They come in various flavors, such as orange, raspberry and strawberry, which are all interchangeable in recipes. Dried cranberries are readily available in grocery and bulk-food stores. Though much sweeter than fresh, they can be substituted for raisins, dried blueberries, cherries or currants in most recipes.

Hawaiian Sunrise Bread

Bring the fragrance and flavor of the Hawaiian islands to your table with this light, angel food–like loaf.

Tips

In this recipe you can add the fruit and nuts directly with the other ingredients — no need to wait for the "add ingredient" signal.

For instructions on toasting coconut, see Techniques Glossary, page 368.

Yes, you're reading it right: The 1.5 lb (750 g) recipe contains the *same* amount of yeast as the 2 lb (1 kg).

Variation

To add multicolored flecks to the loaf, try adding "confetti-style" coconut.

1.5 LB (750 G)		
1¼ cups	water	300 mL
¼ cup	skim milk powder	50 mL
1 tsp	salt	5 mL
1 tbsp	granulated sugar	15 mL
1 tbsp	shortening	15 mL
3 cups	all-purpose flour or bread flour	750 mL
⅓ cup	shredded unsweetened coconut, toasted	75 mL
⅓ cup	glacé pineapple chunks	75 mL
¼ cup	coarsely chopped Macadamia nuts	50 mL
1 tsp	bread machine yeast	5 mL

2 LB (1 KG)		
1½ cups	water	375 mL
⅓ cup	skim milk powder	75 mL
1¼ tsp	salt	6 mL
1 tbsp	granulated sugar	15 mL
1 tbsp	shortening	15 mL
3½ cups	all-purpose flour or bread flour	875 mL
½ cup	shredded unsweetened coconut, toasted	125 mL
½ cup	glacé pineapple chunks	125 mL
⅓ cup	coarsely chopped Macadamia nuts	75 mL
1 tsp	bread machine yeast	5 mL

1. Measure ingredients into baking pan in the order recommended by the manufacturer. Insert pan into the oven chamber.
2. Select **Sweet Cycle**.

Cinnamon Nut Twists

● *Baking sheet, lightly greased*

1 1/4 cups	water	300 mL
1	egg	1
3/4 tsp	salt	3 mL
1/4 cup	honey	50 mL
2 tbsp	butter	25 mL
3 3/4 cups	all-purpose flour or bread flour	925 mL
1 1/4 tsp	bread machine yeast	6 mL

CINNAMON NUT FILLING

3/4 cup	finely chopped walnuts	175 mL
1/2 cup	packed brown sugar	125 mL
1 tsp	ground cinnamon	5 mL
1/4 cup	butter	50 mL

Tip

To form the dough, pick up a strip with a hand at each end; twist each end in opposite directions. Press the ends onto the baking sheet to prevent it from untwisting during proofing.

Variation

Substitute hazelnuts for the walnuts and 1/2 tsp (2 mL) nutmeg for the cinnamon.

1. Measure dough ingredients into baking pan in the order recommended by the manufacturer. Insert pan into the oven chamber. Select **Dough Cycle**.

2. *Filling:* Combine walnuts, brown sugar and cinnamon; set aside. Melt butter. Cool slightly before using.

3. Remove dough to a lightly floured board; cover with a large bowl and let rest for 10 to 15 minutes.

4. Divide dough in half. Roll out each half into a 12-inch (30 cm) square. Brush one square with half the melted butter. Sprinkle half of the filling mixture over half the dough. Fold over the other half and carefully pinch to seal. Cut crosswise into 10 strips, 6 inches (15 cm) long. Twist each strip twice. Place on prepared baking sheet. Cover and let rise in a warm, draft-free place for 30 to 45 minutes, or until doubled in volume. Meanwhile, preheat oven to 350°F (180°C).

5. Bake in preheated oven for 12 to 15 minutes, or until twists sound hollow when tapped on the bottom.

Cinnamon Walnut Swirl Loaf

Each slice is a perfect pinwheel. Your guests will wonder how you formed this loaf.

Tip

Poke the risen dough with a long skewer in several places before baking to prevent a large bubble from forming under the top crust.

Variation

Try this recipe with date filling: In a bowl combine 4 oz (120 g) chopped dates, 2 tbsp (25 mL) sugar and 1 tsp (5 mL) ground cinnamon. No need to cook this filling.

• 9- by 5-inch (1.5 L) loaf pan, lightly greased

1 cup	milk	250 mL
1	egg	1
³⁄₄ tsp	salt	3 mL
3 tbsp	granulated sugar	45 mL
2 tbsp	butter	25 mL
3 cups	all-purpose flour or bread flour	750 mL
1¹⁄₄ tsp	bread machine yeast	6 mL

DOUBLE WALNUT FILLING

1 cup	chopped walnuts	250 mL
³⁄₄ cup	ground walnuts	175 mL
¹⁄₂ cup	granulated sugar	125 mL
2	egg whites	2
2 tsp	water	10 mL
¹⁄₄ tsp	ground cinnamon	1 mL

1. Measure ingredients into baking pan in the order recommended by the manufacturer. Insert pan into the oven chamber. Select **Dough Cycle**.

2. *Filling:* In a saucepan over low heat, combine filling ingredients; cook, stirring, for 10 minutes, or until sugar dissolves. Set aside and allow to cool.

3. Remove dough to a lightly floured board; cover with a large bowl and let rest for 10 to 15 minutes. Roll out to a 16- by 8-inch (40 by 20 cm) rectangle.

4. Spread filling to within ¹⁄₂ inch (1 cm) of edges. Starting at short side, tightly roll like a jellyroll. Place in prepared pan. Cover and let rise in a warm, draft-free place for 30 to 45 minutes, or until doubled in volume. Meanwhile, preheat oven to 350°F (180°C).

5. With a long skewer, poke several holes in risen dough. Bake in preheated oven for 40 to 50 minutes, or until loaf sounds hollow when tapped on the bottom.

Peanut Butter Banana Swirl Loaf

Tip

If the top of this loaf is browned after 30 minutes of baking, but the bottom is still too light and soft, remove the loaf from the pan and set it directly on the oven rack to brown for the last few minutes of baking.

Variations

Pancake syrup (either light or regular) or packed brown sugar can be substituted for the maple syrup.

For a milder flavor, add 1 to 2 tbsp (15 to 25 mL) mashed banana to the filling.

● *9- by 5-inch (1.5 L) loaf pan, lightly greased*

1/2 cup	water	125 mL
1 cup	mashed ripe banana	250 mL
1/4 cup	skim milk powder	50 mL
3/4 tsp	salt	4 mL
3 tbsp	maple syrup	45 mL
2 tbsp	butter	25 mL
3 cups	all-purpose flour or bread flour	750 mL
2 tsp	bread machine yeast	10 mL

PEANUT BUTTER FILLING

1/2 cup	peanut butter	125 mL
1/3 cup	packed brown sugar	75 mL
1/2 cup	unsalted peanuts	125 mL

1. Measure loaf ingredients into machine's baking pan in the order recommended by the manufacturer. Insert pan into the oven chamber. Select **Dough Cycle**.

2. *Filling:* In a bowl, combine peanut butter and brown sugar. Set aside.

3. Remove dough to a lightly floured surface. Cover with a large bowl and let rest for 10 to 15 minutes.

4. Roll out to an 18- by 8-inch (45 by 20 cm) rectangle. Spread the filling to within 1/2 inch (1 cm) of edges. Sprinkle with peanuts. Beginning at short side, roll jellyroll-style. Tuck ends under. Place, seam-side down, in prepared loaf pan. Cover and let rise in a warm, draft-free place for 30 to 45 minutes, or until doubled in volume. Meanwhile, preheat oven to 350°F (180°C).

5. With a long skewer, poke several holes through the risen dough. Bake in preheated oven for 40 to 50 minutes, or until bread sounds hollow when tapped on the bottom.

Pecan Crisps

• *Baking sheet, lightly greased*

Take these crunchy treats to work and set them out to share during coffee break. Just don't mention the calories!

Tip

Be sure to follow the instructions to cover the rolls with waxed paper before rolling. Otherwise, the dough will stick to the rolling pin.

Variation

Bake these crisps muffin-style: place the twelve 1-inch (2.5 cm) slices in individual cups of a muffin tin (no need to roll). Cover and let rise until doubled in volume. Bake as directed.

1 cup	milk	250 mL
1	egg	1
1 1/4 tsp	salt	6 mL
3 tbsp	granulated sugar	45 mL
1/4 cup	butter	50 mL
3 1/2 cups	all-purpose flour or bread flour	875 mL
1/2 tsp	ground cinnamon	2 mL
1 1/2 tsp	bread machine yeast	7 mL

CINNAMON FILLING

1/4 cup	butter, melted	50 mL
1/2 cup	packed brown sugar	125 mL
1/2 cup	granulated sugar	125 mL
1 tsp	ground cinnamon	5 mL

PECAN TOPPING

2/3 cup	granulated sugar	150 mL
2/3 cup	chopped pecans	150 mL
1 tsp	ground cinnamon	5 mL
2 tbsp	butter, melted and cooled	25 mL

1. Measure crisps ingredients into machine's baking pan in the order recommended by the manufacturer. Insert pan into the oven chamber. Select **Dough Cycle**.

2. *Filling:* In a small bowl, combine melted butter, brown sugar, granulated sugar and cinnamon. Set aside.

3. *Topping:* In another small bowl, combine granulated sugar, pecans and cinnamon. Set aside.

4. Remove dough to a lightly floured surface. Cover with a large bowl and let rest for 10 to 15 minutes.

5. Divide dough in half. Roll each half into a 12-inch (30 cm) square. Spread each with half the filling, right to the edges. Roll jellyroll-style. Pinch to seal seams. Cut each into twelve 1-inch (2.5 cm) slices. Place cut-side up on prepared baking sheet, at least 3 inches (7.5 cm) apart. Cover slices with a sheet of waxed paper. Flatten with a rolling pin until $\frac{1}{8}$ inch (2 mm) thick. Brush with cooled butter and sprinkle with pecan topping. Cover with waxed paper and re-roll lightly with a rolling pin. Meanwhile, preheat oven to 400°F (220°C).

6. Bake in preheated oven for 10 to 15 minutes, or until crisps are golden brown.

Giant Pecan Sticky Buns

● 9- by 13-inch (3 L) baking pan, lightly greased

If you need some inspiration to make these sticky buns, take a look at the picture facing page 313. You'll be in the kitchen in a minute.

Tip

Evenly distribute pecan halves, placing upside down in the pan.

Variation

Make mini-buns by rolling half the dough to a 20- by 7-inch (30 by 18 cm) rectangle and cutting into 1-inch (2.5 cm) slices. Shorten the baking time.

1 cup	water	250 mL
1/4 cup	skim milk powder	50 mL
3/4 tsp	salt	3 mL
2 tbsp	packed brown sugar	25 mL
1 tbsp	shortening	15 mL
3 1/4 cups	all-purpose flour or bread flour	800 mL
3/4 tsp	bread machine yeast	3 mL

PECAN PAN GLAZE

1/4 cup	melted butter	50 mL
1/4 cup	packed brown sugar	50 mL
1/4 cup	corn syrup	50 mL
1/2 cup	pecan halves	125 mL

RAISIN PECAN FILLING

1 cup	raisins	250 mL
1/4 cup	chopped pecans	50 mL
1/4 cup	packed brown sugar	50 mL
1 tsp	ground nutmeg	5 mL
1/4 cup	soft butter	50 mL

1. Measure bun ingredients into baking pan in the order recommended by the manufacturer. Insert pan into the oven chamber. Select **Dough Cycle**.

2. *Pan glaze:* In a bowl, combine butter, sugar and corn syrup. Spread in prepared pan. Place pecan halves top-side down (see Tip, at left); set aside.

3. *Filling:* In a bowl, combine all filling ingredients except butter; mix well. Set aside.

4. Remove dough to a lightly floured board; cover with a large bowl and let rest 10 to 15 minutes.

5. Divide dough in half. Roll out each half to a 20- by 7-inch (50 by 18 cm) rectangle. Spread one rectangle with half the soft butter to within $1/2$ inch (1 cm) of the edges. Sprinkle half the filling over the dough. Beginning at the long side, roll jellyroll-style. Pinch to seal seam. Cut into 10 pieces. Place in one half of prepared pan, cut side up. Repeat procedure with remaining dough. Cover and let dough rise in a warm, draft-free place for 30 to 45 minutes, or until doubled in volume. Meanwhile, preheat oven to 375°F (190°C).

6. Bake in preheated oven for 25 to 35 minutes, or until buns sound hollow. Immediately turn upside down on a serving platter. Allow to stand for 5 minutes before removing pan.

Banana Pecan Sticky Buns

• *8-inch (2 L) square baking pan, lightly greased*

1 cup	mashed ripe bananas	250 mL
2	egg whites	2
¼ cup	skim milk powder	50 mL
½ tsp	salt	2 mL
3 tbsp	granulated sugar	45 mL
2 tbsp	shortening	25 mL
1 cup	whole wheat flour	250 mL
2 cups	all-purpose flour or bread flour	500 mL
2 tsp	bread machine yeast	10 mL

FILLING

¼ cup	packed brown sugar	50 mL
½ tsp	ground cinnamon	2 mL
¾ cup	raisins	175 mL
2 tbsp	soft butter	25 mL

PAN GLAZE

¼ cup	maple syrup	50 mL
½ cup	chopped pecans	125 mL

1. Measure dough ingredients into baking pan in the order recommended by the manufacturer. Insert pan into the oven chamber. Select **Dough Cycle**.

2. *Filling:* In a bowl, combine brown sugar, cinnamon and raisins; set aside.

3. *Pan glaze:* In a bowl, combine glaze ingredients and spread in prepared pan; set aside.

4. Remove dough to a lightly floured board; cover with a large bowl and let rest for 10 to 15 minutes.

5. Roll out dough to a 14- by 9-inch (35 by 23 cm) rectangle. Spread dough with soft butter to within $1/2$ inch (1 cm) of the edges. Sprinkle filling over the dough. Beginning at the long side, roll jellyroll-style. Pinch to seal seam. Cut into 9 pieces $1^1/2$ inches (3.5 cm) wide. Arrange the buns, cut-side up, in prepared pan; cover and let rise in a warm, draft-free place for 30 to 45 minutes, or until doubled in volume. Meanwhile, preheat oven to 350°F (180°C).

6. Bake in preheated oven for 25 to 35 minutes, or until buns sound hollow. Immediately turn upside down on a serving platter. Allow to stand for 5 minutes before removing pan.

Hazelnut Chocolate Bread

Here's a flavor combination that every sweet tooth will love — chocolate, hazelnuts and orange!

Tips

For instructions on removing hazelnut skins, see Techniques Glossary, page 369.

Melt the chocolate in the microwave just until soft.

Yes, you're reading it right: The 1.5 lb (750 g) recipe contains the *same* amount of yeast as the 2 lb (1 kg).

Variations

Substitute a cherry-flavored liqueur, such as Cherry Heering, for the hazelnut liqueur.

Replace the hazelnut liqueur with additional orange juice concentrate.

1.5 LB (750 G)		
1 cup	water	250 mL
2 tbsp	frozen orange juice concentrate, thawed (see Tip on page 283)	25 mL
1 tbsp	hazelnut liqueur	15 mL
2 tsp	orange zest	10 mL
1 oz	unsweetened chocolate, melted	30 g
1 tsp	salt	5 mL
1/4 cup	granulated sugar	50 mL
1 tbsp	butter	15 mL
3 cups	all-purpose flour or bread flour	750 mL
1/4 cup	chopped hazelnuts	50 mL
3 tbsp	unsweetened cocoa powder	45 mL
1 1/2 tsp	bread machine yeast	7 mL

2 LB (1 KG)		
1 1/4 cups	water	300 mL
2 tbsp	frozen orange juice concentrate, thawed (see Tip on page 283)	25 mL
2 tbsp	hazelnut liqueur	25 mL
1 tbsp	orange zest	15 mL
1 oz	unsweetened chocolate, melted	30 g
1 1/4 tsp	salt	6 mL
1/3 cup	granulated sugar	75 mL
1 tbsp	butter	15 mL
3 1/2 cups	all-purpose flour or bread flour	875 mL
1/3 cup	chopped hazelnuts	75 mL
1/4 cup	unsweetened cocoa powder	50 mL
1 1/2 tsp	bread machine yeast	7 mL

1. Measure ingredients into baking pan in the order recommended by the manufacturer. Insert pan into the oven chamber. Select **Sweet Cycle**.

Chocolate Banana Loaf

A child's dream combination — bananas and chocolate! Serve with a glass of cold milk and the after-school snack is complete.

Tip

Freeze mashed overripe bananas in 1-cup (250 mL) containers. Thaw and bring to room temperature before adding.

Yes, you're reading it right: The 1.5 lb (750 g) recipe contains the *same* amount of yeast as the 2 lb (1 kg).

Variation

Substitute peanut butter chips for the chocolate chips and add 1/2 cup (125 mL) shelled unsalted peanuts.

1.5 LB (750 G)		
1 1/4 cups	mashed ripe bananas	300 mL
1	egg	1
1/4 cup	skim milk powder	50 mL
1 1/4 tsp	salt	6 mL
1 tbsp	honey	15 mL
1 tbsp	butter	15 mL
3 cups	all-purpose flour or bread flour	750 mL
1/3 cup	chocolate chips	75 mL
1 1/2 tsp	bread machine yeast	7 mL

2 LB (1 KG)		
1 1/2 cups	mashed ripe bananas	325 mL
2	eggs	2
1 1/2 tsp	salt	7 mL
1/4 cup	skim milk powder	50 mL
2 tbsp	honey	25 mL
2 tbsp	butter	25 mL
3 1/4 cups	all-purpose flour or bread flour	800 mL
1/2 cup	chocolate chips	125 mL
1 1/2 tsp	bread machine yeast	7 mL

1. Measure ingredients into baking pan in the order recommended by the manufacturer. Insert pan into the oven chamber.
2. Select **Sweet Cycle**.

Chocolate Fudge Loaf

Double the goodness with double the chocolate.

Tips

If there are no chocolate squares in the cupboard, substitute 3 tbsp (45 mL) unsweetened cocoa powder, and 1 tbsp (15 mL) butter for each 1 oz (30 g) square.

To melt chocolate, cut square in half; microwave on 50% power, just until soft.

Yes, you're reading it right: The 1.5 lb (750 g) recipe contains the *same* amount of yeast as the 2 lb (1 kg).

Variation

Try $1/2$ cup (125 mL) mint or white chocolate chips for a change.

1.5 LB (750 G)

1 cup	water	250 mL
1 oz	bittersweet chocolate, melted and cooled	30 g
1	egg	1
$1\frac{1}{2}$ tsp	salt	7 mL
3 tbsp	honey	45 mL
3 cups	all-purpose flour or bread flour	750 mL
$1/3$ cup	buttermilk powder	75 mL
2 tbsp	unsweetened cocoa powder	25 mL
$1\frac{1}{2}$ tsp	bread machine yeast	7 mL
$1/2$ cup	chocolate chips	125 mL

2 LB (1 KG)

$1\frac{1}{4}$ cups	water	300 mL
$1\frac{1}{2}$ oz	bittersweet chocolate, melted and cooled	45 g
1	egg	1
$1\frac{1}{2}$ tsp	salt	7 mL
$1/4$ cup	honey	50 mL
$3\frac{1}{2}$ cups	all-purpose flour or bread flour	875 mL
$1/2$ cup	buttermilk powder	125 mL
3 tbsp	unsweetened cocoa powder	45 mL
$1\frac{1}{2}$ tsp	bread machine yeast	7 mL
$3/4$ cup	chocolate chips	175 mL

1. Measure all ingredients *except chocolate chips* into baking pan in the order recommended by the manufacturer. Insert pan into the oven chamber.
2. Select **Sweet Cycle**.
3. Add chocolate chips at the "add ingredient" signal.

Chocolate Raspberry Danish

This not-too-sweet breakfast treat will tempt even the fussiest eater. The chocolate-orange combination is irresistible served warm from the oven.

Tip

Pour icing or chocolate syrup into a squeeze bottle to drizzle across the warm Danish.

Variation

Kids enjoy making Danish into fun shapes. For instructions on shaping, see Techniques Glossary, page 368.

● Baking sheet, lightly greased

1¹/₃ cups	water	325 mL
3 tbsp	frozen orange juice concentrate, thawed (see Tip on page 283)	45 mL
1¹/₂ tsp	salt	7 mL
3 tbsp	granulated sugar	45 mL
3 tbsp	butter	45 mL
4¹/₄ cups	all-purpose flour or bread flour	1050 mL
¹/₄ cup	unsweetened cocoa powder	50 mL
1 tsp	bread machine yeast	5 mL
¹/₄ cup	raspberry jam	50 mL

1. Measure all ingredients *except raspberry jam* into baking pan in the order recommended by the manufacturer. Insert pan into the oven chamber. Select **Dough Cycle**.

2. Remove dough to a lightly floured surface. Cover with a large bowl and let rest for 10 to 15 minutes.

3. Roll out the dough into a 16- by 12-inch (40 by 30 cm) rectangle. Cut into 12 strips, each 1 inch (2.5 cm) wide and 16 inches (40 cm) long. On prepared baking sheet, beginning in the center, coil each strip into a circle, keeping the dough strips ¹/₄ inch (5 mm) apart. Tuck the ends under. Cover and let rise in a warm, draft-free place for 30 to 45 minutes, or until doubled in volume. Meanwhile, preheat oven to 375°F (190°C).

4. Spread each center with ¹/₂ to 1 tsp (2 to 5 mL) raspberry jam.

5. Bake for 20 to 30 minutes, or until Danish sound hollow when tapped on the bottom.

Sour Cherry Almond Kuchen

Kuchen is a fruit- or cheese-filled, yeast-raised cake that originated in Germany.

Tips

Thaw frozen sour cherries completely before adding; otherwise, the cold dough will take too long to rise.

Mash the almond paste with a fork. Don't worry about a few lumps; overmixing can make the filling too runny.

Variations

Substitute an equal amount of fresh, pitted sour cherries for the frozen. Dried sour cherries are neither as attractive nor as tasty in this recipe.

Substitute an equal amount of fresh blueberries or sliced apples for the sour cherries.

• Baking sheet, lightly greased

1 cup	milk	250 mL
1 tsp	almond extract	5 mL
1	egg	1
1 tsp	salt	5 mL
2 tbsp	granulated sugar	25 mL
1/4 cup	butter	50 mL
3 1/2 cups	all-purpose flour or bread flour	875 mL
1 tsp	ground cardamom	5 mL
1 tsp	bread machine yeast	5 mL

ALMOND FILLING

5 oz	almond paste	150 g
1	egg white, slightly beaten	1
1 cup	frozen sour cherries, thawed, well drained	250 mL
1/2 cup	slivered almonds, toasted	125 mL

1. Measure ingredients into baking pan in the order recommended by the manufacturer. Insert pan into the oven chamber. Select **Dough Cycle**.

2. *Filling:* In a bowl, combine almond paste and egg white; mix lightly with a fork. Set aside.

3. Remove dough to a lightly floured board; cover with a large bowl and let rest for 10 to 15 minutes.

4. Divide dough in half. Roll out each half to a 15- by 9-inch (38 by 23 cm) rectangle. Spread one rectangle with half of filling mixture to within $1/2$ inch (1 cm) of edges. Sprinkle with half the cherries and almonds. Beginning at the long side, roll jellyroll-style. Pinch to seal seam. Cut in half lengthwise, using sharp scissors to prevent crushing. Twist halves together, keeping cut-sides up, with filling visible. Place on prepared baking sheet. Shape into a ring. Repeat with the remaining half of the dough. Place to make a figure 8. Pinch ends together. Cover and let rise in a warm, draft-free place for 30 to 45 minutes, or until doubled in volume. Meanwhile, preheat oven to 375°F (190°C).

5. Bake in preheated oven for 30 to 35 minutes, or until kuchen sound hollow when tapped on the bottom.

Radar Kuchen

● *Baking sheet, lightly greased*

Here's a traditional German treat that your kids will love — twists of yeast dough, deep-fried, then dusted with icing sugar. The name comes from the German word raeder *(wheels), which refers to the cutting wheel used to shape the dough.*

1 cup	water	250 mL
2	eggs	2
1/4 cup	skim milk powder	50 mL
1 1/2 tsp	salt	7 mL
1/4 cup	granulated sugar	50 mL
1/4 cup	shortening	50 mL
3 3/4 cups	all-purpose flour or bread flour	925 mL
2 tsp	bread machine yeast	10 mL

LEMON GLAZE

1 cup	sifted icing sugar	250 mL
1 tbsp	lemon juice	15 mL
1 tbsp	water	15 mL

Tip

Start heating oil only when you are ready to fry the twists. Watch carefully!

Variation

Dust warm twists with sifted icing sugar instead of lemon glaze.

1. Measure ingredients into baking pan in the order recommended by the manufacturer. Insert pan into the oven chamber. Select **Dough Cycle**.

2. Remove dough to a lightly floured surface. Cover with a large bowl and let rest for 10 to 15 minutes.

3. Divide dough in half. Roll out each half to a 9- by 8-inch (23 by 20 cm) rectangle. Cut the dough into 3- by 2-inch (7.5 by 5 cm) rectangles. Cut a 1 1/2-inch (3 cm) slit lengthwise down the center of each rectangle. Tuck one end into the slit, gently pulling the end partway through. Cover and let rise in a warm, draft-free place for 30 to 45 minutes, or until doubled in volume. Meanwhile, preheat deep fryer to 350°F (180°C).

3. Deep-fry the kuchen for 30 to 40 seconds per side, or until golden brown. Drain on paper towels.

4. *Glaze:* In a small bowl, combine icing sugar, lemon juice and water; mix until smooth. Drizzle over warm kuchen.

Date Orange Bundles (page 284)

Overleaf: Summer Sunflower (page 318)

Nanaimo Bar Loaf

Tip

Some bread machines bake hotter than others. These may partially melt the chocolate chips in this recipe, giving the loaf a marbled look.

Yes, you're reading it right: The 1.5 lb (750 g) recipe contains the *same* amount of yeast as the 2 lb (1 kg).

Variation

Substitute white chocolate, butterscotch or peanut butter chips for the chocolate chips.

1.5 LB (750 G)		
1 cup	water	250 mL
1 tsp	salt	5 mL
3 tbsp	granulated sugar	45 mL
2 tbsp	shortening	25 mL
3 1/4 cups	all-purpose flour or bread flour	800 mL
1 tbsp	unsweetened cocoa powder	15 mL
1/2 cup	unsweetened flaked coconut	125 mL
1/2 cup	chopped pecans	125 mL
1/3 cup	chocolate chips	75 mL
1 1/2 tsp	bread machine yeast	7 mL

2 LB (1 KG)		
1 1/4 cups	water	300 mL
1 1/4 tsp	salt	6 mL
1/4 cup	granulated sugar	50 mL
2 tbsp	shortening	25 mL
3 3/4 cups	all-purpose flour or bread flour	925 mL
1 tbsp	unsweetened cocoa powder	15 mL
2/3 cup	unsweetened flaked coconut	150 mL
2/3 cup	chopped pecans	150 mL
1/2 cup	chocolate chips	125 mL
1 1/2 tsp	bread machine yeast	7 mL

1. Measure ingredients into baking pan in the order recommended by the manufacturer. Insert pan into the oven chamber.

2. Select **Sweet Cycle**.

Giant Pecan Sticky Buns (page 302)

Tips for Making
Perfect Shapes Every Time

- Follow the recipe instructions exactly. The quality of the finished product will depend on exact sizes, thicknesses and baking times.

- Measure lengths with a steel or plastic (not wooden) ruler. Wash it in the dishwasher between uses.

- Make all cuts using sharp scissors rather than a knife; this prevents the dough from being flattened.

- Work with one portion of dough at a time. Keep the remaining portions covered to prevent them from drying out.

- When making wreaths or braids, tuck all ends under; this helps to retain the desired shape during baking.

- For filled shapes, seal all seams and place dough seam-side down on the baking sheet. This holds the filling inside the dough during baking and prevents undesirable cracks from forming.

- In filled, rolled breads such as *Peanut Butter Banana Swirl Loaf* (see recipe, page 299), there is a tendency for large air bubbles to form under the top crust. To help prevent this (and the dough separating from the filling), poke several holes through the risen loaf with a long wooden skewer.

- To ensure that shapes don't disappear while baking, check after 10 to 15 minutes in the oven. If the features of the shapes have disappeared, remove the product from the oven and quickly re-cut or re-poke the shape to sharpen the features. Continue baking until done, then loosen the shapes from the baking sheet immediately. Use a long, flat metal spatula to slide the baked shapes onto a large rack to cool completely.

Donuts

It's said that donuts were invented when a hungry boy poked his finger into his mother's round fried yeast cakes. Everybody will love these homemade delights.

Tip

To fill jelly donuts, use a pastry bag with a ¼-inch (5 mm) hole in the end; press a little jelly or pie filling into the donuts through the slit. A cookie press or cake decorator with a straight tube can be used instead of the pastry bag.

Variation

To make jelly donuts, cut rolled dough with a 3½-inch (8 cm) round cookie cutter. Deep-fry; drain on paper towels. With a sharp, thin knife, pierce donuts from one side almost to the other and fill.

• *Baking sheet, lightly greased*

¾ cup	water	175 mL
2	eggs	2
¼ cup	skim milk powder	50 mL
1 tsp	salt	5 mL
¼ cup	granulated sugar	50 mL
⅓ cup	shortening	75 mL
3¼ cups	all-purpose flour or bread flour	800 mL
2 tsp	bread machine yeast	10 mL

1. Measure ingredients into baking pan in the order recommended by the manufacturer. Insert pan into oven chamber. Select **Dough Cycle**.

2. Remove dough to a lightly floured board; cover with a large bowl and let rest for 10 to 15 minutes.

3. Roll out to ½-inch (1 cm) thickness. Cut the dough with a 3½-inch (8 cm) donut cutter. Place on prepared baking sheet. Cover and let rise in a warm, draft-free place for 30 to 45 minutes, or until doubled in volume. Meanwhile, preheat deep fryer to 350°F (180°C).

4. Deep-fry for 30 to 45 seconds on each side, or until golden brown. Drain on paper towels. Dust warm donuts with sifted icing sugar.

Three Little Piggies

• *Two baking sheets, lightly greased*

1 1/2 cups	water	375 mL
1/4 cup	skim milk powder	50 mL
1 1/4 tsp	salt	6 mL
3 tbsp	packed brown sugar	45 mL
3 tbsp	shortening	45 mL
2 cups	whole wheat flour	500 mL
1 3/4 cups	all-purpose flour or bread flour	425 mL
1 1/2 tsp	bread machine yeast	7 mL
6	raisins	6

These nursery-rhyme characters are a great favorite in our house. Kids will have as much fun making them as eating them.

Tip

Check the piggies after 10 minutes of baking. If an ear or a tail needs to be repositioned, remove the baking sheet from the oven and gently (but quickly), move the piece(s) back into place.

Variation

Make piggie sandwiches: Carefully slice the piggies horizontally and fill with your choice of sandwich ingredients.

1. Measure all ingredients *except raisins* into baking pan in the order recommended by the manufacturer. Insert pan into the oven chamber. Select **Dough Cycle**.

2. Remove dough to a lightly floured surface. Cover with a large bowl and let rest for 10 to 15 minutes.

3. Divide dough into 10 portions. While making and assembling the "piggy parts," keep any dough you're not working with covered.

4. *Heads:* Roll out 3 portions into 5-inch (12.5 cm) circles. Place 1 circle on the center of a prepared baking sheet and the remaining circles well spaced on the other prepared baking sheet.

5. *Ears:* Pat 3 portions into 4- by 3-inch (10 by 7.5 cm) rectangles. Cut each in half diagonally to make 6 triangles. Tuck the short side of each triangle under the top of the heads, cut-side facing out. Fold the ends over, toward the center of the heads, to make typical floppy pig ears.

6. *Hooves:* Cut 2 portions into 3 pieces each. Form into 6 teardrop shapes. With a sharp knife, cut a small slit in the side of the teardrop to form a cloven hoof. Tuck the hooves securely under the bottom of the head.

7. *Tails:* Cut 1 portion into 3 pieces. Roll each into a long, thin 8-inch (20 cm) rope. Curl, then place between the ears, tucking one end under the head to secure.

8. *Snouts:* Divide the last portion into 3 pieces. Roll out each to a 2-inch (5 cm) circle. Position on the center of each head. Poke 2 fingers deep into the center to form nostrils. Add raisins for eyes.

9. Cover and let assembled dough shapes rise in a warm, draft-free place for 30 to 45 minutes, or until doubled in volume. Meanwhile, preheat oven to 350°F (180°C).

10. When dough has risen, poke the nostrils again. Bake in preheated oven for 20 to 30 minutes, or until piggies sound hollow when tapped on the bottom.

Summer Sunflower

● *Baking sheet, lightly greased*

Tip

To space "petals" evenly,
imagine the face of a
clock, and place petals
at 12, 3, 6 and 9; then
place remaining petals.

Variation

While sunflower is
still hot from the oven,
spoon a generous
portion of apricot
jam into the center
of each petal.

1/2 cup	water	125 mL
1/4 cup	fresh orange juice	50 mL
2 tsp	orange zest	10 mL
2	eggs	2
1 1/4 tsp	salt	6 mL
1/4 cup	granulated sugar	50 mL
3 tbsp	butter	45 mL
3 3/4 cups	all-purpose flour or bread flour	925 mL
1 1/2 tsp	bread machine yeast	7 mL

TOPPING

1	egg yolk, lightly beaten	1
3 to 4 tbsp	sunflower seeds	45 to 60 mL
	Raspberry jam	

ORANGE GLAZE

1 cup	sifted icing sugar	250 mL
2 tbsp	frozen orange juice concentrate, thawed (see Tip on page 283)	25 mL

1. Measure ingredients into baking pan in the order
   recommended by the manufacturer. Insert pan into
   the oven chamber. Select **Dough Cycle**.

2. Remove dough to a lightly floured surface. Cover
   with a large bowl and let rest for 10 to 15 minutes.

3. Roll out dough into a 12- by 9-inch (30 by 23 cm)
   rectangle. With a 3-inch (7.5 cm) donut cutter, cut
   into 12 donut shapes.

4. Arrange 3 donut holes in the center of the prepared baking sheet, making sure the sides of the holes touch. Arrange the remaining 9 donut holes to form a ring around the center 3, making sure the sides of the donut holes touch.

5. Place the donut shapes around the outside and touching the donut holes, stretching to form long, narrow sunflower-shaped petals.

6. *Topping:* Brush the donut holes with egg yolk and generously sprinkle with sunflower seeds.

7. Cover and let rise in a warm, draft-free place for 45 to 60 minutes, or until doubled in volume. Meanwhile, preheat oven to 350°F (180°C).

8. Bake in preheated oven for 20 to 30 minutes, or until sunflower sounds hollow when tapped on the bottom. While still hot, fill the petals with raspberry jam.

9. *Glaze:* In a small bowl, beat together sifted icing sugar and orange juice. Drizzle over the petals of the warm sunflower.

Soft Pretzels

• *Baking sheet, lightly greased*

Pretzels like these are usually available only from big-city street vendors or at rural county fairs. Now you can make them at home with your bread machine.

1¼ cups	water	300 mL
1¼ tsp	salt	6 mL
2 tbsp	granulated sugar	25 mL
1 tbsp	shortening	15 mL
3½ cups	all-purpose flour or bread flour	875 mL
1 tsp	bread machine yeast	5 mL

TOPPING

1	egg	1
1 tbsp	water	15 mL
¼ cup	sesame seeds or sea salt	50 mL

Tip

Allowing the dough to rest for an extra 5 minutes makes it easier to handle.

Variation

For an authentic old-world flavor, use beer (at room temperature) instead of water in the pretzel recipe.

1. Measure pretzel ingredients into baking pan in the order recommended by the manufacturer. Insert pan into the oven chamber. Select **Dough Cycle**.

2. Remove dough to a lightly floured surface. Cover with a large bowl and let rest for 10 to 15 minutes.

3. Divide dough into 12 equal portions. Roll each into a 16-inch (40 cm) rope. On prepared baking sheet, form each rope into a circle. Grasping one end in each hand, cross the left end over the right and twist once, then bring the top of the circle over the twisted ends. Meanwhile, preheat oven to 350°F (180°C).

4. *Topping:* In a small bowl, whisk together egg and water. Brush unrisen dough with topping. Sprinkle with sesame seeds or salt.

5. Bake in preheated oven for 20 to 25 minutes, or until pretzels sound hollow when tapped on the bottom.

Tips for Handling Coffee Cakes

Here are a few suggestions for keeping coffee cakes fresh.

1. Cooling
Remove coffee cake from the pan as soon as it is baked. Turn right-side up and cool completely on a wire rack before wrapping airtight.

2. Freezing
Coffee cakes freeze well. Make several, divide into quarters or eighths and then freeze in mix-and-match packages. Wrap airtight in plastic wrap and then either over-wrap with aluminum foil or place in zippered plastic bags. For individual servings, cut and wrap in plastic, then place in airtight freezer bags. Freeze, un-iced, for up to 6 weeks.

3. Thawing
To prevent the coffee cake from drying out, thaw in the refrigerator, wrapped in the original wrapper.

4. Icing/Glazing
For a more attractive finish, ice and decorate with slivered nuts and fruit after thawing.

Serve this autumn treat warm accompanied by a wedge of aged Cheddar cheese.

Tip

Press apple wedges firmly into the dough to keep them in place during rising and baking.

Variation

Substitute 1 cup (250 mL) fresh or thawed frozen cranberries for the apples in the filling and topping.

Dutch Apple Coffee Cake with Cinnamon Streusel Topping

● *13- by 9-inch (3 L) baking pan, lightly greased*

1 cup	milk	250 mL
1/4 cup	unsweetened applesauce	50 mL
1	egg	1
3/4 tsp	salt	3 mL
1/4 cup	granulated sugar	50 mL
2 tbsp	butter	25 mL
3 1/2 cups	all-purpose flour or bread flour	900 mL
1 1/4 tsp	bread machine yeast	6 mL

APPLE FILLING

3	Granny Smith apples, cut into 1/2-inch (1 cm) wedges	3
1/4 cup	packed brown sugar	50 mL
1 tsp	ground cinnamon	5 mL

STREUSEL TOPPING

2 tbsp	soft butter	25 mL
1/4 cup	flour	50 mL
1/4 cup	packed brown sugar	50 mL
2 tbsp	slivered almonds	25 mL
1/4 tsp	ground cinnamon	1 mL

1. Measure cake ingredients into baking pan in the order recommended by the manufacturer. Insert pan into the oven chamber. Select **Dough Cycle**.

2. *Filling:* In a bowl, gently toss together filling ingredients; set aside.

3. Remove dough to a lightly floured board; cover with a large bowl and let rest for 10 to 15 minutes.

4. Divide dough in half. Roll out each into a 13- by 9-inch (33 by 23 cm) rectangle. Place one rectangle of dough in prepared pan. Press half the apple filling mixture into the dough in lengthwise rows. Gently top with the remaining dough. Press remaining filling mixture into dough in lengthwise rows.

5. *Topping:* In a bowl, combine topping ingredients. Sprinkle evenly over cake. Cover and let rise in a warm, draft-free place for 30 to 45 minutes, or until doubled in volume. Meanwhile, preheat oven to 375°F (190°C).

6. Bake in preheated oven for 35 to 40 minutes, or until coffee cake sounds hollow when tapped on the bottom. If necessary, cover loosely with foil for the last 10 to 15 minutes to prevent excess browning.

Apricot Walnut Coffee Cake

Welcome new neighbors with this fresh-from-the-oven coffee cake.

Tip

Snip dried apricots into ¼-inch (5 mm) pieces with sharp scissors.

Variation

Substitute chopped fresh dates or dried apples for half of the apricots in this filling.

● *Baking sheet, lightly greased*

¾ cup	peach or apricot yogurt	175 mL
⅓ cup	water	75 mL
1	egg	1
¾ tsp	salt	3 mL
¼ cup	granulated sugar	50 mL
2 tbsp	butter	25 mL
3⅓ cups	all-purpose flour or bread flour	825 mL
1½ tsp	bread machine yeast	7 mL

APRICOT WALNUT FILLING

¼ cup	packed brown sugar	50 mL
½ tsp	ground cinnamon	2 mL
1 cup	finely chopped dried apricots	250 mL
¾ cup	finely chopped walnuts	175 mL
¼ cup	soft butter	50 mL

APRICOT GLAZE

¼ cup	apricot jam	50 mL

1. Measure cake ingredients into baking pan in the order recommended by the manufacturer. Insert pan into the oven chamber. Select **Dough Cycle**.

2. *Filling:* In a bowl, combine brown sugar and cinnamon. Toss gently with apricots and walnuts; set aside.

3. Remove dough to a lightly floured board; cover with a large bowl and let rest for 10 to 15 minutes.

4. Roll out the dough to a 16- by 8-inch (40 by 20 cm) rectangle. Spread softened butter over dough; sprinkle with two-thirds of the filling. Roll jellyroll style. Using sharp scissors, cut the roll in half lengthwise. Beginning in the center of prepared baking sheet, loosely coil 1 strip of dough, cut-side up. Loosely coil the second strip of dough around the first strip, tucking the end under. Sprinkle with the remaining filling. Cover and let rise in a warm, draft-free place for 30 to 45 minutes, or until doubled in volume. Meanwhile, preheat oven to 375°F (190°C).

5. Bake in preheated oven for 35 to 40 minutes, or until coffee cake sounds hollow when tapped on the bottom. If necessary, cover loosely with foil for the last 10 to 15 minutes to prevent excess browning.

6. *Glaze:* Warm apricot jam in the microwave for 10 to 20 seconds and drizzle over warm coffee cake.

Freshly picked blueberries make this coffee cake a special treat.

Tip

Thawed frozen blueberries or pie filling can be substituted for the freshly picked. You may need to adjust the amount of sugar in the filling. Taste the berries and sweeten if necessary.

Variation

Substitute other seasonal fruits, such as raspberries or strawberries, for the blueberries.

Blueberry Nutmeg Round with Lemon Glaze

● *Two 10-inch (25 cm) springform pans, lightly greased*

1 1/4 cups	sour cream	300 mL
2 tsp	lemon juice	10 mL
2	eggs	2
3/4 tsp	salt	4 mL
1/4 cup	honey	50 mL
2 tbsp	butter	25 mL
3 3/4 cups	all-purpose flour or bread flour	925 mL
1/4 tsp	ground allspice	2 mL
2 tsp	lemon zest	10 mL
1 1/4 tsp	bread machine yeast	6 mL

BLUEBERRY FILLING

4 cups	fresh blueberries	1 L
4 tsp	lemon zest	20 mL
1/2 tsp	ground allspice	2 mL

LEMON GLAZE

1 cup	sifted icing sugar	250 mL
4 to 5 tsp	fresh lemon juice	20 to 25 mL

1. Measure dough ingredients into baking pan in the order recommended by the manufacturer. Insert pan into the oven chamber. Select **Dough Cycle**.

2. *Filling:* In a bowl, combine filling ingredients; set aside.

3. Remove dough to a lightly floured board; cover with a large bowl and let rest for 10 to 15 minutes.

4. Divide dough in half. Stretch each half into prepared pan. Make a cut around the entire edge, 1 inch (2.5 cm) deep and ¾ inch (1.5 cm) from the edge. Sprinkle half the filling over inner circle of each piece of dough. Cover and let rise in a warm, draft-free place for 30 to 45 minutes, or until doubled in volume. Meanwhile, preheat oven to 375°F (190°C).

5. Bake in preheated oven for 35 to 40 minutes or until coffee cakes sound hollow when tapped on the bottom. If necessary, cover loosely with foil for the last 10 to 15 minutes to prevent excess browning.

6. *Glaze:* In a small bowl, stir together glaze ingredients until smooth. Drizzle over warm coffee cakes.

Cranberry Walnut Kaffeekuchen

This variation of traditional German kaffeekuchen (or coffee cake) is ideal served for breakfast or dessert.

Tip

Spread the filling right to the edge of the dough. Place the springform pans on baking sheets to catch any overflow in the oven.

Variation

For two different desserts, reduce the cranberry filling by half and use for only one of the cakes. For the second cake, try the filling from *Blueberry Peach Streusel Cake* (see recipe, page 280), using half the quantity given in the recipe — or use any filling you like.

• *Two 10-inch (25 cm) springform pans, lightly greased*

$1/2$ cup	water	125 mL
$1/2$ cup	fresh orange juice	125 mL
2 tsp	orange zest	10 mL
1	egg	1
$1^1/2$ tsp	salt	7 mL
$1/4$ cup	granulated sugar	50 mL
2 tbsp	butter	25 mL
3 cups	all-purpose flour or bread flour	750 mL
$1/3$ cup	buttermilk powder	75 mL
$1/2$ tsp	ground allspice	2 mL
$1^1/2$ tsp	bread machine yeast	7 mL

CRANBERRY FILLING

3 cups	fresh cranberries	750 mL
1 cup	maple syrup	250 mL

WALNUT TOPPING

$2/3$ cup	granulated sugar	150 mL
$2/3$ cup	all-purpose flour	150 mL
4 tsp	orange zest	20 mL
2 tsp	ground ginger	10 mL
$1/2$ cup	butter	125 mL
2 cups	chopped walnuts	500 mL

1. Measure cake ingredients into baking pan in the order recommended by the manufacturer. Insert pan into the oven chamber. Select **Dough Cycle**.

2. *Filling:* In a saucepan, combine cranberries and maple syrup. Bring to a boil. Simmer for 4 to 6 minutes, or until the cranberries open. Remove from heat; set aside.

3. *Topping:* In a large bowl, combine sugar, flour, zest and ginger. With a pastry blender, cut in the butter until crumbly. Add walnuts; set aside.

4. Remove dough to a lightly floured surface. Cover with a large bowl and let rest for 10 to 15 minutes.

5. Divide dough in half. Press one portion of the dough into one of the prepared pans. Top with half the cranberry filling and sprinkle with half the walnut topping. Repeat with the second pan. Cover and let rise in a warm, draft-free place for 45 to 60 minutes, or until doubled in volume. Meanwhile, preheat oven to 350°F (180°C).

6. Bake in preheated oven for 40 to 45 minutes, or until kaffeekuchen is golden brown. Serve warm or cold.

Hazelnut Plum Ladder Loaf

Late fall is the perfect time to find fresh plums. This coffee cake complements a caffè latte or the raspberry aroma of a café leray.

Tip

For a deep plum color and flavor, use red or purple varieties of sweet plums.

Variation

When fresh plums are unavailable, substitute a high-quality plum preserve or a commercial pie filling, either "Double Fruit" or "Extra Light" varieties.

● *Baking sheet, lightly greased*

1 1/4 cups	milk	300 mL
1	egg	1
3/4 tsp	salt	4 mL
1/4 cup	granulated sugar	50 mL
2 tbsp	butter	25 mL
3 3/4 cups	all-purpose flour or bread flour	925 mL
1 1/4 tsp	bread machine yeast	6 mL

HAZELNUT PLUM FILLING

2 cups	ripe plums, pitted and halved	500 mL
1/2 cup	sliced hazelnuts	125 mL

STREUSEL TOPPING

2 tbsp	all-purpose flour	25 mL
2 tbsp	slivered hazelnuts	25 mL
1 tbsp	packed brown sugar	15 mL
1 tbsp	soft butter	15 mL
1/4 tsp	ground nutmeg	1 mL

1. Measure loaf ingredients into baking pan in the order recommended by the manufacturer. Insert pan into the oven chamber. Select **Dough Cycle**.

2. *Filling:* In a bowl, gently combine plums and hazelnuts; set aside.

3. Remove dough to a lightly floured board; cover with a large bowl and let rest for 10 to 15 minutes.

4. Divide dough in half. Roll out each half into an 18-by 9-inch (45 by 23 cm) rectangle. Spread half of the filling ingredients in a 3-inch (7.5 cm) wide strip lengthwise down the center third of rectangle. With scissors, snip diagonally from edge of dough to edge of filling. Make cuts 3 inches (7.5 cm) long and 1 inch (2.5 cm) apart along both sides of rectangle. Fold strips over filling, alternating sides. Tuck in ends. Place on prepared baking sheet. Repeat with the second half of dough. Cover and let rise in a warm, draft-free place for 30 to 45 minutes, or until doubled in volume. Meanwhile, preheat oven to 375°F (190°C).

5. *Topping:* Mix topping ingredients and sprinkle over the risen dough.

6. Bake in preheated oven for 35 to 40 minutes, or until loaves sound hollow when tapped on the bottom. If necessary, cover loosely with foil for the last 10 to 15 minutes to prevent excess browning.

Raspberry Almond Streusel Coffee Cake

The Swedish enjoy baked sweets, rich in almonds, with their coffee. Join this tradition with our streusel coffee cake.

Variations

Choose a "lite" "Double Fruit" jam for the freshest taste.

Substitute chopped pecans for the almonds in the topping.

• 13- by 9-inch (3 L) baking dish, lightly greased

1¼ cups	milk	300 mL
1	egg	1
¾ tsp	salt	3 mL
¼ cup	granulated sugar	50 mL
2 tbsp	butter	25 mL
3¾ cups	all-purpose flour or bread flour	925 mL
1¼ tsp	bread machine yeast	6 mL

RASPBERRY FILLING

¼ to ⅓ cup	raspberry jam	50 to 75 mL

STREUSEL TOPPING

2 tbsp	soft butter	25 mL
¼ cup	all-purpose flour	50 mL
¼ cup	slivered almonds	50 mL
2 tbsp	packed brown sugar	25 mL
½ tsp	ground nutmeg	2 mL

1. Measure cake ingredients into baking pan in the order recommended by the manufacturer. Insert pan into the oven chamber. Select **Dough Cycle**.

2. *Topping:* In a bowl, combine topping ingredients until crumbly; set aside.

3. Remove dough to a lightly floured board; cover with a large bowl and let rest for 10 to 15 minutes.

4. Press dough into prepared baking dish. With the handle of a wooden spoon, press holes into the dough three-quarters of the way through. Do not press to the bottom of the pan. Fill each hole with a ¼ tsp (1 mL) of raspberry jam. Sprinkle prepared streusel topping over coffee cake. Cover and let rise in a warm, draft-free place for 30 to 45 minutes, or until doubled in volume. Meanwhile, preheat oven to 375°F (190°C).

5. Bake in preheated oven for 35 to 40 minutes, or until coffee cake sounds hollow when tapped on the bottom. If necessary, cover loosely with foil for the last 10 to 15 minutes to prevent excess browning.

Springtime Rhubarb Crunch Coffee Cake

The first harvest of rhubarb heralds the arrival of spring. Here, its tart flavor is combined with oatmeal, giving this coffee cake added crunch.

Tip

For the most attractive filling, choose thin stalks of ruby red strawberry rhubarb.

Variation

Substitute fresh or frozen thawed strawberries for half the rhubarb.

● *13- by 9-inch (3 L) baking pan, lightly greased*

1 cup	milk	250 mL
1	egg	1
3/4 tsp	salt	3 mL
1/4 cup	granulated sugar	50 mL
2 tbsp	butter	25 mL
3 1/4 cups	all-purpose flour or bread flour	800 mL
1 tsp	bread machine yeast	5 mL

RHUBARB FILLING

5 cups	fresh or thawed frozen rhubarb chunks	1.25 L
1/3 cup	all-purpose flour	75 mL
3/4 cup	granulated sugar	175 mL
2 tsp	lemon zest	10 mL

OATMEAL TOPPING

1 1/2 cups	rolled oats	375 mL
1/3 cup	packed brown sugar	75 mL
1/4 cup	soft butter	50 mL
1 tsp	ground nutmeg	5 mL

1. Measure ingredients into baking pan in the order recommended by the manufacturer. Insert pan into the oven chamber. Select **Dough Cycle**.

2. *Filling:* In a small saucepan over low heat, combine rhubarb and flour; cook until tender. (Or combine in a bowl and cook in microwave.) Drain excess liquid. Add sugar and lemon zest; stir to dissolve sugar. Cool before using; set aside.

3. Remove dough to a lightly floured board; cover with a large bowl and let rest for 10 to 15 minutes.

4. Stretch into prepared baking pan. Spread filling evenly over dough to within $\frac{1}{2}$ inch (1 cm) of the edges.

5. *Topping:* In a bowl, combine topping ingredients until well mixed; sprinkle over cake.

6. Cover and let rise in a warm, draft-free place for 30 to 45 minutes, or until doubled in volume. Meanwhile, preheat oven to 375°F (190°C).

7. Bake in preheated oven for 35 to 40 minutes, or until cake sounds hollow when tapped on the bottom. If necessary, cover loosely with foil for the last 10 to 15 minutes to prevent excess browning.

Toppings and Glazes

Drizzle glaze over cake while it is still warm. It will coat and drip attractively down the edges of the cake. If the cake is too hot, however, the glaze will simply disappear into the cake. Before applying icings, baked goods should cool completely. Use a pastry tube for creative icing patterns.

Try some of these toppings and glazes:

Cinnamon Streusel
Combine until crumbly $1/4$ cup (50 mL) soft butter, $1/4$ cup (50 mL) packed brown sugar, $1/4$ cup (50 mL) all-purpose flour, $1/3$ cup (75 mL) raisins and $1/2$ tsp (2 mL) ground cinnamon.

Almond Glaze
Combine until smooth $3/4$ cup (175 mL) sifted icing sugar, 4 to 5 tsp (20 to 25 mL) milk and $1/4$ tsp (1 mL) almond extract.

Orange Glaze
Combine until smooth 1 cup (250 mL) sifted icing sugar and 4 to 5 tsp (20 to 25 mL) orange juice concentrate.

Corn Syrup Glaze
For a sticky bun taste, brush with 2 tbsp (25 mL) corn syrup just before baking.

Lemon Glaze
Combine until smooth 1 cup (250 mL) sifted icing sugar and 4 to 5 tsp (20 to 25 mL) fresh lemon juice.

Raspberry Almond Streusel
Coffee Cake (page 332)

Beyond Breads

As you might expect, a bread machine is wonderful for baking breads and loaves. But it can do so much more — like make fresh pasta, cakes and cookies, even jams and jellies. Try these recipes and discover all the possibilities for yourself.

Lemon Cake (page 344)

Tips for Making Perfect Pasta

- Depending on the bread machine you use, some recipes for pasta dough in this chapter may be a little too dry. In such cases, try adding 1 to 2 tsp (5 to 10 mL) extra water.

- Some bread machines can produce smooth, workable dough in a single **Pasta Cycle**, while others require 2 or 3 cycles. Repeat cycle as often as necessary to ensure that all dry ingredients are incorporated.

- When using the **Dough Cycle**, allow bread machine to knead just as long as necessary to ensure that all dry ingredients are incorporated.

- Rolling and cutting the dough is much easier with a pasta machine — and the instructions in our recipes assume you will be using one. If you don't have a pasta machine, however, you can make do with a rolling pin and a sharp knife.

- Keep pasta dough in a plastic bag until it is rolled and cut. It loses moisture and dries out quickly, making it difficult to work through the pasta machine.

- Roll pasta dough to a thickness of $1/16$ to $1/8$ inch (1 to 2 mm). Thicker pasta dough is easier to work with.

- When using a pasta machine, work with only a small amount of dough at a time. Continue to feed through the smooth rollers of the pasta machine until dough is smooth, shiny and pliable. Depending on the consistency of the pasta dough produced by your bread machine, this may require 8 (or more) repetitions.

- Cook fresh pasta in a large amount of boiling water only until it is al dente (tender but firm). Cooking will take longer for thicker pasta.

- If not serving immediately, rinse cooked pasta under cold water to stop further cooking. Drain and refrigerate for up to 3 days or freeze for up to 1 month.

Basic Fresh Pasta (Spaghetti)

2/3 cup	water	150 mL
1	egg	1
2 tbsp	extra virgin olive oil	25 mL
1 tsp	salt	5 mL
2 1/2 cups	semolina flour	625 mL

Tips

A pasta machine is invaluable for making straight, uniformly shaped pasta. But if you don't have one, you can always use a rolling pin and a sharp knife.

Store fresh cooked pasta in the refrigerator for up to 3 days. Reheat pasta in boiling water for 1 to 2 minutes, being careful not to overcook it.

Variations

Substitute pasta flour for the semolina flour.

Try using a flavored olive oil instead of the plain variety.

1. Measure ingredients into baking pan in the order recommended by the manufacturer. Insert pan into the oven chamber. Select **Pasta** or **Dough Cycle**.

2. With a rubber spatula, scrape down sides of baking pan and kneading blade. Remove dough to a lightly floured surface.

3. Divide dough into 4 to 6 portions; place in a plastic bag to prevent drying. Position the rollers of pasta machine at the widest point. Using one portion at a time, roll the dough, then fold it either lengthwise or crosswise. Continue rolling and folding dough until smooth, shiny and elastic. If dough is sticky, dust with flour.

4. Begin to roll dough thinner by positioning the rollers closer and closer together. Continue until the pasta is between $1/8$ and $1/4$ inch (2 and 5 mm) thick. Replace the smooth roller with a spaghetti cutter and cut dough to desired length and width.

5. Cook in a large pot of boiling salted water for 3 to 5 minutes, or until al dente.

Fresh Spinach Pasta (Fettuccine)

Spinach adds color, flavor and extra nutrients to this pasta. Use the dough to make fettuccine (as here) or any other type you wish.

Tips

Fresh pasta cooks much faster than dried pasta. If you're not careful, it will turn from al dente to mush before you know it.

A pasta machine is invaluable for making straight, uniformly shaped pasta. But if you don't have one, you can always use a rolling pin and a sharp knife.

Variation

Use fresh or frozen cooked spinach for this recipe; just be sure it is well drained.

$1/3$ cup	water	75 mL
2	eggs	2
$1/4$ cup	finely chopped drained cooked spinach	50 mL
2 tbsp	extra virgin olive oil	25 mL
$1/2$ tsp	salt	2 mL
$2 1/2$ cups	semolina flour	625 mL

1. Measure ingredients into baking pan in the order recommended by the manufacturer. Insert pan into the oven chamber. Select **Pasta** or **Dough Cycle**.

2. With a rubber spatula, scrape down sides of baking pan and kneading blade. Remove dough to a lightly floured surface.

3. Divide dough into 4 to 6 portions; place in a plastic bag to prevent drying. Position the rollers of pasta machine at the widest point. Using one portion at a time, roll the dough, then fold it either lengthwise or crosswise. Continue rolling and folding dough until smooth, shiny and elastic. If dough is sticky, dust with flour.

4. Begin to roll thinner by positioning the rollers closer and closer together. Continue until the pasta is between $1/8$ and $1/4$ inch (2 and 5 mm) thick. Replace smooth roller with a fettuccine cutter and cut dough to desired length and width.

5. Cook in a large amount of boiling salted water for 3 to 5 minutes, or until al dente.

Fresh Tomato-Herb Pasta

Tips

Use dry (not oil-packed)
sun-dried tomatoes.

A pasta machine is
invaluable for making
straight, uniformly
shaped pasta. But if
you don't have one,
you can always use
a rolling pin and a
sharp knife.

1/3 cup	water	75 mL
2	eggs	2
3 tbsp	tomato paste	45 mL
1/4 cup	finely snipped sun-dried tomatoes	50 mL
2 tbsp	extra virgin olive oil	25 mL
1/2 tsp	salt	2 mL
2 1/2 cups	semolina flour	625 mL
3 tbsp	packed snipped fresh basil leaves	45 mL

1. Measure ingredients into baking pan in the order recommended by the manufacturer. Insert pan into the oven chamber. Select **Pasta** or **Dough Cycle**.

2. With a rubber spatula, scrape down sides of baking pan and kneading blade. Remove dough to a lightly floured surface.

3. Divide dough into 4 to 6 portions; place in a plastic bag to prevent drying. Position the rollers of pasta machine at the widest point. Using one portion at a time, roll the dough, then fold it either lengthwise or crosswise. Continue rolling and folding dough until smooth, shiny and elastic. If dough is sticky, dust with flour.

4. Begin to roll thinner by positioning the rollers closer and closer together. Continue until the pasta is between 1/8 and 1/4 inch (2 and 5 mm) thick. Replace smooth roller with a cutter and cut dough to length and width desired.

5. Cook in a large amount of boiling salted water for 3 to 5 minutes, or until al dente.

Tips for Making Cakes and Cookies in Your Bread Machine

- Before attempting these recipes, read your bread machine manual for any information about making cakes and cookies. Follow any instructions carefully.

- Add the ingredients in the order recommended in the recipe.

- Cut soft shortening, cream cheese and butter into 1-inch (2.5 cm) cubes before adding.

- All ingredients should be at room temperature or warmed according to the recipe instructions. Refrigerated eggs can be warmed in the shell by placing them in a bowl of hot (but not boiling) water for 5 minutes.

- To ensure even mixing, scrape the corners, sides and bottom of the baking pan with a rubber or plastic spatula to incorporate all dry ingredients.

- To bake completely, some cakes must be left in the bread machine baking pan, using the **Keep Warm Cycle** or **Bake Cycle**. The cake is done when a long wooden skewer inserted into the center of the cake comes out clean.

- Cool cakes in baking pan for 10 minutes, then turn out onto a wire rack to cool completely.

- If using your bread machine to bake a commercially prepared cake mix, choose the large 15- to 18-oz (400 to 550 g) size. The "pudding-in-the-mix" type works best.

Banana Quick Bread

½ cup	milk (room temperature)	125 mL
1 cup	mashed ripe bananas	250 mL
2	eggs	2
½ tsp	salt	2 mL
1 cup	granulated sugar	250 mL
½ cup	vegetable oil	125 mL
2 cups	all-purpose flour	500 mL
2 tsp	baking powder	10 mL
1 tsp	baking soda	5 mL
½ cup	chopped walnuts	125 mL

Fast and easy to prepare, this bread makes a great snack for the family or a nice housewarming gift for a new neighbor.

Tips

Test for doneness by inserting a long wooden skewer into the center of the quick bread. If it comes out clean, the bread is fully baked.

For a moist "quick bread" texture, cool overnight before slicing.

Some bread machines may require up to 50 minutes on the **Keep Warm Cycle** before the quick bread is baked. For specifications on the length of this cycle, and for information on how to use it, check the user's manual for your bread machine.

1. Measure ingredients into baking pan in the order recommended by the manufacturer. Insert pan into the oven chamber. Select **Cake Cycle**.

2. Halfway through mixing time, using a rubber spatula, scrape down sides of baking pan and the kneading blade.

3. When signal sounds indicating the end of cycle, test for doneness with a wooden skewer. If ready, remove baking pan from bread machine. If not, keep in bread machine on **Keep Warm Cycle** for 10 to 30 minutes or on **Bake Cycle** until baked.

4. Set baking pan on a cooling rack for 10 minutes. Turn cake out onto a serving plate and set aside to cool completely.

Lemon Cake

1	package (18 oz/510 g) yellow, golden or lemon pudding cake mix	1
1 cup	water	250 mL
3	eggs	3
1/3 cup	vegetable oil	75 mL
1 tbsp	fresh lemon juice	15 mL
2 tsp	grated lemon zest	10 mL

LEMON SYRUP

1/2 cup	granulated sugar	125 mL
3 tbsp	fresh lemon juice	45 mL

Need a quick dessert for unexpected dinner guests? This one bakes while you eat. Serve with fruit or ice cream.

Tip

Using a cake mix may seem like "cheating" — but with all the fresh lemon flavor in this recipe, no one will ever know your secret! We always keep a cake mix in the cupboard for emergencies.

Variation

For an orange version of this cake, substitute orange juice and zest for the lemon, both in the cake and the syrup.

1. Measure cake ingredients into baking pan in the order recommended by the manufacturer. Insert pan into the oven chamber. Select **Cake Cycle**.

2. Halfway through mixing time, using a rubber spatula, scrape down sides of baking pan and kneading blade.

3. When signal sounds indicating the end of cycle, test for doneness with a wooden skewer. If ready, remove baking pan from bread machine. If not, keep in bread machine on **Keep Warm Cycle** for 10 to 30 minutes or on **Bake Cycle** until baked.

4. *Syrup:* In a small saucepan over low heat, combine sugar and lemon juice. Heat, stirring constantly, until sugar is dissolved.

5. With a long wooden skewer, poke several holes through the cake as soon as it is removed from the bread machine. Spoon warm syrup over the hot cake. Set baking pan on a cooling rack for 30 minutes. Turn cake out onto a serving plate and set aside to cool completely.

Pineapple Coconut Cake

Here's a delicious made-from-scratch cake prepared in the bread machine. It's quick and easy — and there's only one pan to wash!

Tip

Test for doneness by inserting a long wooden skewer into the center of the cake. If it comes out clean, the cake is fully baked.

Variations

For a different texture, replace flaked coconut with shredded coconut.

Add ½ cup (125 mL) chopped pecans.

1 cup	granulated sugar	250 mL
½ cup	shortening or vegetable oil	125 mL
2	eggs, slightly beaten	2
¾ tsp	orange extract	4 mL
1	can (8 oz/227 mL) crushed pineapple, with juice	1
1 tsp	salt	5 mL
2¼ cups	all-purpose flour or bread flour	550 mL
4 tsp	baking powder	20 mL
¾ cup	unsweetened flaked coconut	175 mL
2 tsp	grated orange zest	10 mL

1. Measure sugar and shortening into baking pan. Add eggs. Insert pan into the oven chamber. Select **Cake Cycle**.

2. Two minutes into mixing time, using a rubber spatula, scrape down sides of baking pan and kneading blade. Stop bread machine after 5 minutes of mixing.

3. Remove baking pan from machine. Add orange extract, pineapple (with juice), salt, flour, baking powder, coconut and zest. Insert pan into the oven chamber. Select **Cake Cycle**.

4. Halfway through mixing time, using a rubber spatula, scrape down sides of baking pan and kneading blade.

5. When signal sounds indicating the end of cycle, test for doneness with a wooden skewer. If ready, remove baking pan from bread machine. If not, keep in bread machine on **Keep Warm Cycle** for 10 to 30 minutes or on **Bake Cycle** until baked. Set baking pan on a cooling rack for 10 minutes. Turn cake out onto a serving plate and set aside to cool completely.

Oatmeal Raisin Bars

• *9-inch (2.5 L) square baking pan, lightly greased*

⅓ cup	melted butter	75 mL
⅔ cup	packed brown sugar	150 mL
2	eggs	2
1 tsp	vanilla	5 mL
1 tsp	salt	5 mL
1 cup	all-purpose flour	250 mL
2 cups	quick-cooking oats	500 mL
1 tsp	baking powder	5 mL
1½ cups	raisins	375 mL

Make these tasty bars for school lunches — just don't tell the kids they're nutritious!

Tips

To blend all the ingredients thoroughly, thick cookie doughs may need to be processed through the **Mixing Cycle** 2 or 3 times.

If your bread machine doesn't have a **Mixing Cycle**, use the **Dough Cycle**; keep an eye on the dough and stop cycle when mixing is complete.

Variation

Oatmeal Raisin Cookies: Drop prepared dough, by the spoonful, onto a lightly greased baking sheet. Bake in preheated oven for 10 to 12 minutes, or until baked. Remove from baking sheet and cool on a rack.

1. Measure ingredients into baking pan in the order recommended by the manufacturer. Insert pan into the oven chamber. Select **Mixing Cycle**.

2. Halfway through mixing time, using a rubber spatula, scrape down sides of baking pan and kneading blade. (If ingredients are not well mixed, restart the **Mixing Cycle**.) Meanwhile, preheat oven to 350°F (180°C).

3. When signal sounds indicating the end of cycle, remove baking pan from bread machine. Press dough into prepared pan.

4. Bake in preheated oven for 30 to 35 minutes, or until bars are firm to the touch and golden.

Raspberry Cheesecake

1 cup	granulated sugar	250 mL
2	packages (each 8 oz/250 g) cream cheese (room temperature)	2
4	eggs, warmed (see Tip, at left)	4
3/4 cup	raspberry-flavored yogurt	175 mL
1/2 tsp	lemon juice	2 mL
1/8 tsp	salt	0.5 mL
2 tbsp	all-purpose flour or bread flour	25 mL
1	package (10 oz/300 g) frozen sweetened raspberries, thawed	1

Can you really make cheesecake in a bread machine? Absolutely! And here's the recipe that proves it.

Tips

Check the manufacturer's instructions for the length of the **Kneading Cycle**. It should be approximately 7 to 8 minutes.

To prevent lumps from forming, soften cream cheese completely before adding to the pan.

To warm eggs, place in a bowl of hot (not boiling) water for 5 minutes.

Variation

Use any fruit-flavored yogurt and a matching fruit topping.

1. Measure sugar and cream cheese into baking pan. Insert pan into the oven chamber. Select **Cake Cycle**. (If available, select the 1.5 lb (750 g) loaf size with a light crust setting.) One minute before the mixing ends, press Stop. With a rubber spatula, scrape sides of baking pan and kneading blade.

2. Add eggs, yogurt, lemon juice, salt and flour. Select **Cake Cycle**. (If desired, remove the kneading blade after the kneading is complete but before the cheesecake begins to bake; this eliminates the kneading blade-sized hole in the cheesecake.) When signal sounds indicating end of cycle, test for doneness. A stainless steel knife inserted in the middle should come out clean. If not completely baked, keep in bread machine on **Keep Warm Cycle** for 10 to 30 minutes or on **Bake Cycle** until baked.

3. Set baking pan on a cooling rack for 10 minutes. Carefully turn cheesecake out onto a serving plate and set aside to cool completely, then refrigerate.

4. *To serve:* In a food processor or blender, purée thawed raspberries. Press through a fine sieve. Spoon purée onto individual serving plates. Top with cheesecake.

Tips for Making Jams and Jellies

• Before attempting these recipes, read your bread machine manual for information about making jams and jellies. Follow any instructions carefully.

• To prevent jam from boiling over, don't exceed quantities given in recipes.

• Use oven mitts when handling hot jam — it's hotter than fat used in deep frying!

• Pour jam into sterilized jars. Store in the refrigerator for 3 to 4 weeks. Don't forget to date the product.

MAKES 2½ CUPS

Apple Jelly

3 cups	unsweetened apple juice	750 mL
1 cup	granulated sugar	250 mL
2 tbsp	unflavored gelatin	25 mL
1 tbsp	lemon juice	15 mL

You don't need seasonal fruit to make this jelly — it's easy to prepare all year round.

Tip

Jelly will appear very thin at first. But don't worry — it will thicken as it cools in the refrigerator.

Variation

Substitute white grape juice or any other type of unsweetened fruit juice for the apple juice.

1. Measure ingredients into baking pan in the order recommended by the manufacturer. Insert pan into the oven chamber. Select **Jam Cycle**.

2. When cycle is complete, wait for 15 minutes before opening lid or removing baking pan. Wearing oven mitts, carefully remove the baking pan from the bread machine. Cool in pan for at least 30 minutes.

3. Pour jelly into sterilized jars and seal. Refrigerate to thicken. Jelly will keep in the refrigerator for up to 4 weeks.

Strawberry Rhubarb Jam

3 cups	fresh rhubarb, cut into ¹/₂-inch (1 cm) pieces	750 mL
3 cups	hulled fresh strawberries	750 mL
2¹/₂ cups	granulated sugar	625 mL

1. Measure ingredients into baking pan in the order recommended by the manufacturer. Insert pan into the oven chamber. Select **Jam Cycle**.

2. When cycle is complete, wait 15 minutes before opening lid or removing baking pan. Wearing oven mitts, carefully remove the baking pan from the bread machine. Cool in pan for at least 30 minutes.

3. Pour jam into sterilized jars and seal. Refrigerate for up to 4 weeks.

Making fruit preserves is usually a major production. But with your bread machine, you can make this flavorful jam in small quantities — just what you need for your morning toast!

Tip

For the smoothest texture, use thin, tender stalks of rhubarb.

Variation

Leave the strawberries whole for a chunky type of jam. For a more jelly-like consistency, chop the fruit into smaller pieces.

Tips for Baking Gluten-Free Breads

- Combine all the dry ingredients in a plastic bag or a large bowl before adding to the baking pan. Gluten-free flours have a fine, powder-like consistency and require extra effort to make sure they don't lump and that they mix properly with other ingredients.

- Mix eggs with the liquid ingredients in the bread machine for 2 to 3 minutes before adding the dry ingredients. This beats the eggs and distributes them in the liquids.

- To avoid lumps, add the dry ingredients slowly to the liquids while the machine is running.

- Scrape the corners and the bottom of the baking pan, as well as the kneading blade, for several minutes while adding the dry ingredients. Continue scraping until the dough is smooth and lump-free. This results in a better-textured loaf.

- Gluten-free dough needs vigorous mixing to ensure a high loaf. We found the kneading action of vertical-style machines is generally more effective than that of horizontal-style machines.

- Remove the kneading blade just after the long knead ends, but before the dough begins to rise. (This prevents over-kneading, which can result in a collapsed loaf.) Gluten-free dough is extremely sticky, so moisten your hands before removing the kneading blade from the baking pan.

- Resist the impulse to add more flour to gluten-free dough, even though it may resemble cake batter. Too much flour will produce a dry, crumbly loaf.

- When baking gluten-free loaves, don't add fruit at the "add ingredient" signal. Stirring in the fruit, by hand, at the end of the kneading cycle, distributes it better.

- If your bread machine has a **Bake Cycle**, begin the loaf on **Dough Cycle**. Then, after the dough has risen, finish the loaf on **Bake**. This controls the amount of kneading and eliminates the requirement for a second knead (which results in a shorter loaf).

- Gluten-free loaves may be flat or slightly sunken. This is unavoidable since, without gluten, the dough does not trap the air that creates a rounded top.

Gluten-Free Sticky Buns

• Two 8-inch (2 L) square baking pans, ungreased

1½ tsp	salt	7 mL
2¼ cups	brown rice flour	550 mL
⅔ cup	potato starch	150 mL
⅓ cup	tapioca starch	75 mL
2½ tsp	xanthan gum	12 mL
1 tsp	ground cinnamon	5 mL
2 tsp	bread machine yeast	10 mL
½ cup	water (warmed to 98°F/37°C)	125 mL
1 tsp	cider vinegar	5 mL
1 cup	mashed ripe bananas	250 mL
¼ cup	honey	50 mL
¼ cup	butter, melted	50 mL
3	eggs, lightly beaten	3

PECAN PAN GLAZE

⅔ cup	butter, melted	150 mL
⅔ cup	packed brown sugar	150 mL
⅔ cup	corn syrup	150 mL
1 cup	chopped pecans	250 mL
1 cup	raisins	250 mL

1. Into a bowl or plastic bag, measure salt, rice flour, potato starch, tapioca starch, xanthan gum, cinnamon and yeast. Mix well and set aside.

2. Into bread machine baking pan, measure water, vinegar, banana, honey and butter; add eggs. Insert pan into the oven chamber. Select **Dough Cycle**.

3. Allow liquids to mix for approximately 1 minute. Gradually add dry ingredients as bread machine is mixing. Try to incorporate within 1 to 2 minutes. Scrape with rubber spatula while adding dry ingredients. When mixing and kneading are complete, remove the kneading blade.

4. *Pan glaze:* In a bowl, combine butter, brown sugar and corn syrup. Spread half the mixture in each baking pan. Sprinkle each with half the pecans and raisins. Dip rubber spatula and a large spoon in water, then drop the soft dough by spoonfuls into the pans. Do not smooth the tops. Cover and let rise in a warm, draft-free place for 40 to 50 minutes, or until not quite doubled in volume. Meanwhile, preheat oven to 375°F (190°C).

5. Bake in preheated oven for 35 to 45 minutes, or until sticky buns sound hollow when tapped on the top. Immediately invert pan over a serving platter. Allow to stand for 5 minutes before removing pan. Serve warm.

Gluten-Free Pumpernickel Loaf

With all the hearty flavor of traditional pumpernickel, this gluten-free version is great for sandwiches. Try it filled with sliced smoked turkey, accompanied by a crisp garlic dill pickle.

Tips

Before beginning this recipe, be sure to read the tips for gluten-free baking on page 351.

If your bread machine bakes both 1.5 lb (750 g) and 2 lb (1 kg) sizes, select the smaller loaf size for this recipe.

Variation

For a milder flavor, omit the coffee and unsweetened cocoa.

1 1/2 tsp	salt	7 mL
3 tbsp	packed brown sugar	45 mL
2 cups	brown rice flour	500 mL
2/3 cup	potato starch	150 mL
1/3 cup	tapioca starch	75 mL
2 1/2 tsp	xanthan gum	12 mL
2 tsp	unsweetened cocoa powder	10 mL
2 tsp	instant coffee granules	10 mL
1/2 tsp	ground ginger	2 mL
1 tbsp	bread machine yeast	15 mL
3 tbsp	molasses	45 mL
1 1/2 cups	water (warmed to 98°F/37°C)	375 mL
1 tsp	cider vinegar	5 mL
2 tbsp	vegetable oil	25 mL
3	eggs, lightly beaten	3

1. Into a bowl or plastic bag, measure salt, brown sugar, rice flour, potato starch, tapioca starch, xanthan gum, cocoa, coffee granules, ginger and yeast. Mix well and set aside.

2. Into bread machine baking pan, measure molasses, water, vinegar and vegetable oil; add eggs. Insert pan into the oven chamber. Select **Rapid Two-Hour Basic Cycle**.

3. Allow liquids to mix for approximately 1 minute. Gradually add dry ingredients as bread machine is mixing. Scrape with rubber spatula while adding dry ingredients. Try to incorporate all dry ingredients within 1 to 2 minutes.

4. When mixing and kneading are complete, leaving the baking pan in the bread machine, remove the kneading blade. Allow the bread machine to complete the cycle.

Banana Seed Bread

1 cup	whole bean flour	250 mL
1 cup	sorghum flour	250 mL
1/4 cup	tapioca starch	50 mL
1/4 cup	packed brown sugar	50 mL
2 1/2 tsp	xanthan gum	12 mL
1 tbsp	yeast	15 mL
1 1/4 tsp	salt	6 mL
1/2 cup	sunflower seeds, raw, unsalted	125 mL
3/4 cup	water	175 mL
1 cup	mashed ripe bananas	250 mL
1 tsp	cider vinegar	5 mL
1/4 cup	vegetable oil	50 mL
2	eggs	2

The combination of sorghum and bean flour enhances the banana flavor of this loaf. Serve it for dessert, or with a slice of Cheddar cheese for lunch.

Tip

Use raw, unroasted, unsalted sunflower seeds. For a nuttier flavor, toast the sunflower seeds first (see Techniques Glossary, page 369, for instructions).

Variation

Pumpkin seeds or chopped pecans can replace the sunflower seeds.

1. In a large bowl or plastic bag, combine the whole bean flour, sorghum flour, tapioca starch, brown sugar, xanthan gum, yeast, salt and sunflower seeds; mix well and set aside.

2. Into bread machine baking pan, measure water, banana, vinegar and oil; add eggs. Insert pan into the oven chamber. Select **Rapid Two-Hour Basic Cycle**. Allow liquids to mix until combined. Gradually add dry ingredients as bread machine is mixing. Scrape with rubber spatula while adding dry ingredients. Try to incorporate all dry ingredients within 1 to 2 minutes.

3. When mixing and kneading are complete, leaving the baking pan in the bread machine, remove the kneading blade. Allow the bread machine to complete the cycle.

Equipment Glossary

baguette pan. A metal baking pan, divided into two sections shaped like long thin loaves. The bottom surface may be perforated with small holes to produce a crisp crust and reduce the baking time.

baking liners. Reusable sheets of nonstick coated fiberglass. Flexible and food-safe, they are used to eliminate the need to grease and flour. Wash, rinse well and dry before storing.

baking stone. Available in different sizes and shapes, baking stones are made of unglazed quarry or ceramic tile (the same material used to line brick ovens.) Use for pitas, pizza and focaccia when a crisp crust is desired. *To use a baking stone:* Preheat on bottom rack of oven set to 450°F (230°C) for at least 15 to 20 minutes before using. *To clean:* Cool completely, scrape off any burnt matter, then wipe stone with a damp cloth.

banneton. A woven basket used for rising bread dough. Dust well with flour before using. The crust will have the pattern of the basket after baking.

clay bakers. These are available in a wide variety of shapes, ranging from loaf pans to bundt pans to flower pots. Before using, grease inside completely. While designed to withstand oven temperatures, they are fragile.

dough scraper. A rectangular-shaped piece of metal or plastic, with or without a handle, used to lift or cut dough or to scrape and clean a work surface.

lame. A tool that features an extra-sharp curved blade used by French bakers to make perfectly shaped slashes on risen dough before baking. This ensures the loaf expands to the right shape as it bakes.

pastry brush. Small brush of nylon or natural bristles used to apply glazes or egg washes to the dough. Wash thoroughly after each use. To store, lay flat or hang on a hook through a hole in the handle.

pastry wheel. A small, sharp-edged wheel anchored to a handle. The edge of the wheel may be plain or serrated, and is used for marking and cutting pastry dough.

peel. Not the outside layer of a fruit or vegetable, but a long-handled flat blade, made of wood or metal, used to move pizza or yeast breads on and off baking stones or baking sheets. This prevents the dough from wrinkling as it slides into the oven and protects the baker from burns. *To use a peel:* Generously flour the peel. Slide it under the risen dough or crust and ease it onto the baking stone or oven rack.

pizza wheel. A large, sharp-edged wheel (without serrations) anchored to a handle. Use it to cut dough for breadsticks, rolls or toasties.

rasp (long grater). A tool used to quickly zest citrus fruit, shred garlic or ginger or finely grate hard cheese. It has a long, narrow, razor-sharp "rasp-like" stainless steel blade.

skewer. A long, thin stick (made of wood or metal) used in baking to test for doneness.

spatula. A utensil with a handle and blade that can be long or short, narrow or wide, flexible or inflexible. It is used to spread, lift, turn, mix or smooth foods. Spatulas are made of wood, metal, rubber or plastic.

thermometer. Bakers use this metal-stemmed instrument to test the internal temperature of bread. Stem must be inserted at least 2 inches (5 cm) into the bread for an accurate reading. When bread is baked, it should register 190°F (95°C).

zester. A tool used to cut very thin strips of outer peel from citrus fruits. It has a short, flat blade tipped with five small holes with sharp edges.

Ingredient Glossary

almond extract. A concentrated flavoring made from almond oil and alcohol. Adding $^1/_2$ tsp (2 mL) intensifies the sweet almond flavor without affecting the loaf.

almond paste. Made of ground blanched almonds, sugar and egg whites, almond paste is coarser, darker and less sweet than *marzipan* (see page 363). Do not substitute one for the other.

almonds. Crack open the shell of an almond and you'll find an ivory-colored nut encased in a thin brown skin. With the skin removed, (for technique, see page 368), the almond is "blanched." In this form, almonds are sold whole, sliced, slivered and ground. Two cups (500 mL) almonds weigh about 12 oz (360 g).

amaranth. Native to Mexico, this purple-leaved plant produces seeds that are used as a cereal or ground into gluten-free flour.

anise seeds/star anise. Anise seeds are similar in shape to caraway or fennel seeds, while star anise seeds are egg-shaped. Both types have a distinctive licorice flavor. Anise can also be purchased as a finely ground powder. For recipes that call for anise seeds, half the amount of anise powder can be substituted.

Asiago cheese. A pungent grayish-white hard cheese from northern Italy. Cured for more than 6 months, its texture is ideal for grating.

baba. A Polish Easter cake that is traditionally baked in a cylindrical mold. It contains currants and raisins soaked in rum or Kirsch. The same dough is used to make savarin, a larger variation of baba. Also known as *baba au rhum*.

babka. A Polish sweet bread similar to coffee cake, made with rum, almonds, raisins and orange peel.

barley. A cereal grain with a slightly sweet, nutty, earthy flavor and a chewy texture, sometimes ground into a flour with low gluten content. Barley in baked products adds to the starch and soluble fiber content. Barley flakes are made from the barley grain and look very similar to rolled oats.

bell peppers. See *peppers, bell or sweet*.

brown sugar. A refined sugar with a coating of molasses. It can be purchased coarse or fine and comes in three varieties: dark, golden and light.

buckwheat. Not related, despite its name, to wheat (which is a grain), buckwheat is the seed of a plant from the rhubarb family. Buckwheat flour is dark and strongly flavored. Roasted whole buckwheat, called kasha, has a strong nutty flavor and chewy texture.

bulgur. Whole wheat kernels with the bran layer removed that have been cooked, dried and cracked into fragments. In bread recipes, it provides a nutty texture and flavor, as well as a somewhat coarse texture. Cracked wheat can be substituted for bulgur.

butter. A spread produced from dairy fat and milk solids, butter can be used interchangeably in bread recipes for shortening, oil or margarine.

buttermilk powder. A dry powder, low in calories, that softens the texture of bread and heightens the flavor of ingredients such as chocolate. It is readily available from bulk- or health-food stores. Keep in an airtight container, since it lumps easily. To substitute for 1 cup (250 mL) fresh buttermilk, use 1 cup (250 mL) water and $1/3$ cup (75 mL) buttermilk powder.

caper. A pickled bud of the caper bush grown in Mediterranean countries. Purchase in grocery stores in 2- to 3-oz (60 to 90 g) glass jars. Use in sauces, salads and to garnish fish and meats. Capers enhance the flavor of smoked salmon.

caraway seeds. Small, crescent-shaped seeds of the caraway plant. They have a nutty, peppery flavor similar to licorice.

cardamom. This popular spice is a member of the ginger family. A long green or brown pod contains the strong, spicy, lemon-flavored seed. It is used in Middle Eastern, Indian and Scandinavian cooking.

cereal. Any grain that yields an edible part, such as wheat, oats, rye, rice or corn. It includes the seeds or a processed product made of these seeds and grains.

cereal, 3-grain. See *Red River cereal*.

cereal, 7-grain. Contains barley flakes, triticale flour, corn flakes, steel-cut oats, rye meal, cracked wheat, flaxseed and hulled millet. And yes, for anyone who's counting, there are 8 ingredients, not 7.

cereal, 12-grain. Contains triticale, steel-cut oats, barley flakes, sesame, buckwheat, rye meal, oats, corn, cracked wheat, millet, flax and sunflower seeds. *Note:* All multigrain cereals can be used interchangeably in bread machine recipes.

Cheddar cheese. Always select an aged, good-quality Cheddar for bread machine recipes. The flavor of mild or medium Cheddar is not strong enough for bread machine baking. Weight/volume equivalents are:

4 oz (120 g) = 1 cup (250 mL) grated;

2 oz (60 g) = $1/2$ cup (125 mL) grated;

$1^1/2$ oz (45 g) = $1/3$ cup (75 mL) grated.

chili peppers. To prepare, see Techniques Glossary, page 368.

coconut. To toast, see under *Oats* in Techniques Glossary.

coffee cake. A sweet dough made with yeast that produces a texture more like cake than bread.

coriander. These tiny, yellow-ridged seeds taste of cardamom, cloves, white pepper and orange. Coriander leaves, also known as cilantro, have a flavor reminiscent of lemon, sage and caraway. To increase flavor in a bread recipe, substitute cilantro for parsley.

cornmeal. The dried, ground kernels of white, yellow or blue corn. It has a gritty texture and is available in coarse, medium and fine grind. Its starchy-sweet flavor is most commonly associated with cornbread — a regional specialty of the southern United States.

corn syrup. A thick, sweet syrup made from cornstarch, sold in clear (light) and brown (dark) varieties. The latter has caramel flavor and color added.

cracked wheat. Similar to bulgur, except that it is made from the whole kernel of the grain and is not pre-cooked. Either cracked wheat or bulgur can be used in bread recipes. Bulgur results in a coarser-textured, heavier loaf.

cranberries. Grown in bogs on low vines, these sweet-tart berries are available fresh, frozen and dried. Fresh cranberries are available only in season — typically from mid-October until January, depending on your location — but can be frozen right in the bag. Substitute dried cranberries for sour cherries, raisins or currants. Perfect when a tart flavor is desired.

currants. Similar in appearance to small, dark raisins, currants are made by drying a special seedless variety of grape. Not the same as a type of berry that goes by the same name.

dates. The fruit of the date palm tree, dates are long and oval in shape, with a paper-thin skin that turns from green to dark brown when ripe. Eaten fresh or dried, dates have a very sweet, light-brown flesh around a long, narrow seed.

dough enhancer. Any of several compounds that can be added to dough to increase its strength and tolerance, extend shelf life and make a lighter-textured bread. Examples of dough enhancers include tofu and vitamin C.

eggplant. Ranging in color and shape from dark purple and pear-like to light mauve and cylindrical, eggplant has a light, spongy flesh that, while bland on its own, is remarkable for its ability to absorb other flavors in cooking.

fennel seeds. Small, oval, green-brown seeds with prominent ridges and a mild anise (licorice-like) flavor and aroma. Available whole or ground, they are used in Italian and Central European cookery, particularly in rye or pumpernickel breads.

Feta cheese. A crumbly, white, Greek-style cheese, with a salty, tangy flavor. Store in the refrigerator, in its brine, and drain well before using.

figs. A pear-shaped fruit with a thick, soft skin. Eaten fresh or dried, the tan-colored sweet flesh contains many tiny edible seeds.

filberts. See *hazelnuts*.

flaxseed. Thin, oval and dark brown in color, flaxseed adds a crunchy texture to breads. Research indicates that flaxseed can aid in lowering blood cholesterol levels. Ground flaxseed (also known as linseed) goes stale quickly, so purchase only the amount needed (or, to grind your own, see Techniques Glossary, page 368); store in the refrigerator.

garlic. An edible bulb composed of several sections (cloves), each covered with a papery skin. An essential ingredient in many styles of cooking. See Techniques Glossary, page 369, for tips on how to roast and peel garlic.

ginger. While fresh gingerroot is used most often in savory dishes, the dried, ground form is favored in baking.

gluten. A natural protein in wheat flour that becomes elastic with the addition of moisture and kneading. Gluten traps gases produced by yeast inside the dough and causes it to rise. The stronger the gluten, the greater the loaf volume. Gluten also aids the dough in supporting added ingredients, such as grains, nuts and dried fruit.

gluten flour. When the gluten content of flour exceeds 80%, it is called gluten flour (or "vital wheat gluten" or just "gluten"). It may be purchased from bulk-food stores and added to breads with low-gluten flours to provide extra height.

golden raisins. See *raisins.*

granola. A mixture of dried fruit, grains and nuts. Available in sweetened or unsweetened varieties, it is often used as an ingredient in hearty breads, or can be eaten alone as a breakfast cereal or snack.

granulated sugar. A refined, crystalline white sugar that is also commonly referred to as "table sugar" or just "sugar."

hazelnut liqueur. Best known as Frangelico, a hazelnut-flavored liqueur made in Italy.

hazelnuts. Also known as filberts, hazelnuts have a rich, sweet flavor that complements ingredients such as coffee and chocolate. Remove the bitter brown skin before using (see Techniques Glossary, page 369).

herbs. Annual and perennial plants whose stems, leaves or flowers are used as a flavoring, either dried or fresh. (See also individual herbs.) To substitute fresh herbs for dried, a good rule of thumb is to use three times the amount of fresh as dried. Taste and adjust the amount to suit your preference.

honey. Sweeter than sugar, honey is available in liquid, honeycomb and creamed varieties. Use liquid honey for bread machine recipes.

jalapeño peppers. See *peppers, jalapeño.*

jule kaga or **julekage.** A Swedish Christmas bread with candied fruits and cardamom flavor.

kalamata olives. A large, flavorful variety of Greek olive, typically dark purple in color, and pointed at one end. They are usually sold packed in olive oil or vinegar.

kamut. A large-kernelled, high-protein variety of wheat that was used in ancient times for bread. (Its name is the ancient Egyptian word for wheat.) It has a distinctively nutty taste and contains more nutrients than most types of wheat.

kasha. See *buckwheat*.

kolachy or **kolaches.** A Christmas breakfast tradition in Eastern European homes (particularly those of Czechs and Poles), these sweet buns are typically filled with poppy seeds, nuts and mashed fruit or jam.

kringle. A Swedish Christmas bread.

linseed. See *flaxseed*.

malt powder. The dried form of malt syrup (although not interchangeable with it), malt powder provides a distinctive flavor, texture and crust color to breads, and also helps the loaf stay fresh longer. It absorbs moisture and becomes lumpy very quickly, so store in an airtight container. Diastolic malt powder is a highly concentrated form of malt powder and can be substituted using much smaller quantities.

malt syrup. A byproduct of the process by which barley is soaked, sprouted and dried. The syrup is obtained from the barley by extraction and evaporation of wort — a substance also used to produce beer and certain distilled spirits.

maple syrup. A very sweet, slightly thick brown liquid made by boiling the sap from North American maple trees.

margarine. A solid fat made by hydrogenating one or more vegetable oils. Do not use low-fat margarines; they contain too much added water to produce quality loaves.

marzipan. A sweet paste made from ground almonds, sugar and egg whites. Used as candy filling and for cake decorations, it is sweeter and lighter in color than *almond paste* (see page 359).

mixed glazed fruit. A mixture of dried candied orange and lemon peel, citron and glacé cherries. Citron, which can be expensive, is often replaced in the mix by candied rutabaga.

molasses. A byproduct of refining sugar, molasses is a sweet, thick, dark brown (almost black) liquid. It has a distinctive, slightly bitter flavor and is available in fancy and blackstrap varieties. Use the fancy variety for breads. Store in the refrigerator if used infrequently.

muesli. A cereal blend of oats, dates, sultanas (light-colored raisins), oat bran, currants, almonds, sesame seeds, walnuts, pecans, dried apples, wheat germ, flaxseed and corn grits. It has a relatively high fat content, so it should be stored in an airtight container in the refrigerator or freezer to prevent it from becoming rancid.

nonfat dry milk. The dehydrated form of fluid skim milk. Use $1/4$ cup (50 mL) nonfat dry milk for every 1 cup (250 mL) water.

oat bran. The outer layer of oat grain. It has a high soluble fiber content, which can help to lower blood cholesterol.

oats. Confusing in its many variations, the term "oats" generally refers to the cereal grass of the oat grain. When the oat husk has been removed, it is called a *groat*. Oats are steamed and rolled into flat flakes called *rolled oats* or *old-fashioned oats*. When coarsely ground oats are cooked and used for baking, it becomes *oatmeal*. *"Instant" oats* are partially cooked and dried before rolling. They are rolled thinner, cut finer, and may have flavoring ingredients added. They are not recommended for use in bread machines. *Steel-cut oats* are made from oat groats that are chopped between two steel blades. They are then heat-processed. Steel-cut oats are used to make the firm, textured porridge known as "Scottish Oatmeal." The appearance of steel-cut oats is similar to bulgur. *"Quick-cooking" oats* are rolled oats that are cut into smaller pieces to reduce the cooking time. For a traditional oat bread texture, use small- or medium-flake oatmeal, but not the "instant-cooking" type. See Techniques Glossary, page 369, for tips on toasting oats.

olive oil. Produced from pressing tree-ripened olives. *Extra virgin* oil is taken from the first cold pressing; it is the finest and fruitiest, pale straw to pale green in color, with the least amount of acid, usually less than 1%. *Virgin* oil is taken from a subsequent pressing; it contains 2% acid and is pale yellow. *Light* oil comes from the last pressing; it has a mild flavor, light color and up to 3% acid. It also has a higher smoke point. Product sold as "pure olive oil" has been cleaned and filtered; it is very mild-flavored and has up to 3% acid.

olives. See *kalamata olives*. To pit, see Techniques Glossary, page 369.

parsley. A biennial herb with dark green, curly or flat leaves used fresh as a flavoring or garnish. It is also used dried in soups and other mixes. Substitute parsley for half the amount of a strong-flavored herb such as basil.

pecans. The nut of the hickory tree, pecans have a reddish, mahogany shell and beige flesh. They have a high fat content and are a milder-flavored alternative to walnuts.

peel (mixed, candied or glacé). This type of peel is crystallized in sugar.

peppercorns. The berries of the pepper plant have a brown color when fully ripe. They are available in black, green, red and white. See Techniques Glossary, page 369, for tips on cracking peppercorns.

peppers, bell or sweet. The sweet-flavored members of the capsicum family (which includes chilies and other hot peppers), these peppers have a hollow interior lined with white ribs and seeds attached at the stem end. They are most commonly green, red, orange or yellow, but can also be white or purple.

peppers, jalapeño. Named for the Mexican city of Jalapa, these short, tapered chili peppers have a thick flesh, are moderately hot and are dark green in color.

pine nuts. The nuts of various pine trees native to China, Italy, Mexico, North Africa and the southwestern United States. A shell covers the ivory-colored meat, which is very rich-tasting and high in fat. There are two principal types of pine nut — one mild and long-shaped, the other stronger-flavored and more triangular in shape. Substitute for any variety of nut in bread machine recipes.

pistachios. Inside a hard, tan-colored shell, this pale green nut has a waxy texture and mild flavor.

pita. A flatbread leavened with yeast to create a hollow center — or "pocket." Middle Eastern pitas tend to be oval, while the Greek type are rounder in shape. See Techniques Glossary, page 369, for tips on heating and making pita chips or crisps.

poppy seeds. The tiny, round, blue-gray seed of the poppy has a sweet, nutty flavor. Often used as a garnish or topping for a variety of breads.

potato starch. This very fine powder is a pure starch made from cooked, dried, ground potatoes. It is gluten-free and produces a moist crumb in baked goods. Potato flour can not be substituted.

pumpkin seeds. Hulled and roasted pumpkin seeds have a nutty flavor that enhances many breads. In Mexico, where they are eaten as a snack and used as a thickener in cooking, they are also known as *pepitas*. Roasting enhances the nutty flavor.

quinoa. Pronounced "keen-wa," this was called the "Mother grain" by the ancient Incas. It is a gluten-free complete protein, containing all eight essential amino acids. As a grain, it is cooked like rice — although in half the time — and expands to four times its original volume. Quinoa is also available ground into flour.

raisins. Dark raisins are sun-dried Thompson seedless grapes. Golden raisins are treated with sulphur dioxide and dried artificially, yielding a moister, plumper product.

Red River cereal. Originating in the Red River Valley (in Manitoba, Canada), its nutty flavor and chewy texture comes from the combination of cracked wheat, rye and flaxseed.

rice flour. This fine, powdery, gluten-free flour is made from white or brown rice.

rye flour. Milled from rye, a cereal grain similar to wheat, this flour can be dark or light in color. Because of its low gluten content, it is always used in combination with wheat flour in bread machine recipes.

rye groats. Rye kernel with their husks removed. To cook, see Techniques Glossary, page 370.

savarin. See *baba*.

semolina flour. A creamy yellow, coarsely ground flour milled from hard durum wheat. It has a high gluten content. Semolina is used either alone or in combination with all-purpose or bread flour to make pasta. The semolina makes it easier to knead and hold its shape during cooking. Sprinkled on a baking sheet, it gives a crunch to Kaisers, French sticks and focaccia.

sesame seeds. Also known as benne seeds, sesame seeds are small, flat, oval-shaped seeds with a rich, nut-like flavor when roasted. Most are available as pearly white with a glossy finish. Purchase the tan (hulled), not black (unhulled), variety for use in a bread machine.

shortening. A partially hydrogenated fat made from either animal or vegetable sources.

skim milk powder. The dehydrated form of fluid skim milk. Use ¼ cup (50 mL) skim milk powder for every 1 cup (250 mL) water.

sour. The "mother" or starter used to ferment the dough for sourdough breads.

soya flour. Made from toasted soybeans, high in fat and protein. This lower-fat flour is milled from raw beans.

soy flour. Coarser in texture and stronger-flavored than soya flour. Gluten-free and not very pleasant-tasting, it must be used in combination with other flours.

spelt. An ancient cereal grain native to Southern Europe, spelt is similar to wheat. The nutty-flavored flour is easily digested and slightly higher in protein than wheat. Use in equal amounts to replace wheat flour. Although not gluten-free, it is often tolerated by those sensitive to wheat flour.

star anise. See *anise seeds/star anise.*

stone-ground flour. Produced by milling grain between two huge stones without separating the germ. It tends to be a coarser grind than other types of flour.

sugar substitute. For baking, the best choice is sucralose, which is made from processed sugar and remains stable at any temperature.

sun-dried tomatoes. Available either dry or oil-packed, sun-dried tomatoes have a dark red color, soft, chewy texture and strong tomato flavor. Use dry-packed, soft sun-dried tomatoes in bread recipes. If only oil-packed are available, rinse under hot water and dry well before using. Use scissors to snip each tomato into pieces.

sunflower oil. A pale yellow, flavorless oil, high in polyunsaturated fats and low in saturated fats.

sunflower seeds. The seeds of the familiar sunflower. With roasting comes the addition of extra salt and oil. Use raw, green, shelled, unsalted, unroasted sunflower seeds in bread machine recipes. If only roasted, salted seeds are available, rinse under hot water and dry well before using.

sweet potatoes. Tubers with orange flesh that stays moist when cooked. Not the same as yams, although yams can substitute for sweet potatoes in bread machine recipes.

tapioca starch. Produced from the root of the cassava plant, this starch is used for thickening. Tapioca flour can be substituted.

tarragon. An herb with narrow, pointed, dark green leaves and a distinctive anise-like flavor with undertones of sage. Use fresh or dried.

unbleached flour. Gives loaves a creamier color; may be used interchangeably with bleached all-purpose or bread flour.

vegetable oil. Common oils used are corn, sunflower, safflower, olive, canola, peanut and soya. They have a high polyunsaturated fat content.

walnuts. A sweet-fleshed nut with a large, wrinkled shell.

wash. A liquid applied to the surface of risen dough before baking, frequently made from milk, water or egg.

wheat berry. The berry is the whole wheat kernel, which includes the endosperm, bran and germ. To cook, see Techniques Glossary, page 370.

wheat bran. The outer layer of the wheat berry or kernel, high in fiber and used as a cereal. Oat bran can be substituted in equal amounts.

wheat germ. The embryo of the wheat berry, wheat germ has a nutty flavor and is rich in vitamins (particularly vitamin E) and minerals. It is oily and must be kept in the refrigerator to prevent rancidity. Wheat germ cannot be substituted for wheat bran.

white flour. A flour made by finely grinding the wheat kernel and separating out the germ and bran. It is enriched with vitamins (thiamine, niacin, riboflavin, folic acid) and minerals (iron).

whole wheat flour. A flour made by grinding the entire wheat berry — the bran, germ and endosperm. Store in freezer to prevent rancidity.

wild rice. Native to North America, this nutty-flavored seed does not come from a rice plant, but from a type of grass. To cook, see Techniques Glossary, page 370.

xanthan gum. Used as an ingredient in gluten-free bread to give the dough strength, thus allowing it to rise and prevent it from being too dense in texture. It does not mix with water, so must be combined with dry ingredients. Purchase from bulk- or health-food stores.

yams. See *sweet potatoes*.

yeast. A tiny, single-celled organism that, given moisture, food and warmth, creates gas that is trapped in bread dough, causing it to rise.

yogurt. Made by fermenting cows' milk using a bacteria culture.

zahtar. A blend of sesame seeds, powdered sumac and dried thyme, this spice is an ingredient in the topping on Middle Eastern flatbread. It is available by mail order or in Middle Eastern specialty food stores.

zest. Strips from the colored, outermost layer of rind of citrus fruit. It is used for flavoring and is frequently candied. To zest, see Techniques Glossary, page 370.

Techniques Glossary

almonds. *To blanch:* Cover almonds with boiling water and allow to stand, covered, for 3 to 5 minutes; drain. Grasp the almond at one end, pressing between your thumb and index finger, and the nut will pop out of the skin. Nuts are more easily chopped or slivered while still warm from blanching. *To toast:* See *nuts.*

bananas. *To mash and freeze:* Select overripe fruit, mash and package in 1-cup (250 mL) amounts in freezer containers. Freeze for up to 6 months. Defrost and warm to room temperature before using.

bagel chips. *To make:* Cut bagels in half to form two half circles, then slice ⅛ inch (2 mm) thick. Brush with olive oil and bake at 400°F (200°C) for 12 minutes, or until crisp.

bell peppers. *To roast:* Place whole peppers on baking sheet, piercing each near the stem with a knife. Bake at 425°F (220°C) for 18 minutes, turn and bake 15 minutes, or until pepper skins blister, or roast on the barbecue until skin chars. Place in a paper or plastic bag. Seal, set aside to cool for 10 minutes to loosen skins. Peel, discard seeds.

chili peppers. *To prepare:* Wear rubber gloves to prevent burning the skin as the oil is released. Avoid touching the eyes. Most of the heat is in the seeds and ribs.

chocolate. *To melt:* Foods high in fat such as chocolate soften and then become a liquid when heated. Microwave on High for 1 minute per 1-oz (30 g) square or until soft. Stir until completely melted.

coconut. *To toast:* follow the directions under *oats.*

drizzle. To slowly spoon or pour a liquid (such as icing or melted butter) in a very fine stream over food.

dust. To coat by sprinkling icing sugar, cocoa or flour lightly over food or a utensil.

flaxseed. *To crack:* Place whole seeds in a coffee grinder or blender. Grind only until the outer shell is broken. *To grind:* Place whole seeds in a coffee grinder or blender. Continue grinding to a fine golden-brown color. Grind only the amount required. If necessary, store extra ground flaxseed in refrigerator.

freezing dough. Seal dough in airtight containers and freeze for up to 4 weeks. Thaw, wrapped, overnight in the refrigerator. See also *refrigerating dough.*

fun shapes. To make *snails*, coil rope of dough tightly; instead of tucking end under, raise it, and flatten to form ears and head. This can quickly and easily be changed to a *rattlesnake* by raising the center tail. *Cats, squirrels* and *bunnies* can be made by cutting off 2- to 3-inch (5 to 7.5 cm) pieces for ears and a tail. A double coil in 2:1 or 2:3 proportion shaped into a figure 8 forms the head and the body.

garlic. *To peel:* Use the flat side of a sharp knife to flatten the clove of garlic. Then the skin can be easily removed. *To roast:* Cut off top of head to expose clove tips. Drizzle with $\frac{1}{4}$ tsp (1 mL) olive oil and microwave on High for 70 seconds, or until fork tender. (Or bake at 375°F/190°C for 15 to 20 minutes.)

glaze. To apply a thin, shiny coating to the outside of a sweet or savory food.

hazelnuts. *To remove skins:* Place hazelnuts in a 350°F (180°C) oven for 15 to 20 minutes. Immediately place in a clean, dry kitchen towel. With your hands, rub the nuts against the towel. Skins will be left in the towel. (Be careful: Hazelnuts will be very hot).

nuts and seeds. *To toast:* Spread nuts or seeds in a single layer on a baking sheet and bake at 350°F (180°C) for about 10 minutes, shaking the pan frequently, until lightly browned. (Or microwave uncovered on High for 1 to 2 minutes, stirring every 30 seconds.) Nuts and seeds will darken upon cooling.

oats. *To toast:* Spread rolled oats in a shallow pan. Bake at 350°F (180°C) for 10 to 15 minutes or until brown; stir often. Store in an airtight container or freeze. Toasting oats gives a nuttier flavor.

olives. *To pit:* Place olives under the flat side of a large knife; push down on knife until pit pops out.

onions. *To caramelize:* In a nonstick frying pan, heat 1 tbsp (15 mL) oil over medium heat. Add 2 cups (500 mL) sliced or chopped onions; cook slowly until soft and caramel-colored. If necessary, add 1 tbsp (15 mL) water or white wine to prevent sticking while cooking.

peppercorns. *To crack:* Use a mortar and pestle, if available. Try a hammer, fry pan or a cup and bowl. You could also try the coarse grind on a pepper mill.

pita. *To heat:* Place pita(s) on baking sheet and bake in preheated oven at 400°F (200°C) for about 8 minutes. For a softer sandwich, wrap in foil before heating. To microwave, place on a plate lined with paper towels and heat on High for 1 to 2 minutes. *To make pita chips or crisps:* Separate the layers of the pita by cutting or pulling apart. Cut both circles into 4 or 8 wedges, depending on the size of the pita. Bake, turning once, in a 350°F (180°C) oven for 10 to 15 minutes, or until lightly browned and crisp (or broil for 2 to 4 minutes, until golden and crisp).

plump. To soak dried fruit in a liquid until the fruit softens and swells from absorbing the liquid. Raisins are plumped in brandy, for example, in the *Italian Panettone* recipe.

proof. The period of time during which shaped yeast products rise before baking. Poke dough with two fingers. When indents remain, dough has doubled in volume.

refrigerating dough. One to 2 hours after dough is refrigerated, dough must be punched down, then punched down every 24 hours. For best results, use within 48 hours. See also *freezing dough.*

roasted vegetable cups. *To make:*
Line the cups of muffin tins with
3-inch (7.5 cm) circles of dough. Fill
each with roasted vegetables. Bake
in a 350°F (180°C) oven for 15 to
20 minutes, or until heated through.

rye groats. *To cook:* Cover with at least
1 inch (2.5 cm) water and let stand
overnight. Drain. Add fresh water to
cover. Simmer, stirring occasionally,
for 20 to 30 minutes or until tender.
Drain and allow to cool before using.
Store in refrigerator or freezer.

sauté. To cook quickly in a small
amount of fat at a high temperature.

shaping a loaf for a loaf pan. Roll out
the dough into an 11- by 8-inch
(28 by 20 cm) rectangle. Roll up,
beginning at the short side, pinching
the seam to seal. Tuck under ends.
Place in loaf pan, seam-side down.

slash. This allows for the expansion
of bread while baking. Hold lame
or sharp knife at a 45-degree angle.
Quickly cut the top of the risen
dough in one long motion. The cuts
must be at least $1/4$ to $1/2$ inch (0.5 to
1 cm) deep. The deeper the cut, the
more open the slash.

spritz. To spray risen dough with water
before and during baking for
a crisp crust.

steam. Preheat fire bricks or lava rocks
in a 9- by 13-inch (3 L) metal baking
pan. Place the dough in oven. Quickly
add 1 cup (250 mL) of cold water to
the pan of bricks. Close the door
quickly to prevent the steam from
escaping. Alternatively, spray the
dough with a fine mist of cold water.

The spray should not touch the
oven sides, back or floor. Repeat in
30 seconds and again 2 to 3 times
during the next 3 minutes. You can
also place a 9- by 13-inch (3 L) metal
baking pan in the oven while it is
preheating. Add a tray of ice cubes
to the preheated pan, then quickly
close the oven door.

vegetables. *To sweat:* In a pan over
low heat, cook vegetables, covered,
in a small amount of fat. The food
softens and releases water. This
allows the flavors to release quickly
when cooked with another food.

wheat berry. *To cook:* In a bowl, cover
with at least 1 inch (2.5 cm) water;
let stand overnight. Drain. Transfer
to a pot and add fresh water to
cover. Simmer, stirring occasionally,
for 30 to 45 minutes, or until
tender. Drain and allow to cool
before using. Store in refrigerator
or freezer.

wild rice. *To cook:* Rinse rice under
cold running water. For each 1 cup
(250 mL) wild rice, add 6 cups
(1.5 L) water to a large saucepan.
Cook, uncovered, at a low boil for
about 35 minutes. Cover, lower heat
and simmer for 10 minutes longer,
or until rice is tender and splitting.
Drain well. Store in refrigerator.
Makes 3 cups (750 mL).

zest. *To zest:* Use a zester, or small
sharp knife to peel off thin strips
of the colored part of the skin. Be
sure not to remove the bitter white
pith below.

Index

National Library of Canada Cataloguing in Publication

Washburn, Donna
    250 best Canadian bread machine baking recipes / Donna Washburn, Heather Butt.

Includes index.
Previously published under title: Canada's best bread machine baking
    recipes and More of Canada's best bread machine baking recipes.
ISBN 0-7788-0100-4

1. Bread. 2. Automatic bread machines. 3. Cookery (Bread)
I. Butt, Heather II. Title. III. Title: Two hundred fifty best Canadian
bread machine baking recipes.

TX769.W377 2004   641.8'15   C2004-902920-7

More Great Books from Robert Rose

Appliance Cooking

- 125 Best Microwave Oven Recipes
  by Johanna Burkhard

- 125 Best Pressure Cooker Recipes
  by Cinda Chavich

- The 150 Best Slow Cooker Recipes
  by Judith Finlayson

- Delicious & Dependable Slow Cooker Recipes
  by Judith Finlayson

- 125 Best Vegetarian Slow Cooker Recipes
  by Judith Finlayson

- America's Best Slow Cooker Recipes
  by Donna-Marie Pye

- Canada's Best Slow Cooker Recipes
  by Donna-Marie Pye

- The Best Family Slow Cooker Recipes
  by Donna-Marie Pye

- 125 Best Indoor Grill Recipes
  by Ilana Simon

- The Best Convection Oven Cookbook
  by Linda Stephen

- 125 Best Toaster Oven Recipes
  by Linda Stephen

- 250 Best American Bread Machine Baking Recipes
  by Donna Washburn and Heather Butt

- 250 Best Canadian Bread Machine Baking Recipes
  by Donna Washburn and Heather Butt

Baking

- 250 Best Cakes & Pies
  by Esther Brody

- 250 Best Cobblers, Custards, Cupcakes, Bread Puddings & More
  by Esther Brody

- 500 Best Cookies, Bars & Squares
  by Esther Brody

- 500 Best Muffin Recipes
  by Esther Brody

- 125 Best Cheesecake Recipes
  by George Geary

- 125 Best Chocolate Recipes
  by Julie Hasson

- 125 Best Chocolate Chip Recipes
  by Julie Hasson

- Cake Mix Magic
  by Jill Snider

- Cake Mix Magic 2
  by Jill Snider

Healthy Cooking

- 125 Best Vegetarian Recipes
  by Byron Ayanoglu with contributions from Alexis Kemezys

- The Juicing Bible
  by Pat Crocker and Susan Eagles

- The Smoothies Bible
  by Pat Crocker

- Better Baby Food
  by Daina Kalnins, RD, CNSD and Joanne Saab, RD

- Better Food for Kids
  by Daina Kalnins, RD, CNSD and Joanne Saab, RD

- 500 Best Healthy
  Recipes
  Edited by Lynn Roblin, RD

- 125 Best Gluten-Free
  Recipes
  *by Donna Washburn
  and Heather Butt*

- America's Everyday
  Diabetes Cookbook
  *Edited by Katherine
  E. Younker, MBA, RD*

- Canada's Everyday
  Diabetes Choice
  Recipes
  *Edited by Katherine
  E. Younker, MBA, RD*

- The Diabetes
  Choice Cookbook
  for Canadians
  *Edited by Katherine
  E. Younker, MBA, RD*

- The Best Diabetes
  Cookbook (U.S.)
  *Edited by Katherine
  E. Younker, MBA, RD*

Recent Bestsellers

- 300 Best Comfort
  Food Recipes
  by Johanna Burkhard

- The Convenience Cook
  by Judith Finlayson

- The Spice and
  Herb Bible
  by Ian Hemphill

- 125 Best Ice
  Cream Recipes
  *by Marilyn Linton
  and Tanya Linton*

- 125 Best Casseroles
  & One-Pot Meals
  by Rose Murray

- The Cook's Essential
  Kitchen Dictionary
  by Jacques Rolland

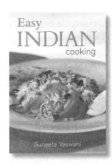

- 125 Best Ground
  Meat Recipes
  by Ilana Simon

- Easy Indian Cooking
  by Suneeta Vaswani

- Simply Thai Cooking
  *by Wandee Young
  and Byron Ayanoglu*

Health

- The Complete
  Natural Medicine
  Guide to the
  50 Most Common
  Medicinal Herbs
  *by Dr. Heather Boon,
  B.Sc.Phm., Ph.D. and
  Michael Smith, B.Pharm,
  M.R.Pharm.S., ND*

- The Complete
  Kid's Allergy and
  Asthma Guide
  Edited by Dr. Milton Gold

- The Complete Natural
  Medicine Guide to
  Breast Cancer
  by Sat Dharam Kaur, ND

- The Complete
  Doctor's Stress
  Solution
  *by Penny Kendall-Reed,
  MSc, ND and Dr. Stephen
  Reed, MD, FRCSC*

- The Complete
  Doctor's Healthy
  Back Bible
  *by Dr. Stephen Reed, MD
  and Penny Kendall-Reed,
  MSc, ND with Dr. Michael
  Ford, MD, FRCSC and
  Dr. Charles Gregory,
  MD, ChB, FRCP(C)*

- Everyday Risks
  in Pregnancy
  & Breastfeeding
  *by Dr. Gideon Koren,
  MD, FRCP(C), ND*

Also Available
from Robert Rose

125 Best
Gluten-Free
Recipes

Donna Washburn and Heather Butt

Robert
ROSE